TIMES OF
Refreshing

100 DEVOTIONS TO ENRICH YOUR WALK WITH GOD

BRENTON M. BARNETT

Aventine Press

TO MY WIFE, WHOSE DEVOTION AND LOVE FOR ME IS MORE THAN I COULD ASK FOR OR IMAGINE.

TABLE OF CONTENTS

INTRODUCTION

"Open my eyes, that I may behold wonderful things from Your law."
-Psalm 119:18

There is a clear Biblical calling for being in God's Word (2 Timothy 3:16-17), for meditating upon His truths (Joshua 1:8), and for letting the Holy Spirit lead and instruct our hearts and minds (John 14:26). We need God's Word as our daily bread (Deuteronomy 8:3, Matthew 6:11), without which our spirits will be weakened such that we will struggle to obey and bear abundant fruit for the kingdom. We need a regular intake of truth, for as Jesus said, "Sanctify them in the word; your word is truth" (John 17:17).

The purpose of this collection of devotions is not so that we can say that we put our time in 100 different times so as to appease God in some fashion or to satisfy our sense of duty. The point of studying God's Word is for spiritual growth so that we learn more about God, grow deeper in our walk with God, and learn to love Him more fully than we had before. Life is about knowing, loving, adoring, worshipping, and enjoying God. He alone can satisfy us. As Psalm 16:11 says, "You will make known to me the path of life; In Your presence is fullness of joy; In Your right hand there are pleasures forever." There is a way that seems right to a man, but it ends in death (Proverbs 14:12). And there is a narrow path, much less traveled, that is the way of life (Matthew 7:14). This path leads to an enjoyment of the constant presence of God in our hearts and lives, and for eternity, it grants us every spiritual blessing in and through Christ (Ephesians 1:3). Satisfaction is what we all seek, and it will never be found in money, fame, or any other earthly thing or pursuit. Ultimately, only God can satisfy, and devotions are meant to remind us of this truth and to help us to better enjoy this reality. Life to the full is about knowing and loving God, and devotions must help us do that. They must teach us through the Scripture rather than just give us some feel good story to make us feel warm and fuzzy for the day. They must really help us learn God's will and ways for our lives so that that we can know Him, love Him, and enjoy Him more deeply, purely, and fully.

It is so easy to grow complacent and to not keep moving forward in our Christian lives. Satan has all kinds of things that he can utilize to weaken us, to distract us, to deceive us, and to keep us from being what God wants us to be. Hosea 6:3 says, "Let us press on to know the LORD." This is how we find refreshment, by pressing on in faith in studying God's Word and in humbly letting the Spirit of God in our hearts teach us, instruct us, convict us, shape us, and lead us. Refreshment comes by repenting of where we have gone wrong and turning to God. Acts 3:19 says, "Therefore repent and return, so that your sins may be wiped away, in order that times of refreshing may come from the presence of the Lord." Sin is our problem, and God's truth is our hope. Refreshment can only be found through the proper application of truth by faith through the Spirit.

James 4:8 says, "Draw near to God and He will draw near to you." Many people want God to be near, but they fail to see that it is their job to make the first move. God says to draw near and then He will draw near in return. My prayer is that many will draw near to God by reading these devotions and choosing to heed the exhortations and commands of Scripture contained therein. I pray that you will be nearer to God by the end of this book than you were at the beginning. Are you willing to draw near, starting now? If so, keep reading.

#1

TEST YOURSELVES

In life there are all kinds of tests that we must pass. We must pass test after test to graduate from high school. Our cars must pass emission tests. We have drug tests, IQ tests, vision tests, hearing tests, allergy tests, and all kinds of tests. We are very concerned about passing these earthly tests because we know that a failure to pass them could be indicative of some serious danger and future failures. Yet we are strangely unconcerned about a future test that all mankind must pass or be sentenced to eternity in hell. There is a serious downside to failing to have our names in the Book of Life. This is one test that we absolutely must pass.

Paul exhorts the Corinthians to test themselves to see if they are indeed of the faith. In 2 Corinthians 13:5, he says, "Test yourselves to see if you are in the faith; examine yourselves! Or do you not recognize this about yourselves, that Jesus Christ is in you--unless indeed you fail the test?" Did they have Christ in them, the hope of their future glory in heaven, or not (Colossians 1:27)? This is the question that they needed to answer. Implied in the notion that we should test ourselves is the fact that we can know if we indeed pass the test or not. The purpose in testing ourselves is thus to know whether or not we are saved so that, if we are not, we can do something about it before it is too late.

We should all come to a place of certainty regarding our eternity. 1 John 5:13 says, "These things I have written to you who believe in the name of the Son of God, so that you may know that you have eternal life." John's motivation in writing the epistle of 1 John was to explain how we can know for sure if we are saved. He wanted believers to be encouraged in their hope of eternal life, and he wanted unbelievers to have the true state of their heart exposed. God's desire is not that we wait it out and hope that we get into heaven. Knowing that we are going to be with Christ for eternity is something that we should anchor our lives upon now. If we do not know Christ, it won't help to find that out come judgment day. We need to know now so that we can repent and receive Him into our hearts as Savior and Lord. *We must test ourselves now so that we can know now.*

John's criteria for being sure of our salvation are as follows: 1) we keep His commandments (1 John 2:4, 29), 2) we love others, especially our brothers and sisters in Christ (1 John 2:9), 3) we do not love the world or the things of it (1 John 2:15), 4) we confess Jesus as Messiah and as God in the flesh (1 John 2:23-24, 4:15), 5) we are being taught by the Spirit (1 John 2:27), 6) we do not practice sin (1 John 3:9), and 7) we practice righteousness (1 John 3:9). These are very basic and black and white criteria. Either we are in Christ or not. Either we love others, or we don't. Either we are led and taught by the Spirit, or we are not (Romans 8:14). Either we are those whose lives are characterized by sin, or we are those whose lives show patterns of righteousness. Either we keep Christ's commandments as a general rule, or we do not. Either we are given to obedience, or we are rebels at heart. Either we love the lusts of the world, or we love Christ. Either we confess Christ as Messiah, or we deny His deity, reject His forgiveness, refuse the draw of the Holy Spirit, and do not submit to His authority. These seven criteria come as a package deal. John is cutting us to the heart to help us see whether we have a fallen heart or a heart that desires the things of God. He is trying to make the point that true saving faith has works as evidence (James 2:17). True Christians will have the fruit of good works, while those who do not truly know Christ will not have any spiritual fruit (Matthew 7:20). Rather, their lives will breed evil, destruction, sin, and hate. We must ask ourselves if we have put our faith in Christ as our Savior and

Lord, and we must see evidence of repentance (Luke 13:5). Repentance is a turning from something and taking a new direction. We should ask ourselves what we have repented from and what we have turned to. There should be a clear difference.

Now Christians do stumble at times (James 3:2), and some have even made shipwreck of their faith (1 Timothy 1:18-20). We may not always love, think, or act as we ought, but there should be obvious evidence that we are not as we used to be. We need to look at the big picture of our lives. Have our lives been different since we turned to Christ? What sin patterns have stopped and what righteous deeds have begun? What do we do that is clear evidence of Christ at work in and through us? Is the love of Christ characteristic of our lives? Do we rejoice when truth prevails? Is it so obvious to others that Christ is our Lord that we end up taking some flack for it? Do our works and behavior deny Christ or affirm a love and devotion to Him? Do we really care about the welfare of others above our own? Is the fruit of the Spirit evident? These are all questions that should have obvious answers.

The point is that we can and should be confident of our salvation. What we need to do is to ask the Spirit of God to testify to our spirits that we are indeed children of God. He will do this as we go through these criteria and questions humbly and honestly if we are indeed born again (Romans 8:16). If we have doubts, we should seal the deal by asking God to forgive us of our sins once and for all and to impart to us the righteousness that can be ours through Christ. Christ bore our sins and the penalty thereof. We must thus receive Him as our Savior and confess Him as our Lord (Romans 10:9-10).

The issue is the state of our hearts. Either Christ is in us, or He is not. It is possible to be sure, one way or the other. Let's test ourselves now so that we can be certain of passing Christ's test come judgment time.

#2

HOLD FAST TO HOPE

1 Corinthians 13:13 says, "But now faith, hope, love, abide these three; but the greatest of these is love." Faith, hope, and love are three concepts that are central to Christian living and belief. Faith is essential to life in Christ, being the grounds for salvation and the means to be able to accomplish anything truly spiritually meaningful in Christ. Love is extremely important, given that it is the mark of true disciples of Christ (John 13:34-35). But hope? What makes hope so great that it is listed as part of these three enduring qualities?

Hope is an essential foundation of Christianity, along with faith and love. Central to true Christianity is a hope in what is not yet seen (Romans 8:24) and a refusal to put our hope in anything that the world says will bring us life. Because of our hope in the eternal, we as Christians are to be focused on trying to live this life in light of our future inheritance in heaven. Our lives on earth should be dictated by a heavenly hope and confidence. This hope and focus on the life to come should be so evident to others that they even ask us about the hope that we have (1 Peter 3:15). No one would marvel at a person who hopes for the next sitcom, paycheck, or promotion. The world's hopes are shallow, shortsighted, unsatisfying, and have nothing to do with eternal life. Our hope in the eternal is what sets Christians apart as we place our focus and hope in heaven.

1 Peter 1:13 says, "Fix your hope completely on the grace to be brought to you at the revelation of Jesus Christ." We can get ourselves into trouble in our Christian lives if we don't put the totality of our hope upon our coming inheritance in heaven. Peter emphasizes that we are to hope fully and completely upon the grace that is coming to us when Christ returns. When Christ returns to take us home, we will be glorified (1 Corinthians 15:42), we will be given new bodies that no longer experience pain (Revelation 21:4), we will be set free from the pulls of our sinful flesh, and we will go on to worship and enjoy God forever in eternal bliss. We will be rewarded for our faithfulness in this life (2 Corinthians 5:10, 1 Corinthians 3:10-15), but it is only the merits of Christ that make it possible for us to enter heaven in the first place (Ephesians 2:8-9). This is why we have put our faith in Him. This is why we love Him because He first loved us (1 John 4:19). And His great love and grace that led us to believe is why we can have such great hope. The God Who started the good work of salvation in our hearts will finish it (Philippians 1:6). He is the author and finisher of our faith (Hebrews 12:2), meaning that He will take what now is a work in progress and make it holy and perfect when we are glorified. He won't quit, grow tired, or bail out on us. We are sealed with the Holy Spirit and guaranteed our inheritance in heaven (2 Corinthians 1:22, Ephesians 1:13, 4:30). This is such a hopeful reality because of its permanence and because God cannot and will not back out on His promises (Titus 1:2). These are sure things, things which should give us great hope. The Christians to whom Peter was writing were enduring persecution and suffering (1 Peter 1:6). Their ability to endure would be related to their ability to keep their hope alive. It might be tempting to deny Christ if we doubt the hope that we have in eternity. It might be tempting to despair if we forget that our coming eternal glory far outweighs any temporal pleasure. Our hope must be fixed upon heaven, and insomuch as that is the case, we can stand firm, be strong in Christ, and be faithful and obedient. Our hope makes a great difference in how we go through this life. Our hope helps keep both our faith and love strong.

Sometimes as believers it can be tempting to misplace the reason for our hope. God's good gifts and provisions in this life are reminders of His good character and love for us, but they are not the ultimate thing that we are to put our hope in. Hebrews 10:23 says, "Let us hold fast the confession of our hope without wavering, for He who promised is faithful." Our ultimate hope is in our confession of faith, our belief in Christ, and in our certainty of His love for us. He has promised us eternity, and He is faithful. Even when we are faithless, still He will remain faithful (2 Timothy 2:13). Should we start hoping in the shallow things of this world to make us joyful, God will still be faithful to us. He will lead us back to Himself and to His promises of eternal life, the only things that can truly keep our hope strong and full.

Those who set their hope entirely on the things of this world rather than upon Christ's return will find themselves enslaved to sin, to bitterness, to fear, and to emptiness. Sin must keep being committed in order for its passing pleasures to be maintained (Hebrews 11:25). Often times, we have to take our sin one step further in order for the same temporary pleasure that it can provide. The temporary nature of sin and its passing pleasures are so contradictory to the permanence of our hope and the faithfulness of our God. This is why Proverbs 11:7 says, "When a wicked man dies, his expectation will perish, and the hope of strong men perishes." In other words, those who set their hope upon the things of this world will lose all hope when eternity comes. They will have chased hope after vain hope in this life, and upon their death, all hope will be gone. The righteous, on the other hand, have hope that will endure, for to them, death is swallowed up in victory (1 Corinthians 15:54). Our hope is secure and eternal, and therefore we don't have to dread death. As Paul says, "To live is Christ and to die is gain" (Philippians 1:21). With that perspective, never is there a reason to lose hope.

Let us hold fast to our Lord and Savior Jesus Christ and His promise of eternal life forever in heaven. He is good to keep His Word, and thus we can put the totality of our confidence in Him.

#3

FOR SUCH A TIME AS THIS

The book of Esther, though it never even mentions the name of God, is clearly about the sovereignty and providence of God in each of our lives. Esther, an orphan child, was adopted by an older cousin named Mordecai. When the King of Persia dismissed Vashti from being Queen, he held a beauty pageant of sorts to find a young woman who would most delight him. Esther, being beautiful, was selected, though she didn't reveal that she was Jewish. She won the favor of the king and became Queen. A man named Haman was promoted in the king's court, and he decided to make the kingdom bow down to him, obviously being on a power trip. Mordecai refused, and thus Haman hated him and wanted him killed. Haman plotted to have all of the Jews killed, and Mordecai communicated the predicament of the nation of Israel to Esther. In Esther 4:14 he says, "For if you remain silent at this time, relief and deliverance will arise for the Jews from another place and you and your father's house will perish. And who knows whether you have not attained royalty for such a time as this?" Mordecai had keen insight into the nature of God. He knew that God would preserve the nation of Israel one way or another because God had promised to make Israel a great nation and bless the rest of the earth through it (Genesis 12:1-3). Thus, his advice to Esther was that maybe God would spare the nation through her. Maybe God had given her great beauty and her position of royalty so that she could be the means through which God would accomplish His will.

Mordecai was a clear believer in the sovereignty and providence of God, for he looked for God's working over their lives and in their circumstances. Yet he was not a believer in fate as if they could stand by and do nothing. Surely, God would preserve Israel one way or another, but Esther and Mordecai had a choice to make. Would they experience the blessing of God as He delivered the nation through their faithfulness, or would they, especially Esther, fail to be strong in the moment which God had ordained for them? This was Esther's chance to make a choice that would impact the history of an entire people and nation. This was her time and her chance, for God had ordered the circumstances of her life for such a time as this.

What we must understand is that Esther is just like us. God is the same yesterday, today, and forever (Hebrews 13:8). Esther's God is our God. Israel was His people, and now we, as believers in Christ, are grafted in as His people (Romans 11:17). How God worked in Esther's life is how God desires to work in our lives. We may not be as good-looking as Esther, we may never have won a beauty pageant, and we may not be in a position of power, let alone Queen of the most powerful nation on earth. Yet, God oversees the events of our lives just as He did the events in Esther's life. Psalm 139:16 says, "And in Your book were all written, the days that were ordained for me, when as yet there was not one of them." From even before we were conceived in our mother's womb, God had a plan for our lives. He knew how He would gift us, what opportunities we would have or the lack thereof, and all of the details of each and every day of our lives. Ephesians 2:10 explains, "For we are His workmanship, created in Christ Jesus for good works, which God prepared beforehand so that we would walk in them." Scripture indicates that there is an intentional connection between how God makes us and the works which He ordains for us. God has a specific plan for our lives that provides the opportunities for us to take advantage of the gifts, abilities, and opportunities that He has given us. He works in the details, ordering circumstances, and establishing our steps (Psalm 37:23). Our calling is to do as Esther did, yielding to the providential hand of God in her life. She didn't ask for her beauty, nor did she earn it. She didn't ask to be an orphan, nor did she have any control over the fact that she was adopted by Mordecai, evidently a God-fearing Jew.

She had no influence over the fact that the king removed the former queen and desired her above all of the other virgins of the land, even though she was a Jew. These were events clearly ordained by God, and she simply cooperated with the hand of God.

God has good works prepared for each of us to do. He wants to use us. In fact, as 2 Chronicles 16:9 says, "For the eyes of the LORD move to and fro throughout the earth that He may strongly support those whose heart is completely His." The question is whether or not we are usable vessels. Esther was humble enough to listen to Mordecai, courageous enough to risk her life for the sake of her fellow Jews, and obedient enough to God to influence the king as she knew she could. She exercised her ability to choose to partner with the providential hand of God. We need to want to be used, and we need to be looking for God's sovereign hand to see where and how we are to serve Him.

There are many times in life, even daily, where God has providentially worked "for such a time as this." Sometimes we get stuck waiting for some dramatic moment where we come through in the clutch and do something great for God. God's call to us is to be faithful in the ordinary everyday things, for even these are ordained by Him purposefully as He provides good works for us to do. We don't know when God will call upon us to make a hard decision or to step out in faith in such a way that many are impacted by our decision. But we will be much more likely to stand strong in such a moment if we have been standing strong all along. We will be much better able to discern the will of God in a time of crisis if we have been seeking Him all along. We must view our lives as those over which God is sovereignly orchestrating circumstances for the purpose of accomplishing His will and advancing His kingdom in and through us.

Esther's life wasn't mere coincidence or fate. It was a cooperating with the God Who ordained it all. Indeed, God has made us all for "such a time as this."

#4

CHECK YOUR MOTIVES

It's not merely what's on the outside that counts, but what is on the inside that leads to what we do on the outside. Proper motivation is important to God, and improper motivation may well be idolatry as we worship self, religious performance, or the approval of others. Some people go through the right religious motions, but there is no joy or life present. Others do the right things to impress others or to make themselves look good. God wants our hearts to be free from chasing our own glory and performing dead works. He wants us to be controlled by His love and motivated by His glory and name.

Ephesians 6:5-8 says,

"Slaves, be obedient to those who are your masters according to the flesh, with fear and trembling, in the sincerity of your heart, as to Christ; not by way of eyeservice, as men-pleasers, but as slaves of Christ, doing the will of God from the heart. With good will render service, as to the Lord, and not to men, knowing that whatever good thing each one does, this he will receive back from the Lord, whether slave or free."

This passage gives us God's criteria for right motives. First, we are to respect those who are authorities in our lives as if we are respecting

God because God has put them there. We don't worship them as god, of course, and we certainly don't do what they say if they tell us to disobey God. But the point is that we honor authority because God has ordained it. Secondly, we remember that when we honor earthly authorities, we are really doing an act of worship to God, honoring Christ by our obedience. Thus, all we do is to be for the glory of God and for His name's sake. In all of our earthly service, we are to serve God in it and by it. Thirdly, we are not to be merely good talkers, putting on an act in front of the boss, but we are to be genuinely obedient and submissive. We are not to try to get others to like us by joining the bandwagon of slacking, laziness, procrastination, and disrespect, but we are to live as those who are slaves of God. The fourth characteristic is the most difficult and most important. We are to act from the heart and with good will. This means that we must have pure motives. This is only possible if Christ is ruling our hearts, giving us the desires of the Lord. This means true surrender, sacrifice, and taking up our crosses daily. It is one thing to clock in and clock out, putting in our time, and it is another thing altogether to rejoice always and never complain, seeking God's glory all the while. This is to be the goal, and it is something we must regularly evaluate ourselves upon. The good news is that, if we act with good motives, we will receive a reward. We may get ridiculed by our peers, but at the end of our stay on earth we can expect a reward from God.

We are not to seek the approval, applause, and recognition of men. If it happens, fine, as long as we direct the glory to God. But we should not count on it. Ultimately, the only rewards that last forever are from God, so those are what we should pursue. And we will only receive those rewards if we learn to obey with sincere motives and willing hearts. *Thus, the best and most God-honoring response to His commands is to do things outwardly that reflect what we are believing and thinking inwardly.* This is what it means to serve God from the heart. *When we get to the point that we want to do what God says and we don't want to do what the world says, we can expect eternal rewards for our obedience.* Paul says of his call to preach the gospel in 1 Corinthians 9:17, "For if I do this voluntarily, I have a reward; but if against my will, I have a stewardship entrusted to me." Paul understood that just doing the right things because we have to or because we are supposed to without a willing, humble, and contrite heart is not sufficient to gain a reward, though it is better than not doing it at all (James 4:17). God sees through self-righteous motives and unwilling hearts. God's desire is that we enjoy His glory by joyous and eager obedience so that we, like Paul when he preached willingly, will get a reward from the Lord. God seeks those who willingly, eagerly, and readily seek His glory in all that they do and say.

If we find ourselves in a place where we have lost our joy and are going through the motions against our will, we must not stop doing right and good. Even if we find ourselves battling self-righteousness, we must keep serving the Lord. We still have a stewardship that we are responsible for. We aren't to go and sit on the sidelines of the fight of faith until our motives change. We need to keep striving for righteousness and the advancement of the kingdom of God, praying all the while for the Lord to change our hearts. As we do this, God will show us how and where we need to repent if we humble ourselves before Him and ask Him to lead us into all truth. He will show us where we are seeking our own glory rather than His, but let us not stop pressing on toward the prize and the upward call in Christ.

When it comes to living the Christian life, it is not acceptable to say that our hearts are not in it. May God enable us to serve because we want to, may we serve faithfully, may we serve Him in all things, may we earn many heavenly rewards, and may we want God to get the glory, always, only, and forever. What's motivating you?

#5

WORK OUT YOUR SALVATION

Some people live under the mistaken notion that salvation does nothing to them or for them except get them out of hell. They think that they are still sinners who are only different post-salvation in that they will be saved from the consequences of their sin. Thus, those who think this way tend to live the rest of their lives on earth with the belief that they are merely sinners who have been saved by grace. Nothing much within them or about them has changed as far as they know, but they can at least rest easy that their continued sinning will be covered by the blood of Christ. Praise God that His blood covers our sin, but the work of Christ on the cross and His triumph over the grave not only gets us into heaven but transforms us in the here and now. Though the fullness of our salvation will not be worked out until we are revealed as the sons of God at Christ's coming, we are in a process of transformation even now. Our salvation has indeed left some permanent changes besides just the fact that we are going to heaven.

Philippians 2:12 commands us to "work out your salvation with fear and trembling." Of course, the next verse reminds us that it is Christ in us doing the work according to His will and good pleasure. Yet our work, as usual, is based in faith. It was our faith by God's grace that saved us, and it is faith that will enable us to be sanctified as we work out our salvation. To work out our salvation means that we will live practically

15

in the here and now more and more in light of who we are in Christ. Thus, if we remain ignorant of all that Christ accomplished on the cross and by overcoming the grave, we may keep the sanctification process from going ahead full-steam as it ought to be.

The Christian is no longer a sinner but a saint. Paul repeatedly wrote to the saints at such-and-such a city (e.g. Romans 1:7, 1 Corinthians 1:2). Never did he address God's people as sinners, though he did call out sin that was present among the saints. We are saints because we have a new identity that is found in Christ. God sees us through the righteousness of Christ. Not only are we "wrapped in a robe of righteousness," so to speak, but God through Christ is working righteousness into our spiritual "DNA." Before we came to Christ, we were born sinners with the fallen spiritual "DNA" of Adam, the first sinner. When we trusted in Christ by faith and repented of our sin, we were born again of the seed of Christ (1 John 3:9) by the Word of God which was planted in our hearts (James 1:21). In other words, we were regenerated and reborn with a new DNA that is not programmed "sinner" but rather hardwired "saint." We are being changed from the inside out. *Righteousness is not just a robe to be worn to cover sin, but it is to be worked in to our very identity, nature, and being.* Salvation leaves with it a change, giving us the ability to no longer be selfish to the core and to have the power and strength in Christ to resist sin and our flesh by faith (James 4:7).

2 Corinthians 5:17 says, "Therefore if anyone is in Christ, he is a new creature; the old things passed away; behold, new things have come." What exactly does this mean that we are new creations in Christ? Romans 6:6 provides some insight when it tells us that our "body of sin" was "done away with," having been crucified with Christ so that "we would no longer be slaves to sin." The old person (also called the old self or old man), which is who we were before salvation, is now dead because he (or she) was crucified with Christ. Our old person with our old ways, ambitions, and bent to sin is now gone, having been put to death along with Christ on the cross. *When Christ rose to new life, He also made it so that we could have new life.* This is what it means to be a new creation- we are literally reborn to become a new person. As a new creation, we ought to be more and more prone to righteousness

and honoring God than to sinning, falling, and faltering. Our old selves were enslaved to the law of sin and death, having no ability to fulfill the law of God. Yet, having been born again, we now have the capacity by faith to obey and resist the pulls of our flesh. We are not finished works in that we will still battle our flesh and its sinful urges, but inside we are new. Our hope is that this new self indwelt by the Spirit of God can overcome the flesh. We will still face temptation, but by faith we can trust God to provide a way of escape (1 Corinthians 10:13). If we were still evil people to the core, we wouldn't even be interested in the escape, but we would rather love our sin. This change in internal desires is evidence of a new heart, one that is no longer desperately wicked and deceitful (Jeremiah 17:9) but one that can be given the desires of God (Psalm 37:4). We as new creations in Christ need to continue to work out our salvation as Christ shows us that His ways are more desirable than the ways of the world.

There is great hope in being new creations in Christ with cleansed hearts. We can even begin to have minds that think with Biblical priorities like Christ (1 Corinthians 2:16). The only thing left to be changed is our bodies, which will be changed when Christ returns and glorifies us (1 Corinthians 15:53). At that point, our human frailty along with our aches and pains will finally be gone. There finally will be no more flesh to battle. But until that day, the fight for faith is on, and we can win it daily by remembering just who it is we are in Christ (1 Peter 4:1-2).

#6

THE FUTILITY OF CHASING THE APPROVAL OF PEOPLE

It is no mystery that many of us have suffered hurt or rejection in some way during our lives. For some, the hurt has come from those who should have loved us the most and the best. Thus, their rejection cuts even deeper, leaving wounds that need to be healed by the unconditional acceptance and love of Christ. Until we find our identity and worth solely in who we are in Christ because of His love for us, we will continue to seek our worth elsewhere, typically chasing the approval of others.

It indeed is the natural way of man to constantly seek the approval of others. Teenagers, for example, look to their peers in particular as a means of gauging their own worth. The high school experience is notorious for ranking individuals based upon clique, dress, extracurricular involvement, and smarts. But it doesn't end with high school; in fact, much of life is based upon performance and rank. Solomon, the wisest man to ever live, said, remarking on life in general, "I have seen that every labor and every skill which is done is the result of rivalry between a man and his neighbor. This too is vanity and striving after wind" (Ecclesiastes 4:4). Every labor, activity, and work of man is, in his natural state, based upon competition with others. Man tries to find his worth based upon human rank, performance, or others' acceptance, but this is never going to satisfy or fulfill the void that rejection and hurt has left in his heart. It is like trying to catch the wind.

When we seek the approval of others as a means to garner self-esteem and worth or to establish our identity, we are out of bounds from a Biblical perspective. In chasing the approval of man, *we are trying to find our worth and identity not based in how God values us but in what others think of us.* This is futile, but it is easy to do nonetheless. This is why people glorify and even deify sports stars, Hollywood icons, rock stars, and politicians for example. We constantly live under the illusion of "if only I did this, had this, made this, knew so-and-so, became like so-and-so, and got this, then I would get so-and-so's approval and then I would be happy." Such is like the ridiculous notion of trying to catch the wind. It can never be done, for it is impossible. In fact, it was ordained and designed to fail. Such is supposed to draw us to the only true source of satisfaction, wholeness, healing, and fulfillment which is Jesus Christ. It is all by God's design.

Hopefully, we have come to the point where we get sick and tired of trying to people-please, worrying about peer pressure, and trying to outdo our neighbor. Hopefully we can see that it is a treadmill that keeps us from ever gaining any ground no matter how hard we work and try. Yet the temptation remains.

John 12:42-43 says, "Nevertheless many even of the rulers believed in Him, but because of the Pharisees they were not confessing Him, for fear that they would be put out of the synagogue; *for they loved the approval of men rather than the approval of God*" (emphasis added). The Pharisees held an elite position of power, authority, and respect. They could make the rules, carry out sentencing, and show everyone how spiritual they were based upon their outward apparel and rituals. To be a Pharisee among the Jews was to be at the top of the pecking order. Yet Jesus constantly rebuked the Pharisees for being hypocrites and for missing the essence of the call of a follower of God- love for God and love for their neighbor. Some of the rulers of the Jews did see their error and come to faith in Christ, yet because of appearances and the love of man's approval, they did not confess Him. They knew that if they confessed their belief in Jesus publicly that they would probably be relieved of their positions in a public display of shame and ridicule. They would likely lose everything, be oppressed, struggle to find work, bring shame to the family name, and potentially endanger their own well-being as well as that of their own families. Some were not willing to give up all of the comfort, show, and "security" of the things of the world for the sake of Christ. They loved the approval of man rather than the approval of God. In other words, it is either one or the other. If we follow God and love Him with all of our hearts, then we must recant our allegiances and compromises with trying to impress others, trying to boost our own self-esteem through making earthly comparisons, and trying to achieve what only God can give. It might be as simple as not wanting to be seen praying because of the ridicule other students or co-workers would bring. Loving man's approval might also lead us to never avoid risking rejection that might accompany sharing the gospel with a stranger or a loved one. But if we love God we must deny ourselves, take up our crosses, and follow Him, even if it means that we are rejected by family and friends.

Paul lost all and counted it joy for the sake of knowing Christ. He would rather enjoy the fellowship of Christ, even if it was fellowship through suffering, than continue to live as an elitist Pharisee of the Pharisees. Paul had it all, having been trained by the best of the best when it came to the teachers of the Law, Gamaliel. Paul, in terms of the rivalry of human nature, had won. He had arrived. Yet upon encountering Christ, he left all the rank, status, and competition behind and became one of the least (Philippians 3:7-8). Identifying with Christ was not an impressive societal mark; being a Pharisee was. Yet Paul chose Christ even though it meant certain persecution, ridicule, and likely death. Paul valued the eternal over the temporal, understanding that in the life to come the last shall be first and the first shall be last (Matthew 20:16). Thus, he rightly understood that seeking God's approval is always worth it in the long run.

Choosing to identify with Christ often will cost us something. However, it is an identity worth having because He will never reject us or cast us out if we are His children. It is a relationship not of competition but of love, grace, and mercy. It is a place of safety, joy, hope, and kindness. Only in Christ can we find healing from rejection and grace to be who Christ has created us to be.

Let us stop chasing the wind and seeking the approval of man. It is time that we desire God's approval more than mere man's, for only God's approval matters and carries any eternal weight whatsoever. So, do we want to please God more or man? That is the question that we must answer.

#7

THE ETERNAL WEIGHT OF GLORY

What is more important, the pleasures of sin in this life, or the riches of eternal life in Christ forever? Weighing these two options side by side should come out to be a no-brainer. The scale clearly tilts in the direction of eternity. After all, the eternal is quite a bit longer than life on earth, and God's rewards are quite a bit nicer than any earthly prize. Plain and simply, the eternal weight of glory is far greater than anything this world has to offer.

The perspective that we need to have is given by Paul in 2 Corinthians 4:16-18 which says,

> "Therefore we do not lose heart, but though our outer man is decaying, yet our inner man is being renewed day by day. For momentary, light affliction is producing for us *an eternal weight of glory far beyond all comparison,* while we look not at the things which are seen, but at the things which are not seen; for the things which are seen are temporal, but the things which are not seen are eternal" (italics mine).

In order to properly value eternity priorities in light of their true value, we must be willing to see beyond the temporal world. We must think

Biblically by viewing this life as a short window of time for doing what God wants us to do. Temporal thinking is easily distracted from the course that God wants us to take. Temporal thinking gets caught up with the circumstances such that the hope of eternity is lost. Paul says that the only way for us not to lose heart when difficult times come is to remember that, though our body decays every day and pain may come our way, we are being renewed inwardly day by day. The inner person is growing more like Christ as we let Christ work in our hearts and minds. Each day our spiritual strength can be fresh and new despite the outward decay of our bodies. Paul had such an eternal perspective that he even thought beyond his own temporal body, thinking of his spirit which would live on. He even viewed the intense affliction that he faced as but momentary and light given that his temporal life was so short compared with eternity.

If we want to begin to think eternally like Paul, we need to think beyond simply what is in front of our faces now. The temporal world is just that, temporary. Things rot, decay, rust, and are destroyed, but that which is eternal lives on. God lives on, our spirits will live on, God's Word will endure, and heaven will be ours. No matter where we live, what we eat, what we wear, where we go to shop, where we go to work, and what we drive or ride to get there, we must see beyond these things. Everything we do, from work to family to leisure to ministry should be done to the glory of God. How we use every minute of the day should be done purposefully in light of the values of heaven. If we don't value heaven's rewards and if we don't care about the judgment seat of Christ, it will be very difficult to let eternity impact our everyday decision-making. But in this case, aging is actually a mercy in that it reminds us as each day passes that this life is fading and that our bodies will one day give out on us. It makes us remember that there is more to this life than just what we see. It helps us walk by faith and think about sending treasure on ahead. This life is temporary, a mere vapor that is here and then gone. *Oh, that we would see the weight of the glory of the eternal and the transience of the temporary!*

We ought to do what God has given us to do in this life to the best of our ability for God's glory. Colossians 3:23 says, "Whatever you do, do your work heartily, as for the Lord rather than for men." We are to come to the point where we become so focused upon eternity and the value of Jesus' approval and the rewards to come that we serve Him with our whole hearts and do everything for Him rather than for people.

Colossians 3:24 continues, "Knowing that from the Lord you will receive the reward of the inheritance. It is the Lord Christ whom you serve." Paul understood Who he served and that his calling was that of a servant. He understood that his life wasn't his own but that he had been bought with a price, namely, Christ's blood (1 Corinthians 6:20). He embraced the role of God's servant willingly, knowing that he would receive the reward of the inheritance. He knew that eternal glory with Christ in heaven was worth doing whatever God wanted him to do in this short timeframe on earth.

The eternal fight is much more interesting than any passing fads on this planet. It carries far more meaning than any earthly crowd-pleasing event or experience. Its importance and value far exceeds any earthly commodity, and its implications extend beyond the grave. There is just no reason why we shouldn't think with an eternal perspective. May God help us to value the weight of glory that is promised to us in eternity through Jesus Christ such that we live only desiring His will in this temporary time and in this fleeting place.

#8

DO YOU WANT TO BE GREAT?

Often times, Christians balk at the thought of becoming great. When we hear things like "be all you can be," "pursue greatness," and "live up to your full potential," we often condemn such thinking as self-centered and worldly. Granted, when the world says things like this, they usually do mean it in such a way. They are telling us to draw our strength from ourselves rather than Christ, they are telling us that life is about us making our mark on the world, and they are assuming that greatness is fame, popularity, wealth, and other false ways of identifying success. We know that the world has it wrong; in fact, they have it totally backward. But is it wrong to aspire to greatness, if we know what true greatness is?

The Scripture teaches that we ought to maximize our stay on earth in light of kingdom priorities (Matthew 6:33). It tells us that we are to want to run in such a way as to win the prize of God and receive the crown of life which is given to those who persevere in faithfulness and steadfastness (1 Corinthians 9:24, Revelation 2:10). God has gifted us all with a special spiritual gift design so that He can empower us to be part of His body advancing the kingdom of God in the hearts of mankind (Ephesians 4:7, Romans 12:6). If God has so gifted us and if He so desires to reward us, it only makes sense that He wants us to be great in His kingdom. Why wouldn't He want us to experience maximum blessing and joy when we get to heaven?

True greatness is living as those who put their values and investments in heaven where moth and rust do not destroy. We are to send on riches for the life to come by denying ourselves in the here and now. We are also to be wise stewards of the gifts and talents that God has given us, not wasting them on selfish things but rather doing what God enables us to do in service for His kingdom.

True greatness is also servanthood. Greatness is not for those who strive to get to the top of the pecking order so that they can rule their earthly kingdom as a means of self-gratification by the indulgence of the privileges of power. Leadership is fine if it is viewed as a stewardship and gift from God. Yet it is not acceptable to "lord it over" others and get some selfish pleasure out of being in authority. Even leaders are to be servants. Matthew 20:25-28 says,

> "But Jesus called them to Himself and said, 'You know that the rulers of the Gentiles lord it over them, and their great men exercise authority over them. It is not this way among you, but whoever wishes to become great among you shall be your servant, and whoever wishes to be first among you shall be your slave; just as the Son of Man did not come to be served, but to serve, and to give His life a ransom for many.'"

God may entrust us with positions of authority and responsibility on earth, and we will be held accountable for how we serve in them. But the key is that we view everything that we do as a chance to serve God and to do things His way. True greatness involves losing what the world says we should be holding dear so that we can find out what life is really all about. Christ's message to the disciples, who had been arguing about who is the greatest, was that their focus was all wrong. Greatness is not how the world views greatness. It is not about how powerful we might become or how much money we might have. It is not about rank and status. Rather, whoever wants to be great in heaven must become a servant now. This means that we must value the needs of others as more important than our own and that we must make kingdom priorities our priorities, doing our part to help fulfill the Great Commission. Our entire life's purpose and our entire existence is to be viewed as that of a servant, first and foremost of God but, secondly, of our brothers and sisters on the earth. Galatians 6:10 says, "So then, while we have opportunity, let us do good to all people, and especially to those who are of the household of the faith." We have opportunity to do good for others only as long as we are alive and functioning on this earth. God may call us home at any moment. At that point our race run for Christ is over, and our eternity is set. We don't get any "do-overs" or second chances. We have one chance to live for Christ in this life, and if we want to be great in the coming kingdom, we must not pursue the world's ideas of greatness but Christ's as we take on the role of a servant, valuing Christ's commission over any other.

Do we want to be great in God's kingdom? If we do, let us live with an eternal perspective, let us send on treasure ahead, let us value others ahead of ourselves, let us seek the kingdom above all things, let us walk by faith, and let us live as servants who value our lives only in light of how God values them. How did Christ value His life? He laid it down so that others might live. If we want to be great in God's kingdom, we must learn to be the servant of all.

#9

THE SUFFICIENCY OF SCRIPTURE

One passage in particular makes an extremely potent case for the sufficiency of the Scripture, and it is the story of the rich man and Lazarus in Luke 16 told by Christ Himself.

The story goes like this. There was a certain rich man who had more than he ever wanted or needed. He lived his life for himself, in wasteful, selfish indulgence, not caring about the poor. Lazarus was a poor beggar who only hoped to get a scrap from the rich man's table, though it is not clear if he ever did. After the rich man and Lazarus die, we get a glimpse of their situations in eternity. Lazarus is with Abraham, symbolizing that he is grafted into the family of God by faith in Christ. He is in heaven. The rich man is in agony in the burning flames of hell. Between the two a great chasm which cannot be crossed is fixed. Though not normally possible, for the sake of the story a conversation is said to take place between Lazarus, the rich man, and Abraham. The rich man (though we should note that he is not rich anymore) knows that his five brothers are as wicked as he was and will no doubt end up in torment as he is, so he begs Abraham to send somebody, even Lazarus, to his brothers. He reasons that if his brothers see a person raised from the dead that they will repent and put their faith in God. His hope is that a miraculous vision will be enough to wake them up from their sinful ways. Yet Abraham explains that unless they hear the law and the prophets, which they already have available to them, they will not repent. Abraham's statement, told by Christ as He gives this story, emphatically makes the point that the Scripture is sufficient. The message from this story is that no sign and wonder will cause a person to repent. No trick or technique that man can conjure up can move a man to want to receive Jesus. Unless people hear and receive what they already have available to them in the Word of God, they cannot and will not be saved. In the story, Abraham puts his full confidence in the law and the prophets, the Old Testament Scripture, which foretold of Christ as Messiah. If the rich man's brothers rejected that, nothing, not even Christ being crucified and rising from the dead would be able to convince them to believe. No miracle, not even the greatest one of all time, would be enough to change their hearts and minds. People continue to reject Christ as God and refuse to receive Him as their Savior despite the many signs and wonders that He did. *Christ knew that only the Word of God could change a person's heart. If Christ even by performing the greatest miracle of all time couldn't convince a person to believe, what really do we have to come up with besides the same thing that He trusted in, God's Word?*

Where would we be without the Word of God? The Word of the Lord will endure forever (1 Peter 1:25), and it contains all that we need for life and godliness (2 Peter 1:3). The Scripture can stand on its own, and it does not go forth void. It accomplishes what God has set it out to do (Isaiah 55:11). It cuts to joints and marrow, judging the thoughts and intentions of the heart (Hebrews 4:12). When we treasure it in our hearts, it keeps us from sinning (Psalm 119:11). It is a lamp unto our feet and a light to our path (Psalm 119:105).

Without God's Word, we would be completely insufficient, but our sufficiency is in Christ and in His Word. 2 Corinthians 3:5 says, "Not that we are adequate in ourselves to consider anything as coming from ourselves, but our adequacy is from God." And God makes us adequate through receiving the teaching and instruction of His Word. Then, and only then, according to 2 Timothy 3:17, are we "adequate, equipped for every good work." *We must understand that it is the work of the Scripture applied to our hearts that enables us, empowers us, and directs*

29

us to be able to effectively and properly love and serve those around us. True life change starts with hearing the Word of God and receiving it in faith.

Let us not take for granted the preaching, the reading, and the proclamation of the Bible. We need to know it, study it, memorize it, and meditate upon it. It is powerful unto salvation for those who don't believe (Romans 1:16), and it is powerful for sanctification for those who do (John 17:17). If we don't know it, we will be naïve, vulnerable to deception, and unable to stand firm. May God give us the desire and discipline to believe in the sufficiency of His Word to such an extent that it permeates all that we do and say.

#10

HOW TO HAVE REAL JOY

There are lots of ideas floating around out there as to how a person can truly be happy, yet the answer is right within us, if we are Christians.

Christ lists nine ways in Matthew 5:1-12 that we can be happy. These ways include being pure in heart, being humble, being gentle, being peacemakers, hungering for righteousness, being merciful, and having an eternal perspective about life. And let us not forget that we are to have joy when we are persecuted and suffer for righteousness' sake and for Jesus' sake. Christ's message to us is that joy is possible at all times and in all areas of life, if we live as He is commanding us to live. Those who were listening to this discourse at the time were hoping that Christ would conquer Rome and set up a Jewish empire. They wanted their circumstances changed so that they could be happy. Yet Christ gave up His life, He did not fix their circumstances, and He did not set up an earthly kingdom. Still He said that they could be happy, if and only if they let the kingdom of Christ rule in their hearts. The happiness that Christ was referring to was clearly not circumstantial in nature. Rather, it was all about investing in heavenly priorities and putting faith in Christ regardless of the circumstances. In Christ alone, we can find fullness of joy. As Psalm 16:11 says, "In His presence is fullness of joy." Jesus alone can make us happy.

The believer's joy is not a fleshly, conjured up type of smiling, niceness, and politeness no matter what. Such is fake and worldly. What Christ is after is a happiness that stems from hope in a Person, even if our face is downcast, even when tears fall, and even when we are in great pain. Joy is an issue of the heart, and it gives us strength in our inner person to carry on in obedience and faithfulness. As Nehemiah 8:10 says, "Do not be grieved, for the joy of the LORD is your strength." True joy transcends circumstances such that, even when we are suffering, we can have joy in our hearts. We may feel pain in the members of our bodies, but we can have joy in our spirits and in our hearts. We may be mocked, ridiculed, persecuted, and harassed, yet we can be happy because we are always in the presence of God. *There is nothing like knowing that our joy remains full even when we have been rendered empty of all that we had thought we needed to sustain our happiness.*

Yet even Christians sometimes fail to experience joy in both good times and bad. Sometimes we get so caught up in the issues of life that we forget to rejoice in the Lord. Rejoicing in the Lord is a choice. This is why Paul commanded us twice in Philippians 4:4 to rejoice in the Lord always. Just because we are in the presence of God (seeing that He indwells our hearts) does not mean that we necessarily will experience joy unless we by faith rest in Him. We must make a choice to let Christ be our joy, to let Him give us joy, and to believe that He will do just that. If we falter in our faith, we will try to manufacture our own joy, which will not last and will fail. *Only when we find our happiness in the person of Jesus as we rest in Him can we experience true joy.* We must rest in Him, love Him, enjoy Him, worship Him, and trust in the fact that our lives are indeed hidden with Christ in God (Colossians 3:3). Constant communion with God is possible through Christ Who works in and through us.

John 15:11 says, "These things I have spoken to you so that My joy may be in you, and that your joy may be made full." John reminds us that we will not have fullness of joy unless we abide in Christ which involves keeping His commands and putting our full trust and confidence in Him. *Obedience to God is central to experiencing the joy of God.* If we do not follow His will and listen to the Holy Spirit in accordance with God's

Word, we will lose out on our joy. There may be some there, seeing that we will still know that we are saved, yet the fullness of joy will be gone because we are not being and doing what God would have us be and do. The darkest times of life are the times of disobedience because there is a lack of joy even if circumstances are easy. In fact, the brightest and most joyous times can actually be when we triumph in faith and obedience during the most difficult and oppressive of times. If we want joy that is supernatural and truly divine, then we must walk in obedience, resting in God all the while.

Sin's pleasures are temporary (Hebrews 11:25), but God's joy endures forever. When we put our confidence in God and choose to have His joy, we can have access to a fruit of the Spirit which is unspeakably wonderful. It transcends the issues of life and draws our minds to heaven. His joy is a pleasure that is forever, and we can experience it even this very moment if we walk in faith and obedience.

#11
RESISTING THE PULL TO NOMINALISM

Too often there seems to be a spirit of apathy, complacency, and a bad kind of spiritual contentment in the church. Granted, there are places where the environment is saturated with the work and filling of the Spirit, but they seem to be the exception rather than the rule. Spiritual nominalism is clearly a problem, and we would do well to think about how we can avoid being pulled into it ourselves.

We can recognize nominalism in our lives if our walks our characterized by a mediocre faith, a subpar holiness, and a habitual indulgence in walking according to the flesh. Nominal Christians tend to let areas of sin go unconfessed, they do not envision what God could do by faith, and they enjoy things that don't make them confront the holiness of God. They do not want to hear about obedience, submission, surrender, the fear of God, and trembling before His Word. Such truths would make them feel uncomfortable. They don't have an appetite for the preaching of the Word. They don't grieve over sin, they are not burdened for evangelism, and they have no passion for being in the presence of God. Their desire to be in God's Word is minimal, and they have little interest in prayer. The authority of God's Word fails to permeate the whole of their lives.

If we want to avoid falling into nominalism, we need to understand what causes it in the first place. When the fear of God is absent among the people of God, sin breaks out like cancer. When the fear of God is present, a thorough self-examination and self-restraint by faith works its way through the people of God as in the story of Ananias and Sapphira in Acts 5 where God executed them both publicly for not giving what they were supposed to give to God. Acts 5:5 says that "great fear came over all who heard it." We tend to forget that God disciplines those whom He loves (Hebrews 12:6). Some Christians are even allowed to become sick or even killed by God if they don't judge the body rightly by allowing sin to go on unchecked and being callous toward the sacrifice of Christ (1 Corinthians 11:30). These punishments are not works of God's wrath, for believers will never face God's wrath because it was poured out upon Christ. But we will encounter God's discipline throughout the course of our lives when we veer off track because God disciplines those children whom He loves (Hebrews 12:6, 10). That God would instruct us and train us in righteousness proves His love toward us because He knows what is best for us. He wants us to have an abundance of eternal rewards, and therefore He will help us to stay on track. We will all face Christ at His judgment seat one day to be recompensed according to our level of faithfulness as believers (2 Corinthians 5:10, 1 Corinthians 3:10-15). Being mindful of our coming judgment and of God's discipline for our rebellion helps remind us to live with a healthy fear of God in our hearts and minds. This motivates us to keep doing right and to keep walking by faith. Nominalism can be right around the corner for those who don't fear God as they should.

Nominalism is also caused by those who do not tremble before God's Word. God says in Isaiah 66:2, "But to this one I will look, to him who is humble and contrite of spirit, and who trembles at My word." Those who fear God will also likely tremble before His Word. Those who do not fear God won't pay much attention to God's Word, and they will likely veer way off course in their spiritual lives. Thus, the fear of God and trembling before His Word go hand in hand. God's Word is our only hope for knowing how to live this life, and we must read it, study it, learn it, know it, obey it, and meditate upon it. Those who tremble before God's Word are those who allow it to do its convicting work such that they take any sin in their lives seriously, dealing with it immediately by confessing it before God. We cannot afford to approach

God's Word casually, but we must view it as the authoritative and life sustaining truth that it is. A casual view of the Bible leads to casual, nominal living which furthers a casual take on the Bible which deepens the falling away from faithfulness. At some point, to avoid the pull of nominalism, we as God's people must turn to God's Word, revering it and trembling at it. Nominalism is just too casual in its view and approach to God. It elevates man and his experience and devalues God and what He has said in His Word. Those who love God's Word and are in it and living obediently can remain filled with the Spirit. This will keep us from falling into nominalism.

Nominalism will erupt in our churches if we refuse to dig into God's Word on Sunday, if we refuse to preach it with authority, if we downgrade the importance of prayer, and if we water down the meaning and admonitions of Scripture. Nominal leaders will create nominal followers. But, it is also true that God can work through revived shepherds to revive the sheep. Nominalism doesn't have to be the state of the church forever, though sadly in too many places it will be.

Let us deal with the state of our own hearts, refusing to become nominal in our faith and choosing rather to be fully devoted to the will and purposes of God. Lukewarm Christians make God sick (Revelation 3:16), so may we be those who are fired up about our Lord.

#12
JUDGE WITH RIGHTEOUS JUDGMENT

In a day and age of tolerance, there is pressure to turn a blind eye to evil deeds. Greater still, there is a pull from society to not even call evil "evil" or good "good." Some will even rebuke Christians who do point out evil on the grounds that the Bible says that we shouldn't judge. We are told to stop judging people and to be more accepting. Society thus wants us to stop differentiating right from wrong and acceptable from unacceptable. They would have us remove all standards of discernment, and they refuse to recognize that Christ will judge them once and for all after they die. Judgment is a reality of the way the world has been designed. We cannot escape from it, and as Christians we have a calling to exercise righteous judgment.

Matthew 7:1 says, "Do not judge so that you will not be judged." Jesus here is not forbidding judgment of any kind. His point is to show that some people judge from a self-righteous, condemning, and hypocritical stance. They point out slivers in the eyes of others not because they care but because they get some cheap thrill from faultfinding as if it makes them feel better about themselves. Some are so self-righteous that they are even blind to their own hypocrisy, being unable to see the log in their own eyes. Jesus is condemning self-righteousness, hypocrisy, and an inability to judge ourselves rightly, which we must do (1 Corinthians 11:29). In no way does Matthew 7:1 forbid discernment. In fact, later in Matthew 7 Christ explains that we can discern true believers from false teachers based upon their fruit. Christ's intention is not to forbid judgment that evaluates between right and wrong, moral and immoral. What Jesus is saying is not to usurp the place of God, Who alone can cast into hell (Luke 12:5).

God sees all, and He will judge sin righteously. Our job is to let God be God and to love and share the gospel with those whom we have discerned through righteous judgment to not be acting righteously. This is the point of John 7:24 which says, "Do not judge according to appearance, but judge with righteous judgment." Righteous judgment sees sin for what it is, and it is not afraid to point it out. But this judgment becomes unrighteous when it stems from "holier-than-thou" motives or when it seeks to condemn rather than to restore. Galatians 6:1 says, "Brethren, even if anyone is caught in any trespass, you who are spiritual, restore such a one in a spirit of gentleness; each one looking to yourself, so that you too will not be tempted." Righteous judgment recognizes that some people are spiritual and some are not, being carnal and mired in sin. If someone who is spiritual finds a brother or sister in sin, they are to restore them in a spirit of gentleness. Clearly this requires discernment and an understanding of right and wrong. Yet it need not cross into unrighteous condemning judgment. A spirit of gentleness and being intentional about seeking restoration are essential to righteous judgment. When we see a fellow Christian sin, we need to confront the sin (after we have dealt with our own hearts) but humbly, graciously, and with an understanding that we are not above the potential to do the very same thing.

Unrighteous, self-righteous judgment is ugly and repulsive to a world desperately in need of Christ. If Christ judged as these folks judge, He would have never come to earth and died for us. But He loved us even while we were yet sinners and died for us (Romans 5:8). The mentality and focus of the Christian ought to be to save sinners and restore believers, not to judge and condemn, though we definitely need to exercise discernment. When Christianity deteriorates into keeping records of wrongs and looking over one another's shoulders in suspicion and even with a hope of catching another in sin, we have fallen far from Christ's call.

In a day and age where judgment has been itself condemned, we need to judge righteously. There is a shortage of discernment in a time that demands an abundance. For the sake of the lost, for our brothers and sisters struggling with sin, for our own spiritual well-being, and for the glory of Christ, let us judge righteously and love unconditionally.

#13

BIBLICAL UNITY

Isn't it strange that when the world claims to desire unity that its emphasis is rapidly becoming diversity? This is because the world cannot solve the problem of disunity, it cannot stop wars, and it cannot bring peace. Only Christ can change a heart and cause a person to esteem others more highly than himself. Only Christ is the answer. Obviously then, the world's approach of tolerance will not work. Tolerance merely accepts the reality that differences, conflicts, disagreements, and contradictions are here to stay. It thus tells people that there is no right or wrong position, belief, or behavior, but that all people are just different. When tolerance becomes the rule, true unity becomes impossible because truth is cast aside. Tolerance stops pursuing truth, opting in exchange for the acceptance of all ideas and practices. The bitter irony of the tolerance and diversity agenda is that it cannot tolerate or embrace as equally valid those who hold to universal truth or who believe in an exclusively right religion. Therein it is self-defeating.

Tolerance emphasizes differences, while the Bible emphasizes unity. Tolerance says that it accepts all things and people, but it is unable to truly love others. It merely tolerates them. Christianity, on the other hand, says that, though others might be different and even wrong about something, they can still be loved. Tolerance doesn't love others enough to tell them that they are wrong, unless of course they are being "intolerant." The bottom line is that if tolerance is practiced in the church, then truth will be minimized, love will be exchanged for acceptance, and true Biblical unity will be forfeited.

John 17:21-23 says,

> "That they may all be one; even as You, Father, are in Me and I in You, that they also may be in Us, so that the world may believe that You sent Me. The glory which You have given Me I have given to them, that they may be one, just as We are one; I in them and You in Me, that they may be perfected in unity, so that the world may know that You sent Me, and loved them, even as You have loved Me."

This passage leaves no doubt that true unity comes by people being in Christ as they repent of their sin and put their faith in Him. Christ prays for His disciples and for all who would come after them (the church) that they would be unified. This unity can only happen if we are grafted into Christ by faith. Unity thus requires an adherence to truth, which is personified by Christ Himself, Who is the truth (John 14:6). True unity is that we be one as Jesus and the Father are one. Jesus and the Father are literally one God, believing the same things, thinking the same things, doing the same things, and so on. There is nothing that is more indicative of oneness than the example of Jesus and the Father. Jesus said that those who have seen Him have seen the Father (John 14:9). True unity then, as Jesus prays, is that we join Their unity, being in Them. It is Jesus in us, the Father in Jesus, and, by implication, us in the Father and in Jesus. We are made part of Christ's body, spiritually speaking. True unity requires that we receive Christ as our Savior and Lord and let Him indwell us. So only through Jesus, Who is the Truth, can unity ever be possible.

If we as God's people want to be unified, we must become more and more like Christ. We do this as we apply His Word and understand it. John 17:17, just a few verses earlier, is a lead-in to Christ's prayer for unity. He gives us, in essence, the key to pursuing this unity among

41

brothers and sisters in Christ. He prays to the Father, "Sanctify them in the word; Your word is truth." True unity will increase as we are conformed to the Word of God in belief and obedience. It is through right understanding of the Scripture that true unity takes place.

Some Christians erroneously encourage a settling for a plurality of viewpoints in the church. Not being conformed to the truth, the church of plurality becomes a church of tolerance. We just agree to disagree. This is the world coming into the church. The fact is that somebody is right and somebody is wrong. Some denominations are right on some things, and others are right on others. The very meaning of the word "denomination" implies inherent division and disagreement. The problem with this is that Christ's prayer is not speaking of merely the invisible unity that the professing body of Christ should possess but a visible unity that the world can see, perceive, and through which it can be impacted. The goal of Christ's prayer is that the world would know and believe that the Father sent the Son and that the Son loved His people. If the church is not unified visibly, then the progress of the gospel is obstructed. The only way that true visible unity will happen is if true invisible unity occurs first. This can only happen, not if we learn to just accept different traditions as all valid and equal versions, but if we pursue the truth according to the infallible Word of God.

This is not mere rhetoric or wishful thinking. Christ prayed for it, and we should to. The fact of the matter is that the Spirit's job is to lead believers into all truth, not just some truth or the truth that pertains merely to the basics of Christian belief (John 16:13). His purpose and mission is to draw us into Christ and God according to the word of the Father. If we are to be one as God and Christ are one, the Spirit must apply the Word of God to our hearts. We must yield ourselves humbly to finding out what Scripture says. Theology books may say one thing, seminaries and their doctrinal systems another, and denominational leaders yet another, but the Bible says the truth. If true unity is ever to be manifested on earth, it will only be in the church of Jesus Christ and only as it conforms to the truth of God's Word.

The world's attempts at unity are feeble and false at best. Only Christ can bring true, full, and lasting unity. If the church wants to be a picture of visible unity, it will be by faith in Christ as we grow in Him according to the truth of the Bible (Ephesians 4:11-13). Perfected unity won't happen until we are glorified, but in the meantime, let us seek Biblical unity by faith in Christ by pursuing a growing understanding of the Bible and by humbly yielding to the Spirit within us as He guides us into all truth.

#14
ESCAPING THE DARK HOLE OF DEPRESSION

Maybe you haven't been all out depressed in your life. Then again, maybe you have. Regardless of where you have been or where you find yourself now, there is hope. Any who have been able to escape depression's grasp can testify to the power and faithfulness of God. There is no need to remain mired in depression, and, better yet, it is possible to keep from getting there in the first place.

Now some people can't relate to depression at all. They just don't understand how some people can get so down on life that they can't even get out of bed. But it all depends on how we are wired. Some people react to stress externally and some people escape internally. Depression is the internal escape, though both means are unbiblical. If we haven't had to encounter depression yet, we will likely one way or another. Yes, even church people suffer from depression. We need to have some understanding of it lest we fall into it ourselves or fail to be the difference in helping to bring a loved one out of it.

Depression's power may well be that those who are succumbing to it can sense it, but they don't know how to stop it. This causes further concern and speeds up the descent into the dark abyss. Fortunately, depression is not so mysterious. In fact, it is a natural fleshly response to difficulty for many people. We all deal with rejection and hardship in life, some more than others. Failures set us back, suffering wears us down, and temptation prods us day after day. Some give into a fleshly indulgence to cope, others lash out in anger and aggression, and others escape into depression. Depression is thus one unbiblical way of handling stress in life. Like Jonah, we do ourselves no good to run from the issues at hand. We must face the trials and the pain head on by the power of Christ, even rejoicing. Fortunately, God pursues us in our trials as He did Jonah, even venturing through our dark valleys with us (Psalm 23:4).

There are times when medications are necessary to overcome depression. Our bodies can develop chemical imbalances that God has graciously provided medicine to resolve. But sometimes things aren't this simple. *Ultimately, depression stems from a preoccupation with self.* There may be triggers of rejection, anger, bitterness, grief, loss, and so on, but these don't necessarily lead to depression even in people prone to it. It is when we don't trust God, when we doubt His love, when we question His character, when we challenge His justice, and when we dwell on ourselves, our situation, our circumstances, and our misfortunes. The road to escape from depression is away from self and toward God and others. Depression may well be defined as a pity party with self as the only participant.

This can be difficult because sometimes we don't realize that we are self-consumed when we really are. It can be as subtle as thinking about why God doesn't answer our prayers, bless us, help us, give something to us, or so on, when we ought to be dwelling on Christ. Isaiah 26:3 says, "The steadfast of mind You will keep in perfect peace, because he trusts in You." Rather than thinking about Christ and our eternal hope (1 Peter 1:13), we begin thinking about ourselves and our situation. Rather than anxiously analyzing, reflecting, and pondering our "hopeless" present, painful past, and overwhelming future, we ought to thankfully give our requests to God in prayer and supplication (Philippians 4:6), forgetting what is behind and pressing on toward the upward call of Christ (Philippians 3:13). *We need to let Him carry the burdens that we were never meant to carry.* Trying to fix things in our own power and solving our dilemmas in our own strength is doomed to lead to defeat and, for some, eventual depression. We must fix our minds on Christ and what is good, right, noble, pure, and so on (Philippians 4:8). We must be thinking of others' welfare ahead of our own even if they seem to be having it much easier than we do. We must think of God rather than ourselves so we don't commit idolatry of self. If we do this, we can be assured that the peace of God will guard our hearts and minds in Christ (Philippians 4:7). Victory through Christ is our promise.

So when we feel the walls closing in and life begins to overwhelm us, we must accept that we can become perplexed, but we must not despair (2 Corinthians 4:8). We may be clueless as to what is going on and totally at a loss as to what to do, but we must not curse God and turn to self. We cannot get to the point of despair. Despair is an accusation against a holy God that He is unjust and unfair, for it means that we believe that He is not worthy of our hope and trust. Christians need not despair because our God cares for us. He may allow difficulty, but it is because He cares. He may not answer our prayers how we want, but it is because He knows better. He may bless somebody in ways that seem disproportionate, but it will only be because He has something good and perfect in the works for us.

If we find ourselves depressed, we must ask ourselves if we have lost faith. We must repent of any doubt, mistrust, resentment, self-preoccupation, or other sin. We must believe that God will bring us through because He loves us and because He is faithful. Even if circumstances confine us to our beds, we can still have joy. Let us not let circumstances steal what only God can provide and what is rightfully ours as children of the Lord. When we feel our feet sinking and our strength failing us, may we let Psalm 40:2 be our comfort: "He brought me up out of the pit of destruction, out of the miry clay, and He set my feet upon a rock making my footsteps firm."

#15

THE MINISTRY OF COMFORT

Suffering is a reality of life, and it is not going to go away any time soon. Only heaven is free of suffering. In the meantime, we will suffer, loved ones will suffer, friends will hurt, and those in our sphere of influence will experience pain, some more severely than others. There will be times when it will be our turn to be comforted, and there will be times when it will be our role to do the comforting. Those who have experienced comfort know how valuable a ministry this is. Those who have not experienced it in their time of need know how badly it is needed. The ability to appropriately and genuinely comfort is a powerful ministry.

The best comforters are those who genuinely care and are able to express their care. It is not necessarily comforting when someone tells us in our time of need, "Well, things could always be worse. After all, there's got to be somebody who has it worse off than you." Maybe there is, and maybe there is not. Suffering, though it is universal, is often very unique to the person. It brings little to no comfort at all to know that things could be worse when things are as utterly bad as they are. Another well-meaning technique that typically fails is to try to help the person solve their problems. There may be a time for this, but we need to be discerning to know when a person has done all that they can do. If indeed they have, then our "friendly" advice comes across as judging their suffering as self-inflicted when we may not mean that at all. If a person asks for help, we can help. If they simply are hurting, we need to comfort them. Comfort and problem-solving are not necessarily the same. The worst technique is to question someone's spirituality or integrity because of their suffering. It is extremely hurtful when a person concludes that we might be in pain or experiencing difficult circumstances because we lack faith or are in sin. If we are in the wrong either way, we shouldn't be offended, but it is not wise to assume that suffering is to be equated with weak faith or sin. Job's "friends" did this by pressing him repeatedly to own up to a wrong that he didn't commit. They thought suffering meant a lack of faith and obedience, which it did not. This didn't bring Job any comfort whatsoever for obvious reasons. He says in Job 21:34, "How then will you vainly comfort me, for your answers remain full of falsehood?" Attempts at comfort are vain if we don't care, if we don't try to empathize, if we judge, and if we play the blame game. Yet there is one more common error. This is another form of vain comfort, and it is to offer hope that God has not promised. Zechariah 10:2 says, "For the teraphim speak iniquity, and the diviners see lying visions and tell false dreams; they comfort in vain. Therefore the people wander like sheep; they are afflicted, because there is no shepherd." Those who should have been teachers and shepherds of the people did not speak the truth of the Word of God but rather their own empty promises of false hope. This is downright cruel to do to a person in suffering. An example would be saying "Things will get better" or "It will be alright." Things may not get better or be alright. In fact, in some instances, things will get worse. This is why we need to speak the truth of God's Word that He is with the person in suffering and not make promises that God has not made.

Christ provides the ultimate example of what it means to comfort. Psalm 23:4 says, "Even though I walk through the valley of the shadow of death, I fear no evil, for You are with me; Your rod and Your staff, they comfort me." The key phrase is that Jesus is with us. He is not absent in our suffering, for He is suffering alongside of us. He is not taking the literal insult or succumbing to the actual disease, but His presence is our comfort. It is good enough just to know that He loves us and cares for us. It is sufficient to know that He is in complete control even when we hurt. It is enough to know that we have Him. Thus, following Christ's example, the best way to bring others comfort (albeit imperfectly when compared to Christ) is for them to know that we support them, that we feel for them, that we care for them, and that we won't abandon them in their time of need. *The state of being comforted is a state of knowing that Someone (and hopefully someone) is there to watch over us and take care of us out of real and genuine love for us.* Comfort thus implies confidence in a person and trust in their loyalty and goodness to us. Those who are fair weather friends are not going to bring us much comfort. The greatest comforters are those who, unlike Job's friends, help get us through the struggle. Why didn't Job's friends mourn with Job? Why didn't they pray for him? Why didn't they bring him food or ointment for his sores? Why didn't they affirm their commitment to him to do what they could to support him and his wife? They offered Job nothing except criticism and judgment, the archenemies of comfort. If we want to be skilled in the ministry of comfort, we must learn to have sympathy, compassion, understanding, and a commitment to bring our friends and loved ones through no matter what it takes. If people sense that our comfort is conditional, it will be just that.

Where is the person who sympathizes? Where is the person who will try to understand and listen? Where is the person who will offer a shoulder to cry on? Where is the person who weeps with those who weep (Romans 12:15)? Psalm 69:20 says, "Reproach has broken my heart and I am so sick, and I looked for sympathy, but there was none, and for comforters, but I found none." David expresses that he has no one to comfort him. Of course, God is there for him, but what a shame it is and what pain it brings when those on earth who should be comforters fail us. It is an awful reality, but it happens, sadly even in the church. So what do we do when we find ourselves comfortless and alone? We must find our comfort in Christ (2 Corinthians 1:3-5) and in His Word (Psalm 119:50), both of which are sufficient, praise the Lord.

Acts 9:31 says, "So the church throughout all Judea and Galilee and Samaria enjoyed peace, being built up; and going on in the fear of the Lord *and in the comfort of the Holy Spirit*, it continued to increase" (italics mine). God is a God of comfort, and it is time that we, His people, learn to be effective ministers of His comfort. May God give us grace in this extremely important ministry.

#16

IN LIFE'S WEARINESS,
DON'T GROW WEARY OF GOD

Life can be very wearying at times for a variety of reasons. Perhaps we have wearied ourselves with our sin (Jeremiah 9:5). Perhaps life has just pushed us physically and emotionally to great lengths, and we are simply tired and worn out. Maybe we have reduced the Christian life to a legalistic system of standards and performance that has made living tiresome. If we have sinned, we must repent. If we are simply languished, there is a time for rest. If we are relying upon self for sanctification, we need to surrender control and come under grace. God's call to the Christian is perseverance and finishing strong. We will battle fatigue, indifference, and the flesh, but we must continue to believe and do good. Galatians 6:9 says, "Let us not lose heart in doing good, for in due time we will reap if we do not grow weary" (see also 2 Thessalonians 3:13). God makes a conditional promise here by saying that we will bear fruit and gain eternal rewards at the proper time if we don't lose heart and grow weary. In fact, if we lose heart in our praying, we are not to expect answers (Luke 18:1-8). Thus, it is of great importance that we know how strength can be sustained and renewed.

The context in Galatians 6 is speaking of sowing to the Spirit versus sowing to the flesh. What God is driving at in His command that we persevere in doing good is that we would continue to bear fruit, both internal and external. We are to be taking care that our heart motivations are right, that our thoughts are pure, and that the fruit of the Spirit is evident in our lives. We are also to be active in serving others by bearing their burdens and showing them good will such that they will see our good works and glorify our Father in heaven (Matthew 5:16). Both internal and external components should be a regular reality for the Christian. If we slough off in either, we will have violated Galatians 6:9, failing to persevere, giving in to spiritual apathy, and losing our first love.

The answer to sustained Spirit-filled living is not merely Christian activity. The church at Ephesus in Revelation 2 continued to stand for truth and defend sound doctrine. They didn't tolerate false teaching, and their good works were abundant. God's issue with them, however, was that they lost their first love. Initially, they did things because they enjoyed God and the pleasure of serving Him, but as time passed, their works became form and function rather than the outworking of love and the abundant life in Christ. The same thing happened to the people of Israel in Malachi's time. In Malachi 1:13, God confronted Israel because they had been saying that His work was "tiresome." God always wants a heart of devotion, love, passion, and commitment. Perseverance isn't simply continuing in doing the "right things," but it is a matter of being driven and controlled by the love of God.

If we have been exasperated or if we have lost heart, the ultimate answer is to look to Jesus. Hebrews 12:3 says, "For consider Him who has endured such hostility by sinners against Himself, so that you may not grow weary and lose heart." When we feel ourselves growing tired of God and ministry, we must consider Jesus. Jesus' life was brutal with many rejections and more suffering than we can conceive of. Yet He endured it, and by His power at work in us, we can persevere in heartfelt service as well. When our strength fails and we feel that we can't go on, Christ is our hope. He never grows tired or weary, and He promises to renew the strength of those who wait upon Him (Isaiah 40:28-31). Relying on willpower alone to sustain us spiritually is not going to suffice, but trusting in God's sufficient grace to work in and through our weakness will (2 Corinthians 12:9-10).

So if we are sensing a spiritual weariness and a loss of joy in the things of God, here is what we must do. We must acknowledge our condition as sin. Isaiah 43:22 says, "Yet you have not called on Me, O Jacob; But you have become weary of Me, O Israel." The issue is that we grow weary of God. Since God is to be the source of our joy and since worship is to be directed toward Him, our issue fundamentally when we lose heart must stem from a spiritual "fatigue" with God. He becomes a bore to us, we put Him on the back burner, or we don't care to commune with Him through reading His Word or prayer. We don't give God the time of day because we have "other interests." It is at this point that we must acknowledge the reality of our spiritual slide and draw near to God Who will, in turn, draw near to us (James 4:8). God alone is the supplier of strength, so when spiritual fatigue enters our lives, we must acknowledge it, repent of it, and let God be our joy. As God becomes our joy, we can trust that strength will soon follow after as we wait upon Him. As Nehemiah 8:10 says, "The joy of the LORD is your strength."

Are you losing spiritual strength? Better said, have you lost your joy in God Himself? Repent, and let God be your joy; His strength and grace will soon follow.

#17

THE SECRET TO BEING CONTENT

Contentment is a tough thing to learn, but our God is able to teach us. Even Paul spoke of having to learn to be content, as if it was a struggle for him. He says in Philippians 4:11-13,

> "Not that I speak from want, for I have learned to be content in whatever circumstances I am. I know how to get along with humble means, and I also know how to live in prosperity; in any and every circumstance I have learned the secret of being filled and going hungry, both of having abundance and suffering need. I can do all things through Him who strengthens me."

Paul had spent much time in desperate need, and at this time, he informed the Philippians that he had an abundance, thanks to faithful giving on the part of the church. Though he was grateful for their gifts, he did not put his ultimate confidence in material possessions, provisions, or even people. There will be times in life when we may have little, and there may be times when we have more than we need. Contentment, like joy, peace, and other gracious provisions of God, is not dependent upon circumstances. When things go well, we must remember that what God gives, He can also take away. Thus, we are to bless the name of the Lord for being God and the source of blessing, not exchanging our confidence in God for material possessions or even God's good gifts themselves (Job 1:21). When things go poorly, we must remember that God is still faithful and on the throne. Thus, whether in times of abundance or in times of lack, our confidence, hope, and trust must be anchored in Christ.

Paul's secret to contentment was that he found his hope, his confidence, and his sufficiency in Christ alone Who would give him strength to do His will (v. 13). The process of learning to be content is a process of coming to believe that, ultimately, God is in control, and we are not. *Contentment rests in the sufficiency of Christ and His Word.* Unless we understand our dependence upon God, believe it, embrace it, and rejoice in it, contentment will elude us. Contentment finds its strength, confidence, and hope in the sufficiency of Christ, in the promises of God, in the unchanging character of God, and in the complete adequacy of the Word of God. When we have all of these things, what more do we need? What can the world provide us that would make us exchange what we have and put our confidence in something else? In Christ we have all of the sufficiency and strength that we need to do His will.

Contentment rests in the good and sovereign purposes of God. If we have a view of God as all-powerful, all-knowing, sovereign, good, and perfectly and impartially loving, then there is no reason not to be content in what He ordains, allows, orchestrates, and provides. As Joseph said to his brothers who had done him great evil, "As for you, you meant evil against me, but God meant it for good" (Genesis 50:20). Because of God's promises, character, and Word, we can always have confidence that all that we experience is meant to work some ultimate good in us and perhaps for many others as well. Indeed, "God causes all things to work together for good to those who love God, to those who are called according to His purpose" (Romans 8:28). No experience, whether good or bad, is purposeless. We are called for God's purposes, and we can trust that God will use all events to work good for those who love God. Christ's cross, the most unfair and brutal thing ever endured on this earth, worked for the greatest good of all time in providing salvation to those who believe. God had a purpose in this, and He has a purpose in our lives also. Knowing this, wherever we are, we can be content as we acknowledge Him and put our trust in Him (Proverbs 3:5-6).

Finally, *contentment rests in God's boundless love*. Paul says in Ephesians 3:17-19, "[That you] being rooted and grounded in love, may be able to comprehend with all the saints what is the breadth and length and height and depth, and to know the love of Christ which surpasses knowledge, that you may be filled up to all the fullness of God." Whether we are in a prison cell or in a palace, we can be content if we know, believe, and trust in God's love. Whether we are in a loving family or a family mired in sin, we can be content knowing that God loves us. Whether we are the most gifted person in the world or partially or totally disabled, we can be content if we rest in the love of God. God's love is to fill us up such that our cup overflows (Psalm 23:5). His love is always available and abundant, and therein we can find contentment.

If we find ourselves panicking or doubting when we have needs, perhaps even using sinful measures to try to meet them, we need to learn contentment. If we find ourselves becoming self-sufficient and prideful when we have more than we need, we need to learn contentment. If we have just what we need, we need to acknowledge God's provision and thank Him. No matter our situation, contentment is worth learning, so may God in His great grace teach it to us.

#18

FULLY FORGIVEN

It is absolutely true that Christ died for sin once for all (Hebrews 7:27). His sacrifice encompasses all sin, past, present, and future. Of course, only those who repent of their sins and place their trust in Christ for forgiveness are able to experience Christ's cleansing. It is a sad thing that many reject the gift of salvation which Christ has offered to them. Yet the glory for those who have received Christ is that we are presented in Christ's righteousness before the Father. Christ's holiness makes us holy before God and able to have a relationship with Him. Ephesians 2:6 says that we are even seated with Christ in the heavenly places. In the assurances of Christ's sacrifice, we are already seated in heaven with Christ. We are thus, in a sense of position, identity, and calling, totally forgiven and holy. When it comes to our salvation, our eternity in Christ is sure because our righteousness is based in what He did, which is a done deal.

Colossians 1:13-14 says, "For He rescued us from the domain of darkness, and transferred us to the kingdom of His beloved Son, in whom we have redemption, the forgiveness of sins." As if speaking of a legal contractual agreement being signed and sealed, we were officially transferred from Satan's ownership to God's and forgiven of our sins. Colossians 2:13-14 echoes this idea, saying,

> "When you were dead in your transgressions and the uncircumcision of your flesh, He made you alive together

with Him, having forgiven us all our transgressions, having canceled out the certificate of debt consisting of decrees against us, which was hostile to us; and He has taken it out of the way, having nailed it to the cross."

We had a debt that we couldn't pay because of our sin, but Christ paid it, nailing the burden of our sins to the cross. The result is that we can, by faith in Christ's work on our behalf and our corresponding repentance, be forgiven of all our sins because our debt is cancelled. This is a permanent, once-for-all forgiveness, which we can praise God for each and every day.

Yet the unfortunate reality of our human condition is that we are not yet perfected; thus, we still sin. We cannot let this go unaddressed, for it grieves the Spirit (Ephesians 4:20), quenches the Spirit (1 Thessalonians 5:19), and keeps us from enjoying the privileges that we have in Christ such as joy, peace, and the manifest presence of God (see Psalm 51:11-12). Furthermore, we will be powerless in terms of bearing true spiritual fruit that endures the fiery test of the judgment seat of Christ (1 Corinthians 3:10-15). Sin needs to be dealt with, and this is why the Spirit convicts our hearts of it. We feel guilty because we are. If we are indeed children of God, it is not that we jeopardize our eternity when we sin, but it is that we dishonor God and jeopardize our rewards in eternity. Sin certainly has consequences, and we need to confess it.

The prodigal son provides a great illustration of the need to confess our sin and receive the forgiveness of Christ. He was always the son of the father, though for a time, he didn't live like it. When he returned to his senses and repented, he recognized that he needed to go and make things right between him and his father. He went home and told his father that he had sinned, and he realized rightly that there was nothing he could do to earn back his father's favor. Yet what he didn't realize was that he had never lost his father's favor, only the benefits of enjoying his fellowship and blessing. His father was deeply grieved, but he still loved his son and wanted him back. He didn't make the son do penance or remove his standing as a son. He received him openly and with celebration. The son was always loved by his father because he was his son. We, who have trusted Christ by faith, will always be His children (John 1:12), and He will always love us (Hebrews 13:5). All that is His is ours (Luke 15:31). We are positionally forgiven in Christ, but we sometimes forget what we have in Jesus and choose to indulge the flesh, follow Satan, and please the world. We run like the prodigal to riotous, self-centered living. Yet when we come to our senses and realize that sin is no fun in the end (Psalm 32:3-4, 1 Corinthians 5:5), we want to return to our Father. Did He ever leave us? No. Did He ever forsake us even if we forsook Him? No way. He is simply waiting to pour out His grace on us and receive us back again. Forgiveness has already been provided for in the blood of Christ. What we need to do is own up to our sin (confess), forsake it (repent), and receive the cleansing (be forgiven) of Christ (see Psalm 32:5, Psalm 51:10, 12, 17). Once we have asked Christ to cleanse our hearts from sin, we simply need to believe that we are received by God in grace and love. There is nothing more that we have to do. We don't have to "redeem ourselves," for we have already been redeemed in Christ. We don't have to perform or earn our way back into God's favor. We simply have to embrace it by faith as we fall into His embrace.

So, positionally, we are clean (John 15:3), but practically and conditionally we can get dirty. When we do sin, let's confess it quickly, repent promptly, and sprint into the forgiving arms of our Lord.

#19

A LESSON IN COMPASSION

Most of us know the story of Jonah. We know that he ran from God, we know that he was in the belly of a fish for three days and three nights, and we know that he preached to Nineveh, at which point the entire city repented. God had told Jonah to proclaim to this wicked city that destruction and judgment was imminent if they would not repent. Upon hearing Jonah's message of judgment, Nineveh repented. This greatly angered and upset Jonah. Why was this? Jonah 4:2 says, "[Jonah] prayed to the LORD and said, 'Please LORD, was not this what I said while I was still in my own country? Therefore in order to forestall this I fled to Tarshish, for I knew that You are a gracious and compassionate God, slow to anger and abundant in lovingkindness, and one who relents concerning calamity.'" Jonah ran from God not only because he was disobedient but because he believed that, if he preached of God's judgment to Nineveh, Nineveh would repent, and God, in turn, would relent of the calamity which He was planning to bring upon them. Jonah wanted to see Nineveh wiped off the face of the earth. He disliked, even hated, these pagan people. They were not his countrymen, but some foreign strangers. What were they to him? Clearly, in his mind, it didn't matter that they were people who would spend eternity in hell if God destroyed them. He wanted to see them get their just due now. He had absolutely no compassion for these wicked people. His refusal to obey God was not about not wanting to preach, being afraid of going to this foreign nation because of what they might do to him, or just that he would rather do something else, being simply selfish. These things were not Jonah's primary issues. He believed, knowing that God is a God of mercy and compassion, that if by chance Nineveh did repent, then he wouldn't get the pleasure of seeing them get wiped out. Jonah had confidence in the power of the Word of God being preached. He dreaded that it might accomplish what God set it forth to do and actually cause this evil nation to repent. He wanted to see these people annihilated, and it was for this reason that he fled.

Once God made it clear to Jonah that He had relented, Jonah was extremely angry and upset to the extent that he asked God to take his life (Jonah 4:3). Still defiantly hoping judgment might come, he went out to some place east of the city where he could wait to see what would happen (Jonah 4:5). This was one angry, bitter, and depressed person all because God had shown mercy to people he didn't particularly like or care for. He wanted to see them destroyed, and the "show" was cancelled.

Jonah, though a prophet of God, needed some instruction and correction from God. The irony is that God had been extremely merciful to Jonah, but Jonah would show no mercy to others. Even as he rebelliously fled to Tarshish, God caused some of the pagan sailors to call upon the name of the Lord and fear Him (Jonah 1:16), working good out of a bad situation. God's mercy to him continued as He appointed a fish to swallow him, lest he drown in the storm. When Jonah repented in the stomach of the fish, God had mercy and ordered the fish to vomit him up on dry land. And despite Jonah's questionable motives, God still used him to bring about a revival of an incredible magnitude. Given that there were 120,000 in Nineveh who didn't know the difference between their right and left hand (likely referring to young, innocent children), we could infer that there were at least several hundred thousand or more people in the entire city. Scripture says that the people of Nineveh, from the greatest to the least, believed in God (Jonah 3:5). But rather than praise God for changing these hearts and sparing their souls and even having the chance to be involved in such a work, Jonah grew angry unto death. God had been so compassionate to him over and over again, but he missed it or refused to acknowledge it. He had no problem with God showing him compassion, but he simply wouldn't be merciful to others.

In the end of the book, God drilled the message home to Jonah. He appointed a plant to miraculously grow up around Jonah to provide shade for him from the scorching sun. This made Jonah happy (Jonah 4:6). God then appointed a worm to eat the plant, causing it to wither, followed by a scorching east wind which made the heat unbearable. Jonah again said to God that he wanted to die, for he missed his plant on which he had had compassion. God's question for Jonah was this:

> "You had compassion on the plant for which you did not work and which you did not cause to grow, which came up overnight and perished overnight. Should I not have compassion on Nineveh, the great city in which there are more than 120,000 persons who do not know the difference between their right and left hand, as well as many animals?" (Jonah 4:10-11).

God was constantly compassionate to Jonah, wanting him to repent and hoping to teach him to have compassion on others. He was so self-centered that he missed his plant, mourning over its death, when he wanted to gloat in the death of hundreds of thousands of innocent lives. As the book closes, it does not tell us whether Jonah repented or not. The message, however, is clear. God is a God of compassion, and He continually pursues us, trying to teach us to be conformed to His ways. Yet we must choose to repent and have compassion on others.

Are we like Jonah? Are there people we so despise that we would love to see them die in their sins? Do we care about their souls and the fact that they, if they do not repent, will spend an eternity in hell? What about the innocent children who suffer because of the sins of others? Do we care? Christianity, at its core, must be compassionate because Christ is compassionate. If we all got what we deserved, including Jonah, we all would be judged and wiped off the face of the earth. But God has been compassionate to us, even giving up His own Son for us while we were yet sinners (Romans 5:8). God loves the unlovely, the unlovable, and those who hate Him. Thus, He gives us Christ. Yet we must repent of our sins, receive His gift, and choose to show compassion on others as He has had compassion on us.

May God compassionately pursue us and teach us to be merciful as He did Jonah.

#20

Resolve to Follow Christ

Sometimes as a new calendar year begins, people make resolutions to be different, to do certain things less, and to commit to doing certain things more. Yet there is nothing inherently miraculous about a new calendar year which will enable us to make accurate resolutions and then keep them. There is nothing inherently wrong with making resolutions, but why should we wait for a new year to be doing so? The Biblical model is to focus on being like Christ daily, being resolute to live as servants of Him all the time.

The reality is that, for many people, New Year's resolutions, or any resolutions for that matter, don't last but a few days or weeks, if even that long. Eventually, old habits and behavior patterns return, and the resolutions are abandoned or forgotten. Yet the sad thing is that once the calendar switches years again, the same resolutions may well be made again only to suffer the same fate of a breakdown of willpower and perseverance. So how does lasting change occur and how can we be sure that our resolutions lead to actual, true growth?

If we choose to make resolutions, we need to be sure that they are Biblical in nature. There is nothing wrong with wanting to be a better spouse or parent, learning a proper work-home balance, or trying to get into better shape. But these resolutions are meaningless if they are not grounded in a conviction by the Holy Spirit as to specific ways in which we need to change. General terms of "betterment," "growth," and "improvement" need to be measured by specific Scriptural admonitions and standards. If our hearts are not burdened over a failure to honor God by submitting to His Word, we may modify our behavior for a time, but we will fail at changing our hearts and having our minds conformed to God's Word.

The process of true growth according to the Bible is called sanctification. It is God working in our hearts by His grace through our faith to convict us of sin, to move us to forsake that sin, and to love and desire His ways. We need to go to God's Word and listen to the Spirit of God at work in our hearts to know where we need to change. David prayed in Psalm 139:23-24, "Search me, O God, and know my heart; Try me and know my anxious thoughts; And see if there be any hurtful way in me, And lead me in the everlasting way." He wasn't simply resolving to try harder to be a better person. He was interested in learning where specifically he fell short of God's holy standards. He wanted to know where he had sin that he needed to be aware of so he could forsake it and thereby grow and change. His resolution was to walk in practical holiness as the Spirit of God led him in the everlasting way of God, as opposed to the ways of the world.

For Christians, making resolutions ought not to be that complex. All we need to do is to be in God's Word so that we can look at it like a mirror and then make the needed changes as God reveals our defects. James 1:22-25 says,

> "But prove yourselves doers of the word, and not merely hearers who delude themselves. For if anyone is a hearer of the word and not a doer, he is like a man who looks at his natural face in a mirror; for once he has looked at himself and gone away, he has immediately forgotten what kind of person he was. But one who looks intently at the perfect law, the law of liberty, and abides by it, not having become a forgetful hearer but an effectual doer, this man will be blessed in what he does."

The point is that God's Word is the mirror to our soul, and as we look into it with humble hearts, God will reveal places of error and fault.

Just as a person looks at himself in the mirror and doesn't present himself publicly until all the blemishes are covered and everything is just as it should be, so too are we to present ourselves spiritually. Romans 12:1 says that we need to present our bodies as living and holy sacrifices unto God. We cannot do this unless we look into the mirror of the Word so that we know where we need to change. Identifying where we need to change is no more complicated than being in God's Word and humbly yielding to the conviction of the Spirit.

The actual changing is really not any more complicated. Change is as simple as confessing our sin, repenting of it, and by faith walking by the Spirit in obedience. Might it be a struggle as Satan battles us and tries to tempt us and destroy our faith? Sure, we can count on more spiritual attacks as we deal with sin. For those who ignore what they see in the mirror, Satan already has won his victory, but as we change, there will be opposition. Yet Christ is able to strengthen us to stand against the wiles of the devil. We need Christ in Whom we have all that we need for life and godliness (2 Peter 1:3). Our willpower alone won't enable us to resist temptation. We need the grace of God and the faith to believe. Christ is our sufficiency, and our ability to be sustained in holiness and obedience is dependent upon our faith in Christ's power, grace, and faithfulness. May God give us grace to believe the truth of Scripture and the strength to walk in it.

Every day is a day to resolutely follow Jesus Christ. He alone can lead us to true and lasting change. May we listen to Him.

#21

EXCEL STILL MORE

When Paul, along with Timothy and Silvanus, wrote the first letter to the Thessalonians, they were overjoyed to hear of the faithfulness and love of their brethren at Thessalonica. This church, into which they had poured their lives, had indeed not succumbed to persecution from the Jews, but it had continued to grow. The writers were sure to gratefully acknowledge the growth of these believers, but almost within the same breath, they eagerly challenged them to excel still more. These missionaries were aware of Satan's schemes of undermining those who were doing well in growing in Christ. They could succumb to pride, to a mere going through the motions without the proper heart attitude, to a loss of their first love of the Lord, or to an attitude of superiority. Though they were making great progress and living to honor God, they were still vulnerable, for they, like us, had not yet been perfected. Only when we go to meet our Savior will our sanctification be complete. In the meantime, challenges will mount, sanctification must continue, and Satan will continue to try to tempt us, discourage us, and lead us astray. Our flesh is ever present with these mortal bodies, rendering with it the capacity to sin. This is why Paul and his brethren did not build up the egos of these people for being so great. They acknowledged their faithfulness and praised God for it, and then they quickly challenged them to keep on keeping on. They were not to stay merely as they were and persist in that same level of faithfulness, but they were to grow, improve, change, and become more and more like Christ.

The Thessalonians were challenged to excel still more in two specific areas. Again, it is not that they were doing poorly; in fact, they were acting very faithfully. It is just that their journey was not over yet, and there was growth that still needed to be accomplished. The first area is revealed in 1 Thessalonians 4:1-2 which says,

> "Finally then, brethren, we request and exhort you in the Lord Jesus, that as you received from us instruction as to how you ought to walk and please God (just as you actually do walk), that you excel still more. For you know what commandments we gave you by the authority of the Lord Jesus."

Paul and his fellow writers went on to describe specific areas in which these believers needed to continue to walk in holiness, ranging from sexual morality to living peaceably with others to working hard at what the Lord had given them to do. Perhaps they could be more faithful at work, perhaps they could be more thankful to God for their employment, perhaps they could treat their husbands or wives better, or perhaps they could sharpen their listening skills and argue less. The Spirit would have to reveal to each specifically where the growth needed to take place, but the message was clear. They knew the commandments of Scripture, and they knew that they were to live under the authority of Christ. They were doing well, but they needed to keep on doing better and better which God would enable them to do as He graciously showed them where and how they could grow.

The second area in which the Thessalonians were encouraged to excel still more is given in 4:9-10 which says,

> "Now as to the love of the brethren, you have no need for anyone to write to you, for you yourselves are taught by God to love one another; for indeed you do practice it toward all the brethren who are in all Macedonia. But we urge you, brethren, to excel still more."

These people were doing a fantastic job of loving one another, God, and all those in their region. This is a tremendous testimony of the essence of being disciples of Christ. Yet, lest they would settle for great instead of greater leading to ultimate perfection as Christ is perfect, they were reminded to keep growing in this area as well.

None of us are what we ultimately could be, should be, or will be. One day Christ will perfect us, but that day has not yet come as long as we have life and breath on this earth. God's will for us, as it was for these early believers, is to keep growing in Christ, not settling for decent, good, or even great. We must seek to excel still more in our understanding of God's Word, in our faithfulness to obey His commands, and in our love for God and others.

This is a tall order, and one in which we are, as in all things, dependent upon the grace of God. We must choose to have faith and honor Christ, but ultimately, we can rest in God's faithfulness to us. This letter closes with Paul and his brethren praying for the believers saying in 5:23-24,

> "Now may the God of peace Himself sanctify you entirely; and may your spirit and soul and body be preserved complete, without blame at the coming of our Lord Jesus Christ. Faithful is He who calls you, and He also will bring it to pass."

Let's do our part to excel still more as we rest in Christ Who will accomplish this in and through us as we yield to Him in faith and obedience. He is faithful, and He will bring it to pass. His grace is sufficient to accomplish this otherwise insurmountable task.

We must not grow complacent. We can't afford even to settle for excellence. Our calling is to excel still more, letting Christ work in us to make us blameless when He comes.

#22

HERE I AM, SEND ME

God is always looking for faithful men and women that He can support and empower to accomplish His will and purposes on this earth (2 Chronicles 16:9). He has given us a commission to be active in making disciples and to teach them all that He has commanded (Matthew 28:19-20). He wants workers, and He asks that we would pray for more workers to go out into the harvest (Luke 10:2). God's method in building His kingdom is by using willing and obedient servants, people who avail themselves to God's call upon their lives. For some, the call may be to foreign missions or to the ministry, but for most of us, we will be called to be ministers of the gospel even though our career paths might look much different. Wherever we are and in whatever we do, God is looking for people whom He can support to build His kingdom. He has missions for us to do, but the question is whether or not we will accept the call.

There is nothing particularly extraordinary about faithful men like Moses, Elijah, Isaiah, etc., at least in and of themselves. James makes that clear when he says, "Elijah was a man with a nature like ours" (James 5:17). He was human just like we are with all the faults and weaknesses and temptations. Yet he, like many other faithful men and women of old (Hebrews 11), was faithful to do what God asked him to do. We would do well to consider what it was that made these individuals take God up on His offer to serve, to be used mightily of

Him, to suffer for Him, and to lay aside the passing pleasures of sin in exchange for the glory of God. They were ordinary human beings, but they let God do extraordinary things in their lives.

Isaiah's commissioning to service gives us some insight into the perspective that is required for a person to come to view their lives as a servant of God and to sacrifice accordingly. In Isaiah 6, Isaiah received a vision of God seated on His high and exalted heavenly throne. That the train of His robe filled the entire temple was a symbol of total power and authority (Isaiah 6:1). Even the seraphim, angels Who minister in God's very throne room, maintained positions of reverence, covering their eyes and their feet while flying so that they wouldn't touch or see the holiness of God (Isaiah 6:2, Exodus 3:5). They called out to one another saying, "Holy, holy, holy is the LORD of hosts. The whole earth is full of His glory" (Isaiah 6:3). The three-fold emphasis of God's holiness is meant to be emphatic to the highest extent. The only right posture as the seraphim demonstrated was to bow, worship, and exalt. Deference to the King of Kings was the only thing that made sense. Add to Isaiah's experience the fact that the foundations of the room were shaking and the room was being filled with smoke, likely symbolizing God's glory indwelling the entire place. Isaiah couldn't take it anymore, being immersed with glory, perfection, and holiness, and he cried out, "Woe is me, for I am ruined! Because I am a man of unclean lips, And I live among a people of unclean lips; For my eyes have seen the King, the LORD of hosts" (Isaiah 6:5). In light of God's perfection and holiness, Isaiah was overwhelmed by his imperfections and sinfulness. It so sickened him that he thought that he was going to die. He recognized that he was unclean and that his people were unclean. But this is exactly what he needed to see. He needed to first see just how holy and wonderful God was before he could see his inadequacies and his need for change and sanctification. Only when we see God for Who He really is can we rightly deal with the true state of our own hearts which God will graciously enable us to do. In Isaiah's case, one of the seraphim took a burning coal from the altar before God and touched it to his mouth (Isaiah 6:6). The coal symbolized the holy cleansing of God sanctifying Isaiah and removing his sin (Isaiah 6:7). This encounter with the grace of God had to be so incredibly relieving and moving that it was something he could never forget and something he was eager to share with his people.

Now up to this point God had not spoken. Isaiah had only seen visions of Him, but then God asked a question. "Whom shall I send, and who will go for Us?" (Isaiah 6:8). The Us clearly refers to all three Persons of the Godhead, for the "I" and "Us" are used in the same sentence for the same God. This just serves to further convey the wonder, majesty, power, and uniqueness of God, and in this environment and asked by such a God, Isaiah's only reasonable answer was to volunteer himself. In Isaiah 6:8 he says, "Here I am. Send me." Interestingly, God didn't force Isaiah to volunteer. He merely asked if there was any who would go, and Isaiah said, "I'm available. I'll go." God doesn't force us to serve, but He works in our hearts so that we desire to volunteer for Him. We should come to see within ourselves the attitude that Isaiah possessed of willingly taking God up on His offer to serve for the kingdom of God.

Isaiah's commissioning ends with God giving Isaiah instructions about how hard his calling is going to be in that those to whom he preached by and large wouldn't listen (Isaiah 1:9-13). Yet, at this point, Isaiah has already committed himself. We are not given any evidence that he wanted to back out, and this is what is so remarkable. He had been so impacted by God's holiness, the depth of his sinfulness, and the grace of God that he was ready and willing to obey God no matter what. He didn't put conditions upon his obedience, but he simply said that he would do what God would ask even though God hadn't yet told him what that would be. Even when he found out that it would be a difficult calling, he didn't back down. When we see God as Isaiah saw God, it is hard not to make ourselves available and it is hard to be dissuaded from our calling, no matter how difficult it might be. A right view of God, of ourselves, of our sin, and of grace is essential for faithfulness to what God has called us to do.

Too often, we wait for someone else to share the gospel with a loved one because we don't want to stir the waters. Sometimes we expect our pastor to do all of the ministry things while we just show up and support him. This is not God's way. He wants us to say with Isaiah that we are available and willing to go and do whatever we are asked. He wants us to have willing hearts and not pass off our responsibilities to someone else. God has created good works for us to do (Ephesians 2:10), and it is our responsibility to do them. We will not be judged one day by what our pastor has done or by what other people do but by what we do. We will give an account for ourselves.

Isaiah, an ordinary man, was willing to obey God and step out in faith to let God do extraordinary things through him. Let us pray that we would come to see and value God as Isaiah did such that we will say with Isaiah, "Here I am. Send me."

#23

PEACE THAT SURPASSES UNDERSTANDING

Many times in life things happen that we don't understand, and we may wonder why. This is particularly difficult if we were of the mindset that this life is supposed to be fair and just, for it is not. Things can be further complicated if we erroneously think that faithfulness to Christ is a guarantee of material blessing and reward in this life. God does exalt the humble, but only at the proper time (1 Peter 5:6), which could well be in the life to come when rewards and honor will endure forever. But if we were expecting God to reward us now or if we thought that God should make all things work out fairly in the present, we might find ourselves struggling if and when things collapse out from under us. What is a Christian to think and do when life isn't fair and hardship befalls the righteous?

First, we as Christians must understand and accept the reality that the rain falls on the just and the unjust (Matthew 5:45). In this life, sometimes the wicked prosper, and other times the righteous reign victorious. Sometimes evil people get away with things, and the righteous are unduly condemned. In this world, we will experience trouble as Christ predicted we would (John 16:33). Our hope is that He has overcome this world, which means in part that He will render to each according to His deeds (Romans 2:6). He will settle all accounts, avenge all wrongs, and make all things fair and just. But in the meantime, things will be out of balance, unfair, and unjust. Thus, we must accept the reality of being in a fallen world, and we must then look forward to the day when Christ will make all things right. We will be rewarded for our faithfulness and stewardship because God sees all. He is a rewarder of those who seek Him (Hebrews 11:6). He will repay both wrongs and rights, so we must keep our focus on what is yet to come.

Secondly, we must by faith trust that God hasn't forgotten us or betrayed us as if He is giving somebody else preferential treatment or answering their requests and not ours. God knows what He is doing, and He shows no partiality (Romans 2:11). God cares for all of His children equally and perfectly. Thus, we must never conclude that God has forsaken us or betrayed us, for He has promised to never leave or forsake us (Hebrews 13:5). He will be with us until the end of the age (Matthew 28:20). The difficult but true reality is that sometimes we must suffer with Him in this life (2 Corinthians 1:5, Colossians 1:24), yet suffering with Christ is far better than suffering without Him. At least we as Christians have the promise that our all-powerful and loving God will cause all things to work for our good as His children (Romans 8:28). God doesn't betray His children, and He will always be with us. He is aware of everything that happens to us, and all that happens to us is for a reason. He will work good out of all things, and He is the One fighting on our behalf (Deuteronomy 3:22). Ultimately, He will see to it that we are not unduly put to shame (Isaiah 49:23).

Thirdly, we must accept the fact that, though God understands all things, we don't understand everything. But we have something that is of a surpassing value to understanding, and that is the peace of God. Paul says in Philippians 4:7, "And the peace of God, which surpasses all comprehension, will guard your hearts and your minds in Christ Jesus." The idea of surpassing comprehension likely has a couple levels of meaning. First, it means that God's peace is so wonderful that it is beyond our ability to understand it with our mere mental faculties and reasoning abilities. Somehow we can just have calm in our spirits and be tranquil internally even when life is chaotic and falling to pieces around us. Yet it also seems Paul is saying something in addition to this. The word translated "surpasses" could also mean "better than" or as it is translated in Philippians 3:8, "surpassing value." Paul is saying that not only is the peace of God so wonderful that it defies our minds' ability to understand it but that the peace of God is even preferable to our trying to figure out our lives and understand our circumstances. We are not God, and we don't have all understanding. However, we can have His peace despite our lack of understanding as we trust God that He will help us know what we need to know. Peace makes it possible for us to have rest even when things don't all make sense to us because we trust God that they make sense to Him. We only see such a small part of the entire picture that we are much better off simply trusting than trying to understand God's every move.

Life on this earth is not always smooth and easy, but God has not forgotten us. In fact, He is always busy at work causing all things to work for our good. In confusing times, we can still have rest and a supernatural peace that is a fruit of the Spirit. This internal tranquility and comfort requires that we trust God, that we rest in His plan, that we cast our cares upon Him, and that we accept the fact that we may not understand what God is doing. His peace, however, is better than knowing His every move, and we need to receive this truth in all humility and thankfulness. God will leave a legacy of goodness and mercy in our lives (Psalm 23:6), but we must trust Him even when we are confused in order to experience peace along the way.

#24

ABIDE IN CHRIST

Jesus spoke frequently to His disciples about abiding in Him. To abide in Him means to remain in Him. There is a sense in which all true believers will abide because Christ is faithful to complete the work He has begun in them (Hebrews 12:2, Philippians 1:6). Thus, Christ can say in John 6:56 that those who eat of His flesh and drink of His blood will abide in Him. In other words, those who truly embrace Him and receive Him as their Savior will be received as His children and will never be cast out of God's family (Hebrews 13:5). Alternatively, those who refuse to receive Him as Savior are said to have the wrath of God abiding on them (John 3:36). So, in one sense, abiding means either belonging to Christ, in which case we will be kept by Him, or remaining under the wrath of God because of unrepentant sin and refusing to receive Christ as Savior.

In John 15:4, Jesus speaks of abiding in a secondary sense when He commands the disciples, "Abide in Me, and I in you." Jesus is not speaking of their salvation but of something else related to their sanctification. In the previous verse, He addressed them as those who were "already clean," meaning that they were already saved. Thus, He is not telling them to abide in Him in the same way as He preached to the unbelieving Jews in John 6:56. Rather, He is speaking of living lives of abundant fruitfulness. We as Christians can either fall to living a life of mediocrity and dead works, or we can be vessels through whom Christ is able to work His power and accomplish His kingdom purposes. Those who abide in Christ in this sense are promised to bear much fruit (John 15:5), to have their prayers answered (John 15:7), and to experience fullness of joy (John 15:11).

All believers are called to bear fruit, though how much will vary based upon a person's faith and obedience (Romans 12:3, Matthew 13:23). Christ's desire, of course, is that we bear much fruit, not just some or a little. If we abide in Him, we will bear much fruit (John 15:5). Fruit-bearing involves becoming like Christ as the Spirit conforms us more and more to the image of Christ (Galatians 5:22-23, Romans 12:1-2). Fruit involves an internal heart transformation to be loving, joyful, at peace, self-controlled, and any other manifestation of Christlikeness. Fruit also involves external behavior and obedience, such as any kind of good work, service, or ministry in the name of Christ and accomplished by His grace and power (Titus 3:14).

Abiding in Christ requires, first, that we obey God by keeping Christ's commandments (John 15:10, 1 John 2:5-6). If we regard sin in our hearts, we cannot be fully filled with the Spirit of God (Ephesians 5:18). We will still have the Spirit, but we will be hindering and suppressing Him such that He cannot accomplish His will within us because of our hardness of hearts (1 Thessalonians 5:19). We will likely grow confused as to His leading, we will struggle in our prayer lives, we will lose our joy and peace, and we will find ourselves striving in our own power. Sinning as believers doesn't separate us from the love of God in terms of our eternity, but it does separate us from being infused with the power and love of God to do effective, God-honoring ministry. There is no guarantee that we will bear genuine spiritual fruit if we serve with unconfessed sin in our hearts (1 Corinthians 9:17). Leaving sin unconfessed and living with secret sins is a quick road to a powerless ministry and a life of dead works. If we want to bear fruit and abide in Christ, we need to obey Him willingly and without secret sins.

Secondly, abiding in Christ requires that we recognize, acknowledge, and by faith live in light of the reality of our dependence upon God. John 15:5 makes it clear that, since Jesus is the vine and we are dependent branches, we need Him. Jesus says, "Apart from Me, you can do nothing." He will give us all of the resources and strength that we need to be able to do the works which He has prepared for us to do (2 Peter 1:3, Ephesians 2:10), but we must yield to Him, surrendering our will and desires to Him (Zechariah 4:6). Any mindset that retains self-sufficiency and not full reliance upon Christ will lead to dead works rather than genuine, Spirit-led, Spirit-filled, and Spirit-generated fruit.

God's desire is that we bear fruit that remains (John 15:16), meaning that it will prove to be of God and not of man. It will be a result of our yielding, submitting, and surrendering to Christ by faith, being willing to obey Him and letting Him have His way in our hearts. This fruit will endure the fiery test of the judgment seat of Christ (1 Corinthians 3:15), and we will be able to have confidence at His coming (1 John 2:28). Dead works give glory to the worker, whereas true fruit gives glory to God. When we truly let Christ work in us, we will be amazed at what He can do. It will be clear that such fruit is a result of God's grace working through human weakness (2 Corinthians 12:9-10), as the disciples certainly experienced themselves, being uneducated and untrained men (Acts 4:13). They were ordinary, but their God was extraordinary, and through them, He did extraordinary things. The same can be true for us.

We can live lives of obedience, joy, and fruitfulness as we abide in Christ, or we can live lives of feeble fruitbearing which will lead to joylessness and few rewards in heaven (1 Corinthians 3:10-15). God wants us to bear much fruit, and He came to give us abundant life (John 10:10). May we live lives filled with His power and love, bearing abundant fruit as our offering of thanksgiving to Him.

#25

DO EVERYTHING WITHOUT COMPLAINING

Philippians 2:14-16 says,

> "Do all things without grumbling or disputing; so that
> you will prove yourselves to be blameless and innocent,
> children of God above reproach in the midst of a crooked
> and perverse generation, among whom you appear as
> lights in the world, holding fast the word of life, so that
> in the day of Christ I will have reason to glory because I
> did not run in vain nor toil in vain."

Paul labored hard among the Philippians to bring them the gospel and
to teach them such that they would grow to maturity in their faith. He
wanted them to persevere by continuing to grow, serve, love, obey,
and...not complain. There are lots of ways that Christians can stand
out from the world, and not complaining is one that we might not often
think about, though it certainly makes sense. The world is constantly
unsatisfied, trying to climb another rung, notch another achievement,
or impress another person. There is zero contentment or gratitude
towards the Lord for what He has given to them. We as Christians
should shine into this darkness as bright lights which thank God, trust
God, praise God, and refuse to grumble about our circumstances.

In Philippians 2:14, the word translated "grumbling" could also mean "murmuring," "muttering," or a "secret displeasure not openly avowed." The word translated "disputing" means "the thinking of a man deliberating within himself." It implies an inward arguing, doubting, or hesitating. We know from God's dealing with the Israelites in the Old Testament, who complained time after time against both Him and Moses, that God hates complaining (Exodus 32:9-10). He is displeased when we, like Israel, lack faith, doubt His power, question His ability or willingness to provide, and hesitate to rest in His love. Whether the people of Israel were captive slaves of Egypt or wanderers in the wilderness headed for the promised land, they complained. Nothing could make that generation happy. There was always something that they found to gripe to God about.

Rather than condemn Israel by thinking that we would never have done such things, we need to look at our own lives. It is easy in retrospect to trust Christ, but it is difficult to trust Him today as the battle wages, as we grow weary, and as temptation comes. We are to learn from Israel, understanding that complaining is not uncommon to man. We must learn, as Paul did, to be content in all circumstances (Philippians 4:11). Part of contentment's work is to teach us not to complain. Sometimes we complain out loud to others about our circumstances, grumbling against what we have to endure on a daily basis. Other times we keep our resentful feelings bottled up inside, acting outwardly like we trust God while inwardly we have a secret displeasure and dispute with Him. Sometimes we can even deceive ourselves into thinking that we are justified in our complaints against God as if He really did do us a disservice or treat us unfairly. Yet there is no reason to doubt or question God's love, and never is our complaining justified.

Israel witnessed miracles, and yet they doubted. We have the testimony of God's love in giving us His Son, and yet we challenge His love. In some ways, we are even more hideous in our complaints. God has kept nothing back in terms of His love in giving us Christ, and yet we still complain. Paul said, if we have food and clothing, with these we will be content (1 Timothy 6:8). Yet how many things can we find to complain about, let alone our food and clothing. We might complain about our tight finances, our health, our lack of free time, how our kids have turned out, or how we didn't get to hear our favorite hymn last Sunday. We might complain about the weather, we might get down about our favorite sports team losing, and we might complain about the traffic. Then there is politics, the leak in the roof, the mortgage payment, another car repair, and the furnace that gives out in the chill of winter. Every new challenge can become a new excuse to complain and grumble. Truly, we are not all that different from Israel.

Complaining and grumbling about our circumstances is a stench to God, and it is something that we have no right to do. Yet there is an alternative to complaining. We can pray and bring our requests before God, for the prayers of the saints arise as incense into the presence of God (Revelation 5:8). God knew what He was doing when He came up with the idea of prayer. He knew we would need it, for we would need a way to humbly and gratefully express our burdens and petitions to God with thanksgiving (Philippians 4:6-7). Rather than complain, we must choose by faith to thank God no matter what, and we must let Him take charge of our burdens and cares as we bring them before Him in prayer (1 Peter 5:7).

Too often, we are so bad in the area of complaining, and we have no excuse. So let us confess our complaining as sin, not arguing against God or becoming bitter against Him, but let us believe that where we are today is a place where God desires to work and to cause all things to result in our good. Rather than complain, let us thank God and offer our requests to Him in prayer.

#26

HOW TO MEASURE SUCCESS

We live in a world where success is defined in innumerable ways, most of which are wrong. Sadly, even the professing church has been prone to increasingly err in its understanding of true, Biblical success. Whether the pressuring voices come from within the church or without, we must not give in to their distortions and perversions of what God says success really is.

Paul says this toward the very end of his life, writing to Timothy in 2 Timothy 4:6-8,

> "For I am already being poured out as a drink offering, and the time of my departure has come. I have fought the good fight, I have finished the course, I have kept the faith; in the future there is laid up for me the crown of righteousness, which the Lord, the righteous Judge, will award to me on that day; and not only to me, but also to all who have loved His appearing."

There is no mention of Paul applauding himself for having become wealthy, nor is there any mention of Paul patting himself on the back for having achieved great fame and notoriety. In fact, he had achieved great fame and power very early on in his life, outdistancing many of his contemporaries in terms of Bible knowledge and understanding

(Galatians 1:14). He was mentored by the best Jewish teacher of all (Acts 22:3), and he was considered a man of high rank. But these things he counted as loss (Philippians 3:7). This was not because there was evil in leading, having status, or even in being wealthy, but it was that he had pursued these kinds of things at the expense of pursuing God. Thus, he chose to abandon the "success" which he had experienced in persecuting Christ in exchange for service to Christ, choosing rather to suffer with Him (Romans 8:17). Paul understood that success is not what we can achieve or gain in terms of worldly things. Sometimes he had much, and sometimes he had little (Philippians 4:12). But in all things he was content, and as he wrote to Timothy, "Godliness with contentment is great gain" (1 Timothy 6:6). Thus, Paul measured success by the state of his heart in relation to God. Godliness, faithfulness, and contentment were paramount in terms of how he wanted his life defined.

False measures of success are often derived from seeking the approval of men rather than that of God (John 12:43). If Paul evaluated his own success based upon what others thought of him, he would have been an utter failure. Of course, we can look back in retrospect and see that his life had an enormous impact in spreading the gospel, but his life was difficult, full of suffering, hardship, starvation, persecution, beatings, freezing in the cold, and being betrayed by many, many people (2 Corinthians 11:23-28, 1 Timothy 1:15). From the world's perspective, he eventually died not as a victor, but as a victim when he was beheaded for Christ's sake. Yet, for Paul, living was Christ, and dying was gain (Philippians 1:21). His view of success and gain was far different from the world's such that even death for Christ's name and glory was victory, progress, achievement, and honor.

From Paul's testimony, we could conclude that success contains the following elements: 1) live life as a living sacrifice, pouring out the love of God to others in service and ministry for the sake of Christ, 2) fight the good fight of faith, continuing to preach the gospel and contending for truth and sound doctrine without compromise even though it could mean persecution or even death (2 Timothy 3:14), 3) finish the course, persevering in godliness so as not to be disqualified from effective ministry due to a lack of discipline (1 Corinthians 9:27), and 4) keep the faith, continuing to serve Christ and abounding in the work of the Lord, never growing tired of loving Jesus (1 Corinthians 15:58). Because Paul was faithful in his testimony, faithful to His calling, faithful in preaching the gospel, faithful to the saints, and faithful to God, he could say with certainty that he would be crowned a victor by Christ in eternal glory. He knew that his life would result in praise, glory, and honor for the sake of Christ because he didn't compromise or pander to the changing desires of people, but he kept teaching the truth of God's Word. He knew what God had called him to do, and he was going to do it even if nobody listened. We can praise God along with Paul that many did respond in faith, and Paul took great joy in this. Yet even good responses were not the fundamental criteria by which he measured his own success. He knew if he was faithful to Christ and to His Word, proclaiming the gospel to the lost and loving them as Christ loved them, he would be deemed successful by Christ, Whose opinion alone matters.

We must not let ourselves get taken in by the pull of society to want to be loved by the world, chasing its misguided definitions of success. In the church, we must not change our teaching or theology in an effort to try to get better "results." All we are called to do is to plant seeds and water them as God provides the opportunities and strength; God alone gives the growth (1 Corinthians 3:6-7). True fruit is something that happens as we obey Christ and abide in Him. We cannot generate our own fruit or redefine what fruit is. If we are faithful to Christ and to His Word, keeping His commands, true spiritual work will be accomplished (Galatians 6:9), and we will be rewarded accordingly (2 Corinthians 5:10).

There is no greater or higher measure of success than the praise of our Savior, saying, "Well done, good and faithful servant" (Matthew 25:23). If we are faithful servants, we are also successful by Christ's standards because we will bear Him abundant spiritual fruit. May it be His glory alone which we seek as we faithfully strive to honor and obey Him no matter the cost or what people might think.

#27

WORTHLESS WORRYING

Worrying can seem like a prison from which we cannot escape, but there is a way out. We must come to understand, admit, accept, and believe that worrying does no good. It accomplishes nothing for us or for anybody else. Worrying is completely useless. Jesus says in Luke 12:25, "And which of you by worrying can add a single hour to his life's span?" Worrying certainly doesn't add value to life or lengthen it. If anything, it diminishes the quality of life and quite possibly its duration because of added stress on our bodies. Worrying is destructive, ineffective, and unnecessary.

There is an underlying assumption by those who worry that they have at least some level of control over their circumstances which, in reality, only God has ultimate control over. There is something inside of them that knows that they are not in control and that they cannot control all that happens in their lives, but they sure want to be able to be in total control. They want to know, fully understand, and control all that is going on, that has gone on, and that will go on. They effectively want to usurp God's position as sovereign, all-powerful, and all-knowing. It is not that they are seeking to replace God, for even this would worry them. But it is that they are struggling to abandon themselves and those whom they care about to God's control. God is in control, and He does care. But those who worry struggle to believe that and appropriate it.

Those who worry tend to mistrust God and have an overly-inflated view of their own ability to make their lives what they want them to be.

To surrender to God does not mean that we submit to fate as if we have no responsibility or choices to make in life. Many times our own difficulties are a result of our own making and irresponsible behavior. We can further muddy the already muddied water from our worrying by not doing our part to make wise choices and to be proactive in seeking God's will, doing what He has already revealed for us to do. Life takes labor, work, effort, strain, and energy. Sometimes those who worry get imprisoned, in effect, by their worry because they stop taking steps of action, maybe because they are too worried. Thus, worry can be a downward spiral of self-imprisonment, leading to a sort of paralysis of the will and mind, resulting in spiritual ineffectiveness, inward destruction, and despair. So we must not worsen matters by not doing what God has already instructed us to do. We are not helpless beings, and we do have a will and a responsibility to act.

The long term and full fix for worry does go beyond merely taking steps of obedience and action. For some, they won't even be able to do this because they are so bound up by worry. Others might find some release from worry for a time, only to fall back into it when they have to face another difficult set of circumstances. Thus, it is important to seek the foundation of the problem in order to find lasting freedom. First, we must recognize that apart from Christ, we can do nothing (John 15:5). We are not adequate in and of ourselves no matter how much we might think we are or how much we want to be. We have no adequacy or sufficiency apart from Christ in us (2 Corinthians 3:5). Jesus says in Luke 12:26, in relation to the futility of our worrying, "If then you cannot do even a very little thing, why do you worry about other matters?" So the first thing we must believe and acknowledge is that we need God, and we have no hope unless we cast ourselves upon His care. It is not just that we can do some things and need His help to do the rest or that we do part and He does part. No, we need Him to do it all. We can't do anything. Thus, things are outside of our power and control ultimately, and we need to rest upon God Who is sufficient, powerful, and able. Second, we must rest not only in our God who is powerful and able but in our God

Who is perfectly and totally loving. He is worthy of our trust because He loves us so much that He even gave us His only begotten Son Whom we didn't deserve, seek, or even ask for. God delights in giving good gifts to His children (Matthew 7:11), and every good and perfect gift is from Him (James 1:17). He works all things for our good (Romans 8:28). This is not a God Who is out to be unfair toward us, unloving, unjust, or evil. God has no evil intent, He does not tempt, and He cannot do us wrong. All that happens to us is necessarily kindest, wisest, and best. Thus, we can rest in God because He is not cruel, vindictive, or malicious. He is good, and His gifts are as well. Third, we must be willing to trust God even when we cannot see or understand what is going on or why. 2 Corinthians 5:7 says, "For we walk by faith, not by sight." There will be times when life's circumstances will seem to indicate that God is absent or that He doesn't really care. We cannot conclude these things, but we must choose to walk by faith. If He gave us His Son, won't He freely give us all things (Romans 8:32)? God gave us Christ, and He is not going to hold back His love to us now. We must remember the cross when we are tempted to start worrying again.

The road to freedom from worry is to trust God, to rest in His love, and to truly believe that He is able and that we are not. Will we let God take the controls of our lives today, knowing and believing that He can do it better than we can? Will we trust Him that He will only do us good all of the days of our lives (Psalm 23:6)? May God take all our worries away as we cast our anxieties upon Him (1 Peter 5:7).

#28

Pause to Praise

Sometimes we can find ourselves getting so consumed with activity and busyness that we fail to give God thanks and praise. Praise is not only for Sunday morning during the singing time, and it is not to be offered only when something good happens to us. Man was created to praise God because God deserves glory all the time (Isaiah 48:11). We exist not for ourselves, not to find out who we are, and not to indulge our lusts. We exist to give God praise, to learn about Who He is, and to give Him glory for Who He is and for what He has done, is doing, and will do. In fact, it may well be that the highest, most elating, and most euphoric experiences that we as human beings can enjoy are those moments when God grasps our attention and shouts to us in our hearts, saying, for example, "Look at what I have made. Isn't it awesome, beautiful, and breathtaking? I thought this up, I designed it, and I brought it into being. Isn't it great?" When we respond in humble acknowledgement, thanksgiving, and praise, we share God's joy about Who He is and what He has done.

For example, consider the stars in the night skies. We know they are there, that they are innumerable, and that they are pretty to look at. But have we ever taken a moment just to praise God for His creative work, His genius, His majesty, His vastness, and His power? It is one thing to say that the sky is big and amazing, and it is another to glorify God for His bigness that transcends even the vastness of the universe. It is one thing to try to get our minds around how big the stars actually are even though they are so small from our viewpoint, and it is another altogether to praise God for thinking up the idea of light and for being the Light. *It is not good enough just to acknowledge that the universe has a designer, but the Designer must be praised.*

The more we study the world and, more importantly, the Bible, the more we will be moved to praise. How can a book written over thousands of years by many different human authors be perfectly consistent, coherent, and complete? Only God could do this, and this should move us to praise. How could God become man, die, and then be raised from the dead? It is amazing, and it should move us to praise. Like the stars on a clear night, the heavens speak forth the glory of God (Psalm 19:1), and the created order should move us to praise. Sometimes we will be able to get a glimpse of the wisdom of God as we see in retrospect just how good He has been to us. Sometimes, we see, like David, how the goodness of God has followed us all the days of our lives (Psalm 23:6). This should move us to praise and to exalt God in our hearts. Every time we encounter God in His Word, in His revelation through the creation, or as the Spirit moves in our hearts about the goodness of God, we should pause to praise Him. In fact, as we come to increasingly understand the love, grace, goodness, and power of God, we won't be able to help but praise. It will be almost instinctive. God wants us to delight in Him (Psalm 37:4) and thereby find our greatest purpose and joy (Psalm 16:11).

The Psalms are full of exhortations to exaltation by writers who can't help but praise God, even when they find themselves in dire predicaments. In fact, the original Hebrew text labeled the book of Psalms as "Praises." Given that this book is the longest in the canon of Scripture, it should be clear to us that God wants praise to be a central part of the believer's life. In fact, Psalm 102:18 says, "This will be written for the generation to come, that a people yet to be created may praise the LORD." One of the main overarching purposes of the Psalms is to motivate us to praise and to instruct us as to how we should praise.

We must continue the praising of God that has been done for thousands of years in song and music, even singing new songs to the Lord as He works in our hearts and leads us to praise (Psalm 33:3). We can praise God through our old favorite songs, as certainly Israel would have done with their Psalms, but we should also be composing new ones. Even in Revelation 5:9, those in heaven sing to God a new song of praise. God doesn't get old, and if He is getting old, stale, and boring to us, we need to recover true, authentic and Biblical praise. Whether through song, prayer, deed, or any other kind of God-glorifying action, we must intentionally pause to praise. Rather than be consumed with ourselves, we must let ourselves be consumed with the glory of God. Rather than boast in ourselves, we should boast in the Lord. As Psalm 34:2 says, "My soul will make its boast in the LORD."

God is great and greatly to be praised (Psalm 48:1, 96:4). May God teach all of us as His children to pause to praise Him, giving Him the glory that is due His glorious name. He has done great things, and He is great. Praise the Lord!

#29
THE BELIEVER'S INTERNAL AGONY FROM SIN

There are many ways to know for sure that we are in Christ, destined for heaven (1 John 5:13). When we see good fruit (Matthew 7:20), when we obey (John 14:21), when we love our brothers and sisters (John 13:34-35), and when we love God rather than the world (1 John 2:15) are just a few of the ways whereby we can know if we are saved. Yet there is another way that, as believers, we will all inevitably experience, though we don't want to have to learn this way. When we let sin go unconfessed and continue to resist the conviction of the Spirit and the truth of the Word of God, we can expect to experience internal double-mindedness, instability, joylessness, and agony.

David was a man after God's own heart, yet he sinned, committing adultery and murder on one occasion. After he committed these grievous sins, he hardened his heart and covered up his sin, refusing to acknowledge it until he was confronted by the prophet Nathan. Perhaps he felt that he had gotten away with his sin in terms of keeping up his image and reputation, but deep down in his heart, he was in agony. His sin probably brought him some short-term pleasure, but the Spirit of God within his heart was working agony in him. Certainly, the sin was not worth the pain and the destructive results, including the punishment

God would bring upon him and upon his newborn child who would die as a result of his sin (2 Samuel 12:10-14).

In Psalm 32 and 51, David recounted his internal feelings and experiences while he kept this sin in his heart. In Psalm 32:3-4, he says, "When I kept silent about my sin, my body wasted away through my groaning all day long. For day and night Your hand was heavy upon me; my vitality was drained away as with the fever heat of summer." David says that his body was literally wasting away day and night because of God's hand of conviction upon him, which he had to willfully resist. His sin caused him to lose his strength and groan. There are severe mental, emotional, and physical consequences to sin for unbelievers and believers, but it is believers in particular who must deal with God's heavy hand of conviction. Unbelievers tend to be more callous to sin given that their consciences are defiled (Titus 1:15-16). Believers, on the other hand, are indwelt by the Spirit of God who will be relentless in convicting us of sin. In a positive sense, this demonstrates that we are indeed God's children, but it also means that we will have a heavier burden to bear. The bottom line is that this agony should be a strong incentive for us not to sin or to hide sin in our hearts.

In Psalm 51:12-13, David says, "Restore to me the joy of Your salvation and sustain me with a willing spirit. Then I will teach transgressors Your ways, and sinners will be converted to You." David had lost the joy which accompanies being a saved child of God for as long as he hid this sin in his heart. His will to do right had grown weak, and he needed God to strengthen him and sustain him so that he could do right and be used of God. Once he finally confessed his sin, he would be able to powerfully and effectively teach others about God and evangelize them. But before God could powerfully use him, he needed to empty himself of his sin and let the Spirit have full control of his heart and life (Ephesians 5:18). Hiding sin in our hearts not only brings internal agony but a loss of spiritual effectiveness.

As Christians, we are ashamed of the sins that we used to take pleasure in (Romans 6:21), and unconfessed sin will bring shame and guilt once again. It is possible that we could self-justify and be deceived such that we develop a certain spiritual dullness when it comes to caring about sin. However, the Spirit will make us uncomfortable with our dullness, for He will never stop convicting and working in our hearts.

If we have sinned against God, we need to ask His forgiveness. If we have sinned against others as well, we also need to ask their forgiveness. James 5:16 says, "Therefore, confess your sins to one another, and pray for one another so that you may be healed." God will always forgive us when we ask, but He wants us to confess our sins to those whom we have sinned against as well. This is part of the spiritual healing process, and it is important for restoring relationships and putting ourselves in a position to be fully empowered by God to do His work.

God is in the business of restoration, forgiveness, compassion, and the giving of joy. Thus, in His mercy, He will work to lead us to brokenness over our sin, allowing us to experience the agony of guilt and shame in the face of a holy, loving God. The upside of this is that it reminds us that we are His and that nothing can separate us from His love (Romans 8:39). The downside is that sin has consequences, and it does us and others great harm. So let us be spiritually healed this day, confessing our sins to God and to those who need our apologies so that we might be restored. Why continue in agony when God wants to replace our sorrow with gladness?

#30

LET YOUR FAITH BE STRETCHED

Faith plays a profound role in our lives as believers. Faith is how we were justified and made righteous in God's sight (Romans 3:28). Through faith we can move mountains (Matthew 21:21). Faith is how we walk, rather than by sight (2 Corinthians 5:7). Faith is how we please God (Hebrews 11:6). Whatever is not from faith is sin (Romans 14:23). God's will for us will always be the road which requires faith.

God has a way of stretching our faith so that it can be increased. He does this by giving us things which make us uncomfortable, which challenge us, and which try the faith which we possess. Tests and trials are ordained by God for our good. They are not malicious as if God delights in seeing us struggle, strain, and suffer. But like a coach or physical trainer pushes an athlete beyond his limits, even to the point of feeling sick, God allows trials to come our way to make us stronger (James 1:2-4). His purpose is good, and He causes all things to work for our good as we are made more and more into the image of Christ (Romans 8:28). So let us not be surprised that, if we desire to grow deeper in our faith, that God would allow difficulty or various challenges into our lives. In order to strengthen us and to teach us to lean only upon Him, God often takes away all that we rely upon so that we come to rely only upon Him. God's call is that we would trust Him with all of our hearts, not some of our hearts and not even most of our hearts. He wants total faith, faith which doesn't doubt, fear, shrink away in shame, or waffle.

He wants to see faith under fire, as Shadrach, Meshach, and Abed-nego demonstrated literally. Their confidence was that God would deliver them, and they were bold, confident, hopeful, and strong. Yet they were not presumptuous, saying that they would stand firm in their faith even if they were consumed in the fiery furnace (Daniel 3:16-18). They knew their God loved them, and they were going to serve Him no matter what, trusting His plan and purpose to be the best for them. When we endure under trial, we will be able to see the work of proven character which God has accomplished in our hearts and lives. The more our faith is stretched and the more we endure, the more like Christ we will become. Additionally, our hope will increase because we will continue to see the power of God in us, for we will know without a doubt that He has been there for us, supporting us, encouraging us, and enabling us (Romans 5:3-5). So it is good for us to suffer and have our faith stretched. It is good for us to be pushed beyond what we think God can do so that we worship a God Who does even beyond what we can ask or imagine (Ephesians 3:20). It is good for us to see the shallowness of our faith so that we ask God to increase it. And how good it is when He does just that, and we learn to rest in His provision and power even more.

Peter feared when he thought he was going to perish in the storm while he and the disciples along with Jesus were at sea (Matthew 8:26). Yet Jesus calmed the storm, rebuking Peter and his brethren for having little faith. Some time later on, Jesus was walking on the water, and Peter asked Him to command him to come to Him on the water. Peter learned, and he was putting his faith to work. He did start doubting as he looked at the waves around him, but Jesus was there to save him. Yet what an increase in faith he demonstrated, and such was clear evidence of God working in Peter's life. In the first instance, he doubted as if there was no hope. Later, he didn't fear, and he wanted to have the opportunity to step out and challenge the fierce waves by faith. And as long as he kept his gaze fixed upon Jesus, he walked on the water, something truly miraculous.

What is impossible with man is possible with God (Matthew 19:26). Yet sadly we too often "limit" God by our lack of faith. We need to learn as Peter did not to fear and doubt when dangers come but to look to Jesus.

We cannot run from God's promises, but we must cast ourselves upon them. It is not good enough to wait for the calm before we act in faith and engage the enemy, following Jesus in service. We must be willing, like Peter, to believe that Jesus can work and that He desires to work through us, even in the most dire of times and even when we feel the weakest.

Peter didn't presume on Jesus and just step on to the water. He asked permission, and once He knew God's will, He acted in faith. *We need to find what God wants us to do, being unafraid and totally expecting God to work, and then we need to do it, keeping our eyes fixed on Christ and not looking at the difficulties around us.*

Stepping out in faith is a vulnerable thing in one sense because it means that we can't control our circumstances fully as we would like. We can't eliminate risk, and others might call us fools. Yet without faith, we cannot please God. To stay as we are and not to grow is sin. We must be willing to let God increase our faith, and He will orchestrate the circumstances of our lives perfectly to do just that.

#31

ENCOURAGE ONE ANOTHER

Sometimes we might get worn down such that we could use a little encouragement to keep us going. As Isaiah 35:3 says, "Encourage the exhausted, and strengthen the feeble." But it is not just those who have been exhausted who need encouragement, but encouragement should be a regular part of life among believers. Hebrews 3:13 says, "But encourage one another day after day, as long as it is still called 'Today,' so that none of you will be hardened by the deceitfulness of sin." There is not a day that goes by that we couldn't benefit from some encouragement or that we should be lacking in giving some encouragement to others. *Encouraging one another matters because it keeps us from being deceived into sinning.* When we get exhausted and in a weakened, worn down state, it is easy to give into sin and stop resisting the devil's temptation. When we are tired, sometimes we decide that we don't care anymore, and our sensitivity to wrongdoing lessens. Encouragement keeps our focus right. It lets us know that we are not alone but that others are supportive of us, praying for us, and caring for us. We need to be active in encouraging one another so that we can keep motivating one another toward love and good deeds (Hebrews 10:24-25).

The Bible gives us some very practical ways that we can encourage others.

1. *We can encourage one another through the giving of gifts.* Ezra 1:6 says, "All those about them encouraged them with articles of silver, with gold, with goods, with cattle and with valuables, aside from all that was given as a freewill offering." A group from Judah went up to rebuild the house of God, and God moved in the hearts of those around them to give to them generously so that they could have an abundance of materials and goods for their journey and for their project. The gifts were a tangible expression of their support, and this was highly encouraging to the laborers.

2. *We can encourage one another through words kindly spoken.* Isaiah 41:7 says, "So the craftsman encourages the smelter, And he who smooths metal with the hammer encourages him who beats the anvil, Saying of the soldering, 'It is good'; And he fastens it with nails, So that it will not totter." This Scripture paints a very simple picture of two people working together, and one says to the other that he is doing a good job. A simple compliment on the quality of one's work goes a long way, and it is a simple yet powerful way to encourage one another.

3. *We can encourage one another through an exhortation to be faithful.* Acts 11:23 says, "Then when he arrived and witnessed the grace of God, he rejoiced and began to encourage them all with resolute heart to remain true to the Lord." Simply encouraging others to keep on keeping on in the Lord can be more of a help than we might think.

4. *We can encourage one another through written words.* Acts 15:31 says, "When they had read it, they rejoiced because of its encouragement." In this case, the congregation was gathered to hear a letter from the apostles, and they were encouraged by it. A simple note expressing thanks, appreciation, or a promise of help can go a long way. These believers saw that the apostles cared about them, and that was very encouraging to them.

5. *We can encourage one another through the preaching of the Word.* Acts 15:32 says, "Judas and Silas, also being prophets themselves, encouraged and strengthened the brethren with a lengthy message." It can be refreshing to hear a lengthy exposition of the Word of God

and to be ministered to by taking in a great quantity of sound Bible teaching. Sharing a good sermon with somebody or sitting under a great Bible teacher can be a refreshing experience as our soul gets to feast upon God's Word.

6. *We can be encouraged by the faith and faithfulness of other believers.* Romans 1:12 says, "That is, that I may be encouraged together with you while among you, each of us by the other's faith, both yours and mine." Just being around other believers who really love the Lord can really bolster our faith. It is highly refreshing to hear testimonies of how God is at work in their lives or how they came to know Christ. Faith and faithfulness can be contagious.

7. *We can be encouraged by regularly being in the Scriptures.* Romans 15:4 says, "For whatever was written in earlier times was written for our instruction, so that through perseverance and the encouragement of the Scriptures we might have hope." God has given us His Word so that we can keep being reminded of how He has worked throughout history, how faithful He is, and how much hope we should have. Being in the Scriptures and meditating upon them is a huge part of staying encouraged in our walks.

8. *We can be encouraged by others who labor with us for the sake of the gospel.* Colossians 4:11 says, "And also Jesus who is called Justus; these are the only fellow workers for the kingdom of God who are from the circumcision, and they have proved to be an encouragement to me." Doing ministry is tough, and to have other faithful believers working alongside of us is a huge means of support. Paul rarely traveled alone on his missionary journeys, choosing rather to enjoy the encouragement of faithful brothers in Christ.

God's call to us is that we encourage one another regularly so that we don't slough off and fall into sin because we have lost heart and lost focus. Even when others fail to encourage us or are unavailable to encourage us, God and His Word are available and sufficient to encourage us. Let us take care that we stay in the Word to be encouraged ourselves so that we can be an encouragement to others. We never know when even a small gesture of encouragement might make a very significant difference.

#32

THE GOD WHO IS NEAR

Sometimes as we go through life we can begin to feel as if God is absent, uninvolved, unhelpful, or that He doesn't care. We might feel that our prayers bounce off the ceiling, we might feel as if God blesses others but not us, and we might come to the false conclusion that God isn't at work in our lives at all. This is a sad, unbiblical, and dangerous place to be spiritually because it is riddled with lies straight from the devil. It is a direct attack against the very nature and heart of God Who loves His us enough that He sent His own Son to redeem us. Our God is good, He cares, and He is at work not just in the world around us but in our lives and even in us.

There is a misconception in Christianity that God is "out there," somewhere high above us, away from us, and imperceptible to us. To an extent this was true in the Old Testament, when God was approached through Moses on behalf of the people, for example. Yet we are under a new covenant, which is a better covenant (Hebrews 7:22), through which Jesus has made it possible for all believers to approach God directly (Hebrews 4:16). Jesus is the mediator of the new covenant (Hebrews 9:15), through which every believer becomes the temple and dwelling place of God (1 Corinthians 6:19). We don't have to go to a temple, a tabernacle, or a church building to find God. We don't have to offer up peace offerings to be sure God still approves of us. God's favor is ours because Christ has been offered up as a pleasing sacrifice to God on our behalf once and for all (Hebrews 9:12). God has drawn near to man in redeeming him so that we can draw near to God by faith as we turn from our sins in surrender to Jesus. We have direct access to God in prayer, and the best part is that He lives in us. The God of the universe, though He fills all things, being omnipresent, lives in each and every believer. We as God's children have died with Christ such that Christ lives out His life and desires in and through us, or at least such should be the case (Galatians 2:20). God is not distant from the believer, for He lives in the believer's heart. He is no farther away than this, and our very lives are found in knowing Him. *As believers, the issue is not in chasing down God in a distant hope that He might fellowship with us, but it is simply believing that Christ lives in us, our hope of glory* (Colossians 1:27). The joy and privilege of the believer in this time is indeed Christ in us, living out His life through us as we die to self and are made alive in Him.

God is very near, very involved, and very personal, being our very life. John 17:3 says, "This is eternal life, that they may know You, the only true God, and Jesus Christ whom You have sent." Most certainly eternal life means that we will live with Christ forever in heaven, never perishing because we will have been given bodies that will be immortal. Yet we must understand that there is a sense in which eternal life is a state of being, or rather a state of knowing. John says outright that eternal life is knowing Jesus Christ personally. Therefore, there is a sense in which eternal life starts at the moment we come to know Christ. Certainly, the fullness of knowing Jesus will manifest itself after we die when we go to be with Christ forever in heaven. But let us not forget that God is very near to us in the Person of Jesus Christ right now if we are have received Him as Savior. The promise of having eternal life implies both an eternal existence in heaven and an eternal relationship with our Lord. We are not in heaven yet, but we do know our Lord already. Of course, our relationship with Him will only get better as we grow to know and love Him more. This relationship will be perfected in heaven in eternity, but we can enjoy this relationship even now. Because we have eternal life, we know Jesus, and He is near to us in our hearts.

God is alive, active, working, and moving in our hearts. As Paul said, describing the one true God, "in Him we live and move and exist"

(Acts 17:28). He is not an image of stone, wood, or some other created material to which we must go and worship, just hoping he listens. *He is alive, and it is in Him that we live, move, and exist. Life in Christ is this personal, this real, and this near when it comes to knowing God.*

When we understand these things, it becomes foolish to dwell on the notion that God is distant or that He doesn't care. Circumstances might be difficult, and prayers may not be answered in the way we would desire. Yet God cares, He endures the trials with us (Psalm 23:4), and He is always there to be our constant Companion and Guide.

Jeremiah 23:23-24 says, "'Am I a God who is near,' declares the LORD, 'And not a God far off? Can a man hide himself in hiding places so I do not see him?' declares the LORD. 'Do I not fill the heavens and the earth?' declares the LORD." God's declaration to us today is that He fills the earth, including the hearts of those who believe (John 1:12). He is a God Who is near, so let us believe this and enjoy our fellowship with the God of the universe today.

#33

KEEP RESISTING THE DEVIL

Sin is typically the easy way out, being often a source of fun, pleasure, or distraction, albeit a temporary and destructive one (Hebrews 11:25). But sin is not God's way, and the call for us as believers is to do what is hard and requires great faith and self-control. We must not deceive ourselves into thinking that sin is ever acceptable. Even if circumstances are ridiculous, horrible, or extremely difficult, we cannot justify or rationalize sinning. The reason for this is described in one very powerful verse. 1 Corinthians 10:13 says, "No temptation has overtaken you but such as is common to man; and God is faithful, who will not allow you to be tempted beyond what you are able, but with the temptation will provide the way of escape also, so that you will be able to endure it." Every Christian needs to be aware of this verse, the truths it implies, and the promises of God which it reveals.

This verse teaches us that temptation is a common, ordinary reality of life on this earth. Believers and unbelievers alike are tempted by the devil. We must expect to be engaged in a spiritual battle for our hearts and our purity before God. Satan doesn't rest, and he seeks to lead us astray, taking advantage of our weak points, mercilessly trying to exploit us and deceive us. We can pray that God will "lead us not into temptation" as the Lord's prayer says (Matthew 6:13), but sometimes God will allow us to be tempted (Luke 22:31-32). This is just the reality of the human experience. Humans all will give in (Romans 3:23), and even Christians will stumble at times (James 3:2). *But the message that Paul says by inspiration of the Holy Spirit is that we don't have to give in.* We do give in because our faith is weak, but our sinning is a choice. We are not helpless because God is faithful, and He will never allow Satan to tempt us beyond what we are able to resist as we place our trust in God. In other words, we are fully responsible for our own sin. We cannot blame the devil, another person, a circumstance, or a feeling. We can't even blame God, even though it wouldn't make sense to do so given that He doesn't do the tempting (James 1:13). We are ultimately responsible because we have the power to choose. Unbelievers are not able to free themselves from the power of sin, though they are responsible for keeping themselves in such a state and failing to receive the grace of God in Christ. Such is their choice. Believers, on the other hand, are able to resist the devil because of the power of Christ in them. They have no excuse because God has given them "everything pertaining to life and godliness" in Christ (2 Peter 1:3). We can never be justified in our sinning because God has made available to us the strength, self-control, and perseverance which we need. When we sin, it is because we choose to sin. The resources to do right are ours in Christ, and we must take advantage of them.

Let us not be surprised when temptation comes our way (1 Peter 4:12). Let us not be taken off guard, but let us be ready to fight. The world needs more Christians who are willing to stand their ground against the devil. Paul says in 1 Corinthians 15:34, "Become sober-minded as you ought, and stop sinning; for some have no knowledge of God. I speak this to your shame." Many will proclaim allegiance to God but then quit standing for truth when the battle gets tough. Some will get excited about serving Jesus on a Sunday morning but then fail to live out Christ during the week. God needs soldiers who don't run from the battle but who stand their ground, and there is a world dying in their sin which needs to see lives changed by Christ as Christians stand against sin.

The promise God gives us is that if we resist the devil, he will flee (James 4:7). God doesn't say that he might flee or that he will only flee in selected instances. It says that if we resist him and stand firm in Christ, he *will* flee. He might wage a war for a good long time, but we have the resources in Christ to stand for as long as we need because God is faithful. He will provide the way of escape and give us strength so that we can endure whatever Satan tries to throw at us.

God's command to us when it comes to battling sin and the devil is in Ephesians 6:10-11 which says, "Finally, be strong in the Lord and in the strength of His might. Put on the full armor of God, so that you will be able to stand firm against the schemes of the devil." God's call for Christians is not to be wimps against sin and the devil but to stand our ground. We need to win in our own lives so that we can be strong to serve others and support them in their fights against sin and the devil. We must keep our shield of faith raised because if we doubt, we will be vulnerable (Ephesians 6:16). We must keep the belt of truth wrapped around us so that lies don't take us down (Ephesians 6:14). We must know the Word of God so that we are able to stand our ground and not be tricked into giving in unnecessarily to the devil (Ephesians 6:17). We must keep our helmet of salvation on so that we remember who we are in Christ and just Who is standing in our court (Ephesians 6:17). Our strength is nothing compared to the devil's, but the devil's strength is nothing compared to Christ's strength which is with us. By faith in God's Word and His promises, we can win the battle. To win, we must put on Christ, trusting in His strength and infallible Word.

Life is tough, and Satan is merciless. But our God is stronger, and He will deliver us from evil. He may not spare us the temptation, but He will enable us to walk away unscathed from sin. May God enable us to walk by faith such that we resist the devil, forcing him to flee, so that we can go on advancing the kingdom of God. Battles will come, and may we, like good soldiers, stand firm.

#34

BIBLICAL PRINCIPLES FOR HEALTHY COMMUNICATION

Too often we experience a breakdown in communication. Marriages can fall apart because of cruel words spoken in an outburst of anger, business deals can be scrapped because of a failure to disclose information, workers can be fired for failing to understand their responsibilities, children can be emotionally traumatized by parents who never listen, and churches can decay without a pastor who is able to teach the Word. Communication is a significant part of who we are as human beings and as believers. In order for us to be able to maintain healthy relationships, we need to follow God's principles for healthy communication. If we fail to communicate effectively and properly, the results can be disastrous. Fortunately, if we heed God's Word, communication can be used for good, deepening and enriching our relationships.

James gives a three-fold exhortation concerning communication. He says in James 1:19, "But everyone must be quick to hear, slow to speak and slow to anger; for the anger of man does not achieve the righteousness of God." **The three points of healthy communication involve being quick to hear, slow to speak, and slow to anger.**

Anger never helps communication; it only complicates it and makes it all that more difficult. In fact, letting anger control us when we should be listening or speaking in an understanding way is totally opposed to God's ways. It is not righteous, and it is destructive. Being slow to anger allows others to feel as if they can share all that they are thinking and feeling. Being slow to anger communicates that a conversation is worth enduring because the relationship is worth saving, preserving, and deepening. It communicates that the other person's dignity matters, that the relationship matters, and that feelings expressed matter.

Being slow to anger is complemented by being slow to speak. It is easy to interrupt others, thereby communicating to them that their point of view doesn't really matter. Even if we are sure that our point of view is correct, we should still let others speak what is on their minds. Then, once they feel that they have been heard, the details can be worked out. Cutting a person off is rude, it doesn't speed up communication, and it is often a sign of arrogance, expressing that our point of view is more important than that of the other person. Being slow to speak also involves measuring our response and thinking through what we say carefully. Too many people just open their mouths, let the words come out, and clean up the mess later. We would be better off thinking through what we will say before we say it. Words should be used wisely and purposefully. This is more of a struggle for some people than others. Some people are naturally quiet, while others are naturally more talkative. The talkative ones need to learn to let others talk and to encourage the quiet ones to speak up. If the quieter ones don't ever try to open up, it is difficult to know them, help them, and enjoy their company. James doesn't say that talking is bad or that being more of a quiet person is bad. Neither does he say that everybody should talk exactly the same amount. Being a good communicator is not necessarily found in the volume of the words spoken or the lack thereof but in the ability to make the words count and to listen well. Good communicators are able to identify when they are talking too much or not enough. They are able to make others feel comfortable, cared about, and as though they are generally interested in them as people. Being slow to speak means controlling what we say, speaking wisely, and making sure others have a chance to say what is on their hearts as well.

Finally, James says that we should be quick to listen. When we get into a conversation, listening needs to be our immediate priority, especially in instances where there is a conflict. Listening is more than just hearing and just spending time with a person. Listening involves really trying to understand others and what they are going through. It is not enough just to be skilled in asking questions, but good listeners ask good questions and pay attention to the responses. How well people listen is highly indicative of how much they care about others. Suppose we spent several hours with some people and shared what was on our hearts only to find out they weren't really moved by what we said or that they had already forgotten what we said. Their failure to listen could be heartbreaking as we come to realize that they don't really care or at least are horrible at showing it. Listening is central to caring, and it is a necessary part of the love that Christians are called to show one another. Good listeners pay strong attention to others when communicating, picking up on what is not being said as well as what is being said. They can learn to see when a person is lying, holding something back, or just needing a shoulder to cry on. Listening well requires our full attention, effort, and care.

Being quick to listen, slow to speak, and slow to anger are three principles that can truly revolutionize our ability to communicate. If we want to imitate our Lord and Savior, Who Himself was a perfect communicator, we need to be willing to work on this area of our lives.

#35

A PROPER VIEW OF SELF

We live in a culture and society that is consumed with self. Self-help books sell left and right, and they even have their own section in the local bookstore. Many are preoccupied with helping themselves to become all that they can be. Yet their error and the error which the books propagate is that the answer to change and growth can be found in us. The Bible doesn't teach this at all, and it takes quite a different approach to dealing with self and how we grow as human beings.

The Biblical solution to self's struggles and failures is for self to die. *The Bible doesn't hold out any hope that self can be helped enough to be what God desires it to be, which is holy.* According to God, self is corrupt, evil, deceitful, destructive, and beyond able to please God and be all that God desires for it to be (Jeremiah 17:9, Romans 3:23). We, left to ourselves, are hopeless cases. We need divine intervention, and we need to be born again (John 3:7). We need to have our old selves die with Christ so that new selves can be raised with Him unto new life in Him (Romans 6:4). This is what happens when we come to Christ in saving faith and as we receive His forgiveness for our sins.

Colossians 3:9-10 says, "Do not lie to one another, since you laid aside the old self with its evil practices, and have put on the new self who is being renewed to a true knowledge according to the image of the One who created him." The beauty of being born again as a believer in Jesus

Christ is that the old nature which was enslaved to sin and unable to please God dies, and we are made new, able then to be renewed into conformity with Christ. 2 Corinthians 5:17 says, "Therefore if anyone is in Christ, he is a new creature; the old things passed away; behold, new things have come." Christians are new creations, consisting of a new self made in Jesus and indwelt by Jesus. It is then through His power and presence that we are able to please God and change in a way which is in conformity with Christ and His desires. The world does not have this help, this hope, or this power because they are still controlled by their old nature. As believers, however, we can grow and change rightly. We do still have the flesh to reckon with, and we still stumble into sin. We are not fully what we will one day be, but we have been freed from sin's bondage and control. We have the resources in and through Christ to walk in purity and holiness. The old self was incapable of this, and thus a world which is trying to patch together the old self is running a hopeless race. The old self is riddled with sin, and it will never be able to please God, which is the ultimate need of man. Self needs more than help; it needs to die with Christ.

As we live the Christian life, we, and the world as well for that matter, do not need to grow in our self-esteem. We do not need to have high regard for our flesh, which is weak and vulnerable (Mark 14:38), but we need to find our confidence and hope in Jesus. It is in and through Him that we have life, joy, satisfaction, worth, and a whole new identity, being adopted into God's family. We should have a high regard for Jesus Christ, Who is exalted above all things, including ourselves. *When we seek to esteem ourselves highly, we will struggle to worship God rightly.* This is not to say that we are to look down on ourselves or hate ourselves; neither is it to say that we are to be consumed or preoccupied with ourselves. We are but dust (Genesis 2:7), a jar of clay (2 Corinthians 4:6-7). God is the glory, and it is Christ in us Who gives us worth, dignity, glory, and confidence. *In Christ, we don't need to concern ourselves with our own esteem level, for our worth and dignity come from knowing Christ and being one with Him.* Colossians 3:3-4 says, "For you have died and your life is hidden with Christ in God. When Christ, who is our life, is revealed, then you also will be revealed with Him in glory." Galatians 2:20 adds, "I have been crucified with

Christ; and it is no longer I who live, but Christ lives in me; and the life which I now live in the flesh I live by faith in the Son of God, who loved me and gave Himself up for me." The message for our hearts is this: life is not about us, but it is about Christ. In fact, our lives are actually said to be one with the life that Christ lives as He lives out His will and desires in and through our hearts and lives. *So life is not about us becoming all that we can be, but it is about Christ being all that He already is in and through us.* When we yield to Christ, reckoning ourselves dead to sin and alive to God, Christ can have His way in our lives. Then, and only then, do we find our fulfillment, our greatest source of happiness, and the true culmination of the human experience.

The old self is a disaster that must die. The new self is being renewed into the image of Christ for His glory. Yet the new self is not what we are to glory in. Rather, our worth, identity, dignity, purpose, and glory is Christ in us. Jesus is our life, and our wholeness can only be found in His unconditional love. If we are struggling with self-hate or self-loathing, we need to see our lives in light of Christ's love for us. We are but jars of clay, but He lives in us and loves us. Therefore, we have worth, dignity, and honor in and through Jesus. Rather than try to increase our self-esteem, we need to further embrace Christ's love for us. Only this will give us what we seek.

#36

FROM LAZY TO LABORER

Proverbs 6:6-11 says,

> "Go to the ant, O sluggard, observe her ways and be
> wise, which, having no chief, officer or ruler, prepares
> her food in the summer and gathers her provision in
> the harvest. How long will you lie down, O sluggard?
> When will you arise from your sleep? 'A little sleep, a
> little slumber, a little folding of the hands to rest'-- your
> poverty will come in like a vagabond and your need like
> an armed man."

Solomon instructs any who are prone to laziness to look at the ant, a
tiny creature which accomplishes an incredible amount of work. What
it can carry and what it can move around in such a short time is certainly
remarkable. The ant is not driven to work like it does because of some
boss or taskmaster, but it just works hard because that is what it does.
There is nothing within the nature of the ant which is indicative of
laziness. The ant is a serious laborer, and it will have no want in time
of need. Obviously, this passage teaches that laziness is a sin and that
those who refuse to work will subsequently find themselves short on
the bare necessities of life, starving and out in the cold. These need to
labor, exert themselves, and accomplish some things in life. But there

is a deeper principle at stake here, and it has great implications for the church of Jesus Christ.

Many of the problems of the modern church could be traced at least in some way to laziness. Doing God's work God's way is extremely challenging, difficult, and laborious. It requires endurance, toughness, fortitude, and even perspiration. It is not comfortable to go knock on doors in the summer heat and share the gospel. It is not easy to go to the mission field and go on the bare minimum of food and provisions. It is a sacrifice to get up early and help set up for a Sunday service. It is tough to admit we are wrong and go to a person and ask for forgiveness, and it is certainly easier to skip reading the Bible and praying than to make time for it. There is work involved to accomplish ministry, and Jesus' desire is for laborers to enter His harvest. Jesus said in Luke 10:2, "And He was saying to them, 'The harvest is plentiful, but the laborers are few; therefore beseech the Lord of the harvest to send out laborers into His harvest.'" The church has a lot of bodies, but we need more laborers. 1 Corinthians 15:58 says, "Therefore, my beloved brethren, be steadfast, immovable, always abounding in the work of the Lord, knowing that your toil is not in vain in the Lord." The idea of toiling for the Lord speaks of an intense labor, something that requires severe sacrifice and energy. Paul is painting a picture that he wants the church to be what Christ asked the disciples to pray for, a body of laborers who are willing to have sorrow, grief, sweat, and trouble if only it will advance the gospel and the name of Christ. These are not fair-weather Christians, but these are willing to do the work that is uncomfortable, which brings persecution, and which involves sacrifice.

Too often the church looks to gimmicks or quick-fixes to accomplish the Great Commission, a sort of get-rich-quick scheme in the church. Yet, just as get-rich-quick schemes are not schemes but scams, so too is any method of trying to accomplish the Great Commission that doesn't involve hard work by faith. The ant understands that hard work is required for a return on its labor, and in the kingdom, believers must labor and toil by God's grace and power if they want to be rewarded. True and lasting spiritual fruit is not easily gained. Yes, it is true that striving in our own effort is a waste of effort, but living by faith and by the Spirit's empowerment is still labor. Just ask Paul or any of the twelve disciples. They studied the Word, they preached, they tarried in prayer, they traveled as missionaries, and they suffered persecution. But they will be rewarded greatly because they were steadfast, immovable, and abounded in God's work.

There is an interesting phenomenon happening in the modern church. Many churches have a smorgasbord of "ministries," but upon closer examination, true ministry really isn't being accomplished, that is, ministry which involves evangelism, prayer, discipleship, counseling, in-depth Bible study, etc. There are typically a lot of activities, but we need more ministry. On the flip side, some churches do things which directly pertain to the Great Commission, and yet they wear people out because they expect them to come to Sunday morning service, Sunday evening service, the prayer meeting, the mid-week Bible study, the community activity on Saturday, and so on. Too much activity for people can drain them spiritually to the point where they lose their first love and merely go through the motions. The answer is not to overwhelm ourselves with activity or to engage in activity not necessarily related to carrying out our commission. Rather, we are to give ourselves where we can and as the Spirit would have us in actual, authentic, hard-work oriented ministry.

There is much in the Bible to remind us that time is short, that our lives are but a vapor (James 4:14), and that we need to walk circumspectly, making the most of the time (Ephesians 5:15-16). God doesn't want sluggards in His army, but He wants workers that put the ants to shame. May God make us effective laborers who truly engage the enemy in battle and advance the truth of the gospel in love.

#37

NO LONGER TO BE CHILDREN

What a joy it is to be adopted into God's family as a child of the King! John 1:12 contains such a wonderful promise that "as many as received Him, to them He gave the right to become children of God, even to those who believe in His name." It is indeed a most wonderful privilege to become a child of God when we receive Christ into our hearts as Savior and Lord. Yet, are we always to be children?

It is tempting to think of ourselves always as children of God, given that we will always be sons and daughters of Him, but the Bible suggests that we are no longer to be children at least in terms of our maturity. Ephesians 4:14-16 says,

> "As a result, we are *no longer to be children*, tossed here and there by waves and carried about by every wind of doctrine, by the trickery of men, by craftiness in deceitful scheming; but speaking the truth in love, we are to grow up in all aspects into Him who is the head, even Christ, from whom the whole body, being fitted and held together by what every joint supplies, according to the proper working of each individual part, causes the growth of the body for the building up of itself in love" (emphasis added).

Thus, believers are not to remain infants in Christ, but they are to grow to maturity in Christ. They are to be fully-grown, fruit-bearing, reproducing disciples of Christ. They will always be children of God in that they are His offspring through Christ, but they are to be grown children nonetheless.

There is nothing wrong with first being a child, for when we come to Christ, we are born again. Thus, we start the Christian life as a spiritual infant, needing milk, the fundamentals of the faith. We need a lot of training and instruction, and we need the basics before the more advanced things can make sense. This is a normal place to be in the process of growth, but it is not where we are to be indefinitely as Christians (1 Corinthians 3:2, Hebrews 5:13).

Paul explains in Ephesians 4:11-12 that God has gifted godly teachers and preachers to build up the body of Christ through sound instruction so that we can grow. Verse 13 explains the desired extent of our growth when it says, "Until we all attain to the unity of the faith, and of the knowledge of the Son of God, to a mature man, to the measure of the stature which belongs to the fullness of Christ." In other words, we are to become imitators of Christ to a full extent. This is the summation of maturity. Of course, this will be a lifelong process of growth and change, but we must recognize that we are to keep growing. The Ephesians were a doctrinally well-taught group, and Paul delved into some heavy teaching concepts with them throughout the Book of Ephesians. The Ephesian Christians were meat-eaters, going beyond bottle-feeding, even past bibs and booster seats, to the point where they could feed themselves and others who needed help. Thus, they had the privilege of plunging deeper into the profound mysteries of God and into the depths of the glory and wonder of the Word of God. This is a place we all should want to be.

Yet, even though the Ephesians were generally mature believers, still they needed to be taught and keep growing as we all do. Too often we as believers tend to skip over the difficult to understand passages or the ones which are more controversial. Yet we should be willing to explore them all, and may God raise up godly teachers after His own heart with the wisdom of Christ who can help us to understand such passages.

116

We ought not to be content with a minimalist grasp of Scripture, but rather we should seek to dig deeper and deeper and deeper. We are not speaking merely of head knowledge, however. The Scripture applied to a tender heart leads to change, sanctification, and obedience. Right theology should lead to right living, if we are sensitive to our Lord. Vain and empty knowledge which goes unapplied can lead to arrogance, but true Holy Spirit-given insight to the Word moves us to obey. Then, as we grow, we are able to share what we know with others. Parents are able to teach their children God's Word and ways, pastors are able to equip their church bodies, and the church grows increasingly stable, discerning, mature, and Christlike.

If the church is all children, then some of the children need to grow up. If there are no children, we need to pray for God to open up doors of opportunity for evangelism so that we can see His blessing of conversions. We must keep growing, reproducing, and equipping others to become like Christ.

There is a time for being a child, but it is a temporary time. We come to Christ as children, but we must grow to maturity in Him as His life, desires, and ways are to shine through us. May God make us more and more like Jesus to His glory as we grow up in Him and dig deeper into His Word.

#38

THE FEAR OF THE LORD

There are many directions a person can take in life, but the Bible says that as we make decisions, either we can be wise or foolish. If we want to be wise, we must start by dealing with our hearts in that we must be sure that we fear the Lord and have surrendered our lives to Him. Proverbs 9:10 says, "The fear of the LORD is the beginning of wisdom, and the knowledge of the Holy One is understanding." Those who fear the Lord are those who have true wisdom, understanding, and insight as to what this world and this life are all about. They are those who do not waffle when it comes to principle and truth, but they stand firm for righteousness and justice, things in which God delights. Those who fear the Lord don't pander to the crowd or seek to people-please, but they seek to please the Audience of One.

In addition to being the beginning of wisdom, the fear of the Lord is also the end of all things, that is, it is the summation of our purpose and life on this earth. Ecclesiastes 12:13-14 says, "The conclusion, when all has been heard, is: fear God and keep His commandments, because this applies to every person. For God will bring every act to judgment, everything which is hidden, whether it is good or evil." Some live for selfish pleasure, others for riches, and others for fame, notoriety, and vain ambition. Those who are wise, however, will live by the guiding principle of the fear of the Lord. They will seek His will above their own, knowing that God sees all and will hold them accountable for how they live. Those who could care less about God's judgment because they don't fear Him won't care to receive the gospel. But those who do fear the just punishment of God for sin have reason and incentive to trust in Christ. The fear of the Lord is the only right posture for living, and it is the only way that leads to wisdom.

Fearing the Lord is a starting point for faith and a guiding motivator for life in Christ. Our entire lives should be lived by fearing God and keeping His commandments. Those who fear God will keep the commands of God, living out Christ's desires on earth. When we fail to fear God and thereby exalt ourselves, we will sin. The fear of God is to be a lifelong posture which will enable us to walk in holiness over the long haul. The Christian life requires much perseverance, and a right view of a holy God will help keep us on the right track. Proverbs 28:14 says, "How blessed is the man who fears always, but he who hardens his heart will fall into calamity." As soon as we start being careless, as soon as we devalue eternal priorities in exchange for temporal pleasure, and as soon as we lose sight of God's nature as a consuming fire (Hebrews 12:29), we will walk arrogantly and lackadaisically into Satan's traps. It is imperative that we recognize that we are engaged in a battle and that we represent the true Sovereign of the universe. There is nothing else and no one else to fear but God. He alone has all power, and nothing happens beyond what He ordains. He deserves our full allegiance, obedience, respect, reverence, awe, and fear. God's manifestations of Himself as recorded in the Scripture as earthquakes, trumpets, fire, thunder, and so on are there to remind us of His awesome power, wonder, and authority (1 Kings 19:11-12, John 12:29). He is the Master of the universe, and we must keep that in mind as we make choices each day.

Jesus says in Matthew 10:28, "Do not fear those who kill the body but are unable to kill the soul; but rather fear Him who is able to destroy both soul and body in hell." Only unbelievers will face God's wrath in hell, so, as believers, we wrongly understand the idea of fearing God if we think God is going to pour out His wrath upon us. As believers, the fear of the Lord shows up most clearly based upon how we view our time on earth. Those who fear God will keep His commandments not because they are afraid of God's wrath but because they know that they have a stewardship before God (1 Corinthians 9:17). They understand that they will have to stand before the judgment seat of Christ and give an account for how they lived their lives (2 Corinthians 5:10). Some Christians will receive an abundance of rewards on that day, while others will suffer great loss as they recognize that they were not nearly as faithful as they could have and should have been (1 Corinthians 3:10-15). When we remember that God sees all, knows all, and is over all, it will prompt us to be careful as to how we use our time, energy, talents, and resources on this earth. If we are keeping God's commandments willingly and joyfully, it is a clear sign that we fear God and can expect rewards. If live for ourselves and think very little upon advancing the kingdom of God, we lack wisdom and don't fear God as we ought to. We need to try to view our lives in terms of how Jesus the Judge views our lives. When we start concerning ourselves with what He thinks, we are fearing God and preparing ourselves for a much happier judgment day.

There is none like our God Whose power, majesty, glory, holiness, and perfection demand our offering our lives in sacrifice and service to Him. We need to remember that we are ultimately accountable to Christ, so may His satisfaction, honor, and glory be our chief delight.

#39

BIBLICAL DECISION-MAKING

There is a lot of teaching on how to find and know the will of God for our lives, but we really need not make it over-complicated. Here are five truths from Scripture to help guide us so that we can make wise choices and honor God with our lives.

1. God leads us according to and never in contradiction to His Word.

2 Timothy 3:16-17 says, "All Scripture is inspired by God and profitable for teaching, for reproof, for correction, for training in righteousness; so that the man of God may be adequate, equipped for every good work." If we want to be sanctified, if we want to be used of God to bless others, if we want to be able to speak truth, if we want to be able to avoid deception, and if we want to be fully equipped and adequate to accomplish God's purposes on earth, we must be in God's Word, studying it and meditating upon it. This is a lifelong journey, and it is not always easy, requiring perseverance and much prayer. Fortunately, God has given us His Holy Spirit to help teach us the truth, for through Him, the Word can make sense and pierce to the depths of our souls (Hebrews 4:12). As we are in God's Word, the Holy Spirit will constantly be working to teach us new things about God and His ways, His principles, and how He wants us to live this life. There are so many decisions that would be greatly simplified if only we knew what God already said in His Word. Those who want to walk in wisdom and make God-

honoring decisions need to be people who are regularly in God's Word and devoted to learning God's principles for how to live this life.

2. God leads us by the work and ministry of the Holy Spirit in our hearts.

Romans 8:14 says, "For all who are being led by the Spirit of God, these are sons of God." Galatians 5:18 echoes this truth, saying," But if you are led by the Spirit, you are not under the Law." Jesus was also led by the Spirit (Luke 4:1), and the leading of the Spirit is thus a mark of the true follower of God. Having the Spirit's leading in our hearts is a clear indicator of God's provision, blessing, and faithfulness in our lives. He does not leave us to be on our own, but He is always there to throw up a red flag if we are veering off course of where we should be. He is there to create an internal prompting in our hearts that we need to do something that we have been praying about and seeking God's principles about. He will always lead according to God's principles and never through some additional revelation, for the Bible is complete. No words are added to God's Word without a curse (Revelation 22:18-19). Thus, the Spirit does not give us new revelation, but He leads us through our spirits by helping us to apply God's Word, to see as God sees, to desire as God desires, and to think as Christ thinks. He shapes our wills to do and want what God wants. We will know when we are grieving or resisting the Spirit, and it will be clear to us when He is leading us in a certain way. The world is led by false spirits of distortion (Isaiah 19:14), but God's people are led by the Spirit of the Lord to give us rest and to bring God glory (Isaiah 63:14). We should never underestimate the Spirit's value in helping us make decisions, and if we choose to ignore His leading, we should expect trouble.

3. God leads us by giving us wisdom when we ask Him in faith.

God calls upon us to ask Him for wisdom in James 1:5-6, saying, "But if any of you lacks wisdom, let him ask of God, who gives to all generously and without reproach, and it will be given to him. But he must ask in faith without any doubting, for the one who doubts is like the surf of the sea, driven and tossed by the wind." Wisdom will be given to those who truly seek it, who truly want it, and who truly believe that God will give it to them. The mere reality that we have to ask for wisdom implies that we will often lack wisdom. Despite our study of God's Word and the fact that we have the Spirit in our hearts, we still need to ask for the wisdom of God. This is because we will constantly need to keep growing and learning as God gives us challenges fit for doing just that. We should never think that we have arrived spiritually such that we have all wisdom or that we fully understand the Bible. God has a way of putting us in places where we will need to ask Him for wisdom such that we will explore the depths and wonders of God's Word further and know the leading of His Spirit better. When we have a tough decision to make and we don't know what to do, we need only to ask God for wisdom in faith. He will provide it. This promise should provide us with great confidence and hope for the future.

4. God leads us through the desires of our hearts if and only if we are fully delighting in Him.

Psalm 37:4 says, "Delight yourself in the LORD; And He will give you the desires of your heart." The key thing here is that we do not do what we want without seeking the will and wisdom of God, for if we start thinking that our desires are always infallible, then we will likely end up fulfilling the desires of our flesh. However, if we are confident that we are indeed fully seeking the delight of God and His glory, then we ought not to entirely discount the desires and affections of our hearts. We should be patient as we test our desires to make sure that they are right and that they align with God's principles in His Word and in His timing for our lives. But let us not completely ignore what we long for in our hearts as if God's purposes are always to spite our desires. That is not the kind of God we serve. He enjoys giving us good and perfect gifts (James 1:17), gifts that even surpass that which we could ask for or imagine (Ephesians 3:20). 1 John 3:21-22 says, "Beloved, if our heart does not condemn us, we have confidence before God; and whatever we ask we receive from Him, because we keep His commandments and do the things that are pleasing in His sight." Those who are walking faithfully before God, keeping His commandments, can truly delight in God. These should not totally ignore the desires of their hearts, but they do need to remember that God in His wisdom and perfection is "greater than our heart and knows all things" (1 John 3:20). Desires are part of the equation, but they must always be tested and submitted to the Spirit of God and to the Word of God because God doesn't make mistakes, though we do.

5. God leads us as we persevere in prayer.

When we are faced with a dilemma and tough predicament, we need to follow Nehemiah's example in Nehemiah 1:4. He says, "When I heard these words, I sat down and wept and mourned for days; and I was fasting and praying before the God of heaven." It is easy to want to act immediately, and God is not oblivious to the timeframes that we might be under. But, as Nehemiah rightly did, we should spend time before the Lord, casting our requests upon Him as we beg and plead with Him for change, for direction, for insight, and for answers. Nehemiah didn't take a step of action until he had clear direction. God blessed his steps and honored his faith, but he first stopped to seek God, praying and fasting for days. It is easy to be impatient with God, but we will save ourselves a lot of trouble and wasted time and effort if we commit to praying first before acting brashly.

There will be times in life where we will be confused and lack wisdom. This is just the reality of this world and this time. Yet we do not have a God Who is confused or lacking anything, and our God desires to give us wisdom so that we can make God-honoring decisions. For the sake of His name and glory, He wants to help us. Let us be those who turn to God in our time of need, listening to His Word, obeying His commands, being sensitive to the Spirit's ministry in our hearts, evaluating our desires before Him, and persevering in prayer. When we are in darkness, God will give us the light that we need (Psalm 119:105).

#40

A GLIMPSE OF HEAVEN

The Bible doesn't give us an abundance of details as to what heaven will be like, but it does give us what we need to know. After all, how could we possibly fathom all that God has stored up for His saints to enjoy and experience? If we could understand heaven fully now, it wouldn't be much to look forward to. But, the God Who is able to do even above and beyond what we can ask or imagine (Ephesians 3:20) will create a new heaven and a new earth that will transcend any feeble attempt by our present earthly imaginations to be able to conceive of what heaven will be like. The best and greatest we can think of or ask for, God will do more. In fact, He will do much more. As such, we have much to look forward to, even though we don't know specifically what all is coming.

What Scripture does reveal to us we should take to heart so that we have hope. The Bible says that heaven is paradise. Christ, when speaking to the thief on the cross who repents, says that he will be with Him that very day in paradise (Luke 23:43). Paul speaks of being caught up into the third heaven into the very presence of God, and he describes it as paradise (2 Corinthians 12:1-4). As good as the Garden of Eve was, heaven will be perfect, a perfect paradise. We know that there will be no more pain, tears, grief, or sorrow because Christ will wipe away all tears (Revelation 21:4). All physical ailments, emotional pain, and sorrow will be gone for we will be in the presence of Christ Himself (Revelation 21:3). Perhaps that is the best part of all, having the eternal

125

opportunity to be in the very presence of our Savior face to face. Yet there is more.

In heaven, we will sing praises to God (Revelation 4:11). We won't be bored or just sitting around because God has much for us to do, learn, see, and accomplish. We will have responsibilities as we reign with Him and serve Him (Revelation 22:3, 5). Our souls will be filled with ecstasy as we get to work with Jesus to bring about His wonderful, glorious, and perfect plan in paradise. We will see those who have died in Christ, and we will be reunited. We won't go to church, per se, because we will worship Christ Himself Who is our temple (Revelation 21:22). There will be transparent streets of gold (Revelation 21:18, 21) and all kinds of precious stones for the foundation of the walls of the city of the New Jerusalem (Revelation 21:19-21). Jesus will light the world (Revelation 21:23), God will be on His throne (Revelation 22:3), and the tree of life will be there (Revelation 22:2), representing our eternal existence with God. There will no longer be any curse, which means that there will no longer be any sin (Revelation 22:3). Finally, our battle against our flesh will be over, and we will be able to live in holiness perfectly. There will be no fear any longer, for Jesus will be our King.

There just isn't any reason why we shouldn't look forward to heaven. We can rest assured that worshipping God in heaven in paradise will not be boring. He will have much for us to do, see, discover, and be responsible for. Psalm 16:11 says, "In Your presence is fullness of joy; in Your right hand there are pleasures forever." *Heaven is thus joy maxed out because we will be in the presence of Christ and we will be able to experience the eternal pleasures which He has stored up for us.* We will be forever with God, which in and of itself is so wonderful it is beyond our ability to fully comprehend. Yet there will be still more joy, pleasure, responsibility, and infinitely more.

It just can't get any better than heaven, so let's fix our hope entirely upon Christ's coming (1 Peter 1:13) as we wait for something beyond and so much better than what our imaginations can conceive. One day very soon, we who are children of God will see our Savior face to face, and our joy will be beyond complete. "He who testifies to these things says, 'Yes, I am coming quickly.' Amen, 'Come, Lord Jesus'" (Revelation

22:20). In a world of many distractions, disappointments, delusions, and deceptions, one thing is for sure. Christ is coming back to reign and to gather His own. May this reality encourage us to be holy, to hope, and to persevere.

#41

THE FILLING OF THE SPIRIT

Ephesians 5:18 says, "And do not get drunk with wine, for that is dissipation, but be filled with the Spirit." Paul is purposefully setting up a comparison here between drunkenness and the filling of the Spirit. Drunkenness, of course, is wrong, whereas the filling of the Spirit is desirable and commanded of us. Drunkenness and the filling of the Spirit do have some things in common, which is why Paul would attempt to compare them. When a person is drunk, he is controlled by alcohol and totally under the influence of it. When a person is filled with the Spirit, the same principles apply in that he is controlled by the Spirit and totally under the Spirit's influence and direction. However, there are obvious differences between the influence of alcohol and the filling of the Spirit. For example, alcohol brings out the bad desires of the heart by lowering inhibitions and restricting good judgment. The filling of the Spirit brings out that which is good and full of life, increasing good judgment and sharpening our relationship with God. When a believer is filled with the Spirit, he is fully surrendered and submitted to the rule and will of God in his heart. Self-seeking is abandoned and exchanged for seeking the pleasure and purposes of God. This is not a bitter obedience or an obedience which looks to exalt self, but this is an obedience that is consumed totally and exclusively with the glory of God. The filling of the Spirit moves a person to obey with joy as he is consumed with the awe, majesty, and perfection of God. This is a state of utmost freedom and usefulness to God, and it is a state where believers are commanded to be regularly, continually, and on an ongoing basis.

The filling of the Spirit is available to all believers from day one as a follower of Christ. If we walk in humility and abide with Christ, we can expect to be filled. If we quench the Spirit or grieve Him with sin or pride, we can expect not to be filled. *All believers have the Spirit within their hearts; the issue is whether or not they are letting the Spirit have all of their hearts.* The filling of the Spirit is not some advanced state of being, some higher plane of thinking, or some mystical out of body experience. Rather, it is a yielding to the Spirit's leading and guiding as we depend upon Him for strength rather than upon ourselves. Those who are filled with the Spirit are able, ready, and willing to receive the truth of God's Word. The result of the Spirit's filling is great faithfulness and fruitfulness as God accomplishes great things through us.

How the command to "be filled" is stated is also important. It implies a yielding to the work of God because it commands us to let God do something to us and in us. It doesn't say "fill yourself" but rather "be filled." We do have a choice in the matter, but it is a choice to let God do what God wants to do. Such is the submissive nature of the filling of the Spirit. The command also implies that we continue to be filled. We are not to live sometimes filled, but we should be filled all the time. Going from filled to empty and back and forth over and over again speaks of a spiritual instability problem stemming from pride and sin. God's call is to be continually filled as we continually walk in humility and obedience. As we come before God empty, humble, and in faith, we can trust that His Spirit will fill us and empower us to do His will.

Acts 4:31 says, "And when they had prayed, the place where they had gathered together was shaken, and they were all filled with the Holy Spirit and began to speak the word of God with boldness." In verse 28, prior to God's answer of the disciples' prayer, we see their heart in the matter when they say, "Do whatever Your hand and Your purpose predestined to occur." This is the key in being filled with the Spirit. There was no question about the humility of the disciples or of their desire to obey. They were fully open and surrendered to what God would have them to be and do. They didn't hold on to sin in their hearts, and they were ready and willing to be obedient. As a result, God answered their prayer, filled them with the Spirit, and empowered them to speak forth the Word of God with boldness. The filling of the Spirit takes weak people and makes them spiritually strong. It takes the timid and makes them bold, and it takes the fearful and makes them courageous.

When we are filled with the Spirit, there is a distinct difference from when we are not in terms of how God works in and through us to build His kingdom. There is a power, wisdom, and strength there that we just know is not our own. What God accomplishes with those who are filled with the Spirit is plain and simply above and beyond what we as humans could do. It is truly a supernatural event, and it is to be this way all the time.

#42

ONE WAY

Those who truly love Christ must have come to Him with an understanding that He is the only hope of salvation. Indeed, He says of Himself in John 14:6, "I am the way, and the truth, and the life; no one comes to the Father but through Me." Jesus is an inclusive exclusivist. In other words, His love is boundless in that He desires all people to repent and come to know Him (2 Peter 3:9). He offers the way to the Father through Himself to all regardless of religion, gender, age, rank, nationality, etc. His desire for salvation to come to all people is one of total inclusivism, absolute non-discrimination, and an utter lack of partiality. He opens the door for all who would receive His Son Jesus Christ. Yet God is also an exclusivist. That is, He offers an exclusive means to salvation through His Son Jesus Christ. He does not allow for any who deny that Jesus is God and the only means for salvation to enter His heaven. He is very specific about what it takes to enter heaven, and central to saving faith is believing that Jesus is the way, the truth, and the life, with emphasis on the singular "the."

The world, on the other hand, offers many ways to worship. In fact, individual faith is quickly becoming a religious smorgasbord, as people pick and choose parts of religions and mix them with other religions as if they are interchangeable parts. This is syncretism, a blending of various religions into a perverted whole. It is a man-centered way of belief as people choose the parts that they like or that are convenient for their sinful lifestyles while casting aside the rest. Jesus hates when we mix truth with lies, so syncretism is not acceptable to Him.

Neither is pluralism. Pluralism teaches that a variety of viewpoints can all be truth, even if they contradict one another. Pluralism teaches that truth is not absolute but relative. This belief results in teaching that says that Jesus is one way to the truth but not the only way to the truth. It allows for some people to believe Jesus is a way to God so long as they allow for other people to believe that their way to God is also true. The problem is that religions contradict one another, with only true Christianity affirming the deity of Christ and salvation by grace through faith through His work on the cross alone. Pluralism creates a totally illogical dynamic of belief by allowing contradictory truths to be accepted as truth. It is like saying that green and red can both be red at the same time and in the same sense even though only red is truly red. Pluralism says that green must be allowed to be red also, as well as yellow, blue, orange, etc. This form of belief is of the devil's making because it denies Jesus' own words when He said that He is the only truth.

It is becoming rarer and rarer to find those who believe the whole counsel of God. We live in a day and age where professing Christians are more likely to deny the exclusivity of Jesus Christ than to believe in it. Too few Christians are willing to take a stand and say that other world religions are in error and in danger of hell fire if they do not repent and turn to Christ as Savior and Lord. It is a highly unpopular thing to do to take a stand for Jesus Christ, but Jesus wasn't popular either. Pilate said "what is truth?" as if ignoring the very idea, blaspheming Christ in the process (John 18:38). Though we have newer terms for this blasphemy, the same lie that the devil has been propagating persists still. It has just been dressed up in more modern sounding terms such as "pluralism" or "tolerance." As Christians we must be willing to hold to the truth that Jesus is the only truth. In fact, He is the very definition and embodiment of truth. This is a very radical position to take, but it is true.

The time has come and will continue to come when "Christian" leaders seek common ground with those who do not share Christian ideals. They will (and have already) joined hands with those who kill babies and redefine marriage. They will glorify social progress (education, eradication of disease and hunger, etc.) over saving faith through Jesus alone. Of course, we should do what we can to educate, to feed empty stomachs, and to curtail disease, but what good is an educated, fed, and healthy world that will die in hell. We must not forget the higher importance of the spiritual, eternal reality. The gospel of Jesus Christ must not be compromised but rather remain the preeminent reality that it is. As Colossians 1:18 says, "That in all things [Christ] might have the preeminence."

Christians must defend the truth and stand upon it (Jude 3). The true church is the pillar and support of the truth (1 Timothy 3:15), but as soon as it denies Jesus as the only way or begins calling Him a liar (i.e. He really did intend a man to marry a man) or a lunatic (i.e. He just didn't know all that we know today), the church is no longer the church.

Any movement away from an exclusive way of salvation is of the antichrist. Any catering to sin, whether homosexuality, abortion, or any other, is of the antichrist. When we forget to mention hell, sin, and repentance, we pave the way for the antichrist. May the church not prepare the way of the antichrist but rather preach the gospel and get ready for Christ's return in glory. We have a beautiful message to carry (Romans 10:15), one of great love and inclusivism through Jesus, so let us not bow to pluralism and fail to stand for the truth (1 Corinthians 16:13, 2 Thessalonians 2:15, 1 Peter 5:12).

Thousands listened to Jesus' teaching, but only a few followed Him through the cross and beyond. Most said His teaching was too difficult. Most today would say it is too exclusive. Are we willing to be part of the ridiculed few?

#43

IF YOU ARE DECEIVED,
YOU DO NOT KNOW IT

Do we honestly think that if Eve realized the severity of the consequences of her choice and that she was being tricked by the devil that she would have eaten the fruit? If she had known that the fruit would destroy the joy and paradise that she had and force her into great pain and strife, do we really think that she would followed the devil's counsel? The obvious answer should be "no." If she had known and seen the truth, she wouldn't have sinned against God. Such is the nature of deception; it is unseen, unrealized, and, thus, dangerously deadly.

We are familiar with rebellion, the sin that God likens to witchcraft (1 Samuel 15:23). We have all rebelled against God at some point or another, when we have seen and known the right thing to do and not done it. Or, we might have known that what we were thinking about doing was wrong and yet done it anyway. In either case, we knew what we were doing, and we were willing to take our chances in going against God. These are willful sins which grieve and quench the Spirit of God and the heart of God. Rebellion isn't hard to identify because it is an "in your face" kind of sin. But deception is far more subtle. It is a sin that doesn't want to be seen for what it is. It is a temptation that wants to masquerade as wisdom and blessing. It is lust that seeks to hide its fangs. Deception is cunning, shrewd, manipulative, and deadly.

It allows darkness to move in close for the kill and to kill while as yet being unrecognized. Deception can accomplish its work because the one being deceived doesn't realize his or her own imminent destruction.

For some reason, we often think of deception merely as rebellion, which it is in that it is sin, but an important distinction remains. *Deception is first unperceived temptation followed by unrecognized rebellion.* It might be that a person comes to their senses soon after they see the results of their decision. The destruction is evidence of their having been deceived, and thus they might come to their senses. Yet others may continue in deception for a long time because they ignore sin, don't care to be introspective, or value voices other than God's Word as higher or at least on par with God's Word. Then there are those who are just naïve that need to be pulled from the fire lest they destroy themselves unwittingly. Surely, we can be destroyed for lack of knowledge (Hosea 4:6). The more knowledge of Scripture we have that is true wisdom, the more discerning we can become and the harder it is for us to be deceived. The less understanding we have, the easier it is for us to be made victims. Deception must be avoided as much as possible as we trust God's Word lest we be made into rebels unaware.

Satan is extremely shrewd, and he masquerades as an angel of light (2 Corinthians 11:14). Not surprisingly, many false religions and cults have begun as a result of a person encountering an angel of light. Yet he is able to make sin look like good even to those who are of the one true faith. Thus, we must be on the alert, aware that we are being preyed upon, and diligent to be in the Word. If something doesn't feel right in our souls, it is likely the Spirit telling us to beware. The Spirit is better at identifying deception than we might be, particularly as we are younger in our faith. As we grow, it is easier to pin chapter and verse on a wile of the devil, but the Spirit can always be relied upon to get our attention when we are in danger. The best response in such an instance is to flee. We should get as far away from evil as we can, and in so doing, we resist the devil such that he is really the one who flees (James 4:7).

In the case of deception and temptation, we need to escape as fast as we can. If we reason with deception, the lies might go deeper still. Satan doesn't need to be argued with and sin doesn't need to be rationalized.

Deception's power is in dialogue; victory, on the other hand, is in rebuke and resistance. All Eve needed to do was to say what God said, believe it, and walk away from the serpent, but she didn't. When the devil tempted Jesus, Jesus used only a few words to respond, and they were Scripture (see Luke 4:1-13). Truth sets free from the web of deception, which might very well contain bits and pieces of Scripture pieced together into a perverted whole. Scripture uncompromised is a freeing thing (John 8:31-32), and it sets the devil to running. Praise God that there is a map and a compass for us to live this life. We don't have to rebel, and neither do we have to be deceived because we have the uncompromised, infallible, always-true, and forever-enduring Word of God to enlighten our paths along with the Spirit of God to illumine our hearts and minds to rightly apply the Word. We have all we need for life and godliness in Christ (2 Peter 1:3), and the issue is if we will listen to His leading.

In life, there are many voices telling us to do something, go somewhere, buy such-and-such, or to become this-and-that. Our minds replay voices, songs, quotes, sermons, books, and so on, but one Voice must stand authoritatively above them all, namely, Jesus Christ through His Word. May the Word of God be what replays through our minds more and more, such that we meditate upon it day and night (Joshua 1:8). Wrong thoughts must be taken captive unto obedience to Christ (2 Corinthians 10:5), and right thoughts must fill our minds (Philippians 4:8). The more we are Word-saturated, Spirit-filled, and Jesus-loving, the harder we will be to deceive. May God anchor us upon His Word, and may He enable us to live free from deception and rebellion to His glory.

#44
SEVEN PRINCIPLES OF GIVING

How we handle our finances is important, and it reflects where our hearts and priorities are at. Here are seven Scriptural principles to guide us as we seek to honor God's command to His church to give of what we have been given.

First of all, our giving should be free. Jesus said in Matthew 10:8, "Freely you received, freely give." All that we have is from God, and He commands us to give freely. We ought not to expect something in return as if we are looking for approval or honor before men, but simply because we have the privilege of being able to give. And giving is a privilege before God, so we ought to take care that we live in financial balance so that we are able to give as God gives to us. To give freely is to give not expecting or even desiring some temporal personal benefit in return. The joy comes from the act of giving in Jesus' name, period, because of the joy and glory it brings to Him. The by-product of this selfless attitude is joy and eternal blessing.

Second, giving is to be in secret. Matthew 6:3-4 says, "But when you give to the poor, do not let your left hand know what your right hand is doing, so that your giving will be in secret; and your Father who sees what is done in secret will reward you." We will have had our reward in full if we are seeking to give for the sake of looking good to others. Those who give to be seen by men have forfeited their eternal reward and their joy in exchange for temporal recognition and renown by mere people. Giving in secret keeps others from having a chance to judge us, envy us, compare with us, or applaud us, and we them. Churches need to be mindful of their times of taking in financial gifts that the system does not contribute to judgment, ranking, competition, etc. Others have no business knowing what we give as a family unit to Christ's work and church, and we have a responsibility not to showcase or flaunt what we give. Neither should we feel embarrassed or worry about being put to shame. *There are few joys on earth as being able to freely give to others without anybody else knowing.*

Third, we are to give according to our ability (Ezra 2:69, Nehemiah 5:8, 2 Corinthians 8:3, 12). We can't give what we don't have, and we are not to put our families at risk of not having a home to live in or food to eat. God understands that life costs money. We must meet our debts and expenses so as to keep a good testimony before men. What good does it do to give to a charity and then fail to pay a bill or bounce a check? We do more good for the kingdom by living in balance and following God's leading over time.

Fourth, there are times that God will move us to give above what we feel able to do (2 Corinthians 8:3). This is not the rule or the norm (see point #3), but there are instances where God will call us to give in such a way that really requires faith on our parts. This is one of God's ways to cause us to experience growth in Christ through an increasing need to rely upon Him in faith. If this is the case, God will make it clear.

Fifth, we will reap in proportion to that which we sow. 2 Corinthians 9:6 says, "Now this I say, he who sows sparingly will also reap sparingly, and he who sows bountifully will also reap bountifully." In other words, those who give generously will themselves be given back to generously by God. No one can say exactly how God will repay a person's generosity or exactly when it will happen, so we must beware of any who claim to know the mind of God in regard to our finances. God honors those who give to His work bountifully, abundantly, and generously. *Generosity within our ability is a sacrifice that leads to great joy and reward.*

Sixth, we are not to give out of duty and against our will but cheerfully. 2 Corinthians 9:7 says that our giving is not to be done "grudgingly or under compulsion, for God loves a cheerful giver." God wants giving to be a happy experience, not a drudgery or mere requirement. The giver is not trying to satisfy the harsh expectations of a deity, nor is he supposed to be giving begrudgingly and against his will. Giving is a "want to" thing. God moves in a person to give joyfully and cheerfully. The word for cheerful could also mean "prompt or ready to act." *In other words, a cheerful giver is both a joyful giver and an eager giver, ready, willing, desiring, and prepared to give.*

Seventh, we give as the Lord leads us individually. 2 Corinthians 9:7 says, "Each one must do just as he has purposed in his heart." We are not to give because our pastor motivated us by giving us a guilt trip about tithing. We are not to give so that we can get God off our backs or to earn His favor. Rather, we are to give because we want to give and because we believe that God would be honored by our giving. If we are not purposing in our hearts to give or if we find that we have no desire to give, we had better ask the Lord why these things are the case. It is one thing to be unsure about a church or a ministry and be hesitant to give to it. It is another thing to be hesitant to give altogether. The important thing is that we are faithful and willing to give where and to the extent that God leads us to give.

Giving is an indescribable gift in and of itself (2 Corinthians 9:15). The world cannot understand this as they do not enjoy giving for the most part; they enjoy getting. The Christian's way is backwards, getting much more joy out of giving than receiving. Jesus Himself said, "It is more blessed to give than to receive" (Acts 20:35). Thus, in giving we truly receive.

#45

HOW TO HANDLE YOUR FEELINGS

Feelings are a very confusing thing if one tries to think about what they actually are and what they actually do. One thing is for sure, feelings are powerful, and they can significantly impact our thinking and our choices. Thus, we must understand what they are and how to best live as human beings whom God made with feelings.

In some circles, it is taught to suppress or ignore feelings as if desire or passion of any kind is dangerous and deadly. This kind of thinking stems from poor theology about the nature of the believer's heart. If we believe the Scripture which says that we are given new hearts (Ezekiel 36:26, Matthew 5:8) and made into new creations (2 Corinthians 5:17) who are no longer slaves to sin (Romans 6:6), then we need not categorically fear our emotions as if they are always evil and destined to lead us astray. The Bible doesn't portray such a negative view of feelings. For example, the bride in Song of Solomon says that her feelings were aroused for her beloved (Song of Song of Solomon 5:4). Jesus felt compassion for the people who followed him for three days and needed food (Mark 8:2). In the early church, everyone kept feeling a sense of awe because of the powerful work of God in their midst (Acts 2:43). Paul felt love and gratefulness when he thought of the believers at Philippi (Philippians 1:7). These are examples of good, normal, and healthy feelings. To suppress such feelings would be to dehumanize ourselves and to ignore part of how God made us. It would be to take love and romance and make it into disinterested boredom. It would be to take care and compassion and make it into impersonal charity. It would be to take an uplifting experience in worship when we are caught up in the wonder of the majesty of our God and supplant it with mechanical ritual and heartless words. To remove feelings from our existence is to kill off a very important part of our being. To be fully human, and thus to live life to the full and to glorify God, we must allow our feelings to operate in a sanctified manner.

Feelings have value and purpose. In fact, feelings are very much interconnected to our thinking. We don't feel things for no reason at all, but there is a cause. If we feel angry, it is likely because someone has agitated us. If we feel afraid, it is likely because we mentally perceive danger, whether real or not. If we feel disinterested, it is because something is not stimulating our mind to be considered worthy of our thoughts and attention. Feelings also lead to different responses by our body, whether flushed cheeks, a rush of energy, a feeling of fatigue, or a variety of other things. Our body, soul, and mind are very much interconnected, and to suppose that feelings can or should just be turned off is not a healthy or Biblical approach.

The way to handle feelings is the same way we handle thoughts, and this works because of the interconnectedness of thinking and feeling. Philippians 4:8 says, "Finally, brethren, whatever is true, whatever is honorable, whatever is right, whatever is pure, whatever is lovely, whatever is of good repute, if there is any excellence and if anything worthy of praise, dwell on these things." Sometimes we will feel things that are legitimate feelings but in the wrong context. A temptation of lust, for example, might excite us before we even have a chance to consciously think about who it was that incited the feelings. This is a normal feeling that is part of being a sexual being, but it is in the wrong context and at the wrong time. Once we are cognizant of the mental state which we are in and of the feelings which we have, we must immediately and almost as a reflex reevaluate them in light of our conscience and Biblical morality. In this instance, the feelings must be dropped which means that we will have to not think on what we just saw and rather think on what is good, right, noble, and pure. Once we discard the thought or, as the Bible says, take the thought captive unto obedience to Christ (2 Corinthians 10:5), the feelings will subside, and the bodily impulses will go away. But we must not let feelings that are in the wrong context lead to a willful decision to sin by thinking wrong thoughts or doing wrong things. We are not slaves to our thoughts, to our choices, or to our feelings because we are no longer slaves to sin. There is always a way of escape from temptation, even if the feelings are strong (1 Corinthians 10:13). We must choose to think rightly, thereby redirecting our feelings. After all, the feelings we will have after doing right are always more fulfilling than the regret of doing wrong.

May God enable us to live in a way such that our feelings are increasingly sanctified such that we delight in obedience, good, and truth and get disturbed by disobedience, evil, and deceit. The more we walk in truth and obedience, the more our feelings will cooperate and prod us onward in the right direction.

#46

FOOL'S FOR CHRIST'S SAKE

In the Book of 1 Corinthians, Paul spends a great deal of time explaining to the Corinthian believers that the wisdom of God is perceived as foolishness by the world (1 Corinthians 1:18). In fact, Paul says that the gospel is not naturally palatable to the world, and it is only because of the mercy of God that some even receive this message of "foolishness" (1 Corinthians 1:21). The way that leads to destruction is wide while the road to life is very narrow. Few find it, and thus few will respond in faith to the gospel of Christ (Matthew 7:13-14). It is the greatest story that will ever be told, and yet the world in its wisdom can't grasp it. The reason for this is that it takes grace to see and divine power to enlighten a natural man to become a spiritual man (1 Corinthians 2:14). It is truly a battle of spiritual power (1 Corinthians 4:20), and our giving the words of truth of the gospel along with committing to prayer are what God asks of us as we go through this world. We don't know whose eyes will be opened and who will respond, so we must go into all the world and preach the gospel. This is our calling, and this is the work that was initiated by Christ and given to the apostles to launch. They laid the foundation (Ephesians 2:20), and now we must keep building (1 Corinthians 3:10).

When we hear the Great Commission, it is often invigorating and exciting as we go to harvest. And we must always have faith to pray for a harvest and to trust God for the salvation of souls. Yet we must understand the nature of the battle of the commission of our Lord. It is not easy, it is not always fun, and it is not for our glory or ambition. If it is for our own gain, we will be prone to distort the gospel, we may lack boldness, and we might rely upon our abilities to advance the kingdom rather than the power of God, something Paul adamantly refused to do (1 Corinthians 2:1-2). What we must understand is that the work of the kingdom is very frustrating, laborious, and difficult. It is also very satisfying and has the potential to yield great joy and reward if done properly and obediently. But in order to have full joy, we must be willing to make a full sacrifice. The work of the gospel is not for the faint of heart but for those full of faith. The reason for this is because of the nature of the battle. We preach a message that the world perceives as foolish and which can only be understood by the intervention of the Lord. Therefore, it will not be an infrequent occurrence that people will look at us like fools who are wasting our lives and their time. We can expect insult and persecution (2 Timothy 3:12), but we can also expect joy and a reward in heaven. If one is willing to accept the hardship now, there can be great gain later.

Paul was willing to accept hardship, and eventually it cost him his life. But it wasn't just in death that he sacrificed; it was in life. In 1 Corinthians 4:9-13 Paul sarcastically rebukes the Corinthians for thinking that they have been willing to pay the price such as he has. He says,

> "For, I think, God has exhibited us apostles last of all, as men condemned to death; because we have become a spectacle to the world, both to angels and to men. *We are fools for Christ's sake*, but you are prudent in Christ; we are weak, but you are strong; you are distinguished, but we are without honor. To this present hour we are both hungry and thirsty, and are poorly clothed, and are roughly treated, and are homeless; and we toil, working with our own hands; when we are reviled, we bless; when we are persecuted, we endure; when we are slandered, we try to conciliate; we have become as the scum of the world, the dregs of all things, even until now" (italics mine).

If we let the gravity of what Paul is saying about the nature of his apostleship sink in, it is severely sobering and humbling. He recognizes that he is a fool for Christ's sake. He had it all before his conversion: fame, glory, the respect of persons, status, and so on. Now, he was rejected, reviled, persecuted, without food, poorly clothed, homeless, thirsty, roughly treated, and so on. This man suffered greatly for Christ's sake, and he worked extremely hard to support himself and to do the work of the gospel. He was a radical, a perceived nutcase, one whom the world thought had become a raving religious madman speaking incessantly of Christ, repentance, and salvation. He went against the grain and took the shame, like Jesus before him, albeit imperfectly. The world rejected Jesus Who came in love, doing good for people. What makes us think they will like us?

Paul's explanation of himself and the apostles as the "scum of the world" and the "dregs of all things" is highly telling. Society regarded the apostles are despicable, worthless, and as foul matter. They were expendable, annoying, and an insult on humanity as they preferred it. The question is, do we love the world, or are we willing to let the world think of us as scum? Seriously, are we willing to be despised as worthless refuse? If we trust in the simple power of the gospel and preach it, we will be treated this way. It will happen. If we start standing for truth and defend the purity of the church, even professing believers might start to despise us. If we want to imitate Christ, we must realize that *part of Christlikeness is to accept the ridicule which Christ accepted.* If we want to be those who truly labor for Christ, we will also have to be fools for His sake. If Christ was willing to be regarded as a fool, so, too, must we.

#47

THE SUFFICIENCY OF CHRIST

Along with a proper understanding of the sufficiency of the Bible, understanding the sufficiency of Christ is a fundamental pillar for living the Christian life and for developing proper theology as we grow in faith. Either Christ has all power and strength, or He does not. Either He is the One we need to depend on, or He is not. Either He can enable us to walk by faith, or He cannot. Sufficiency is an all-or-nothing concept, and we must decide whether we accept that Christ is indeed our all in all or if we are trying to cipher away some of His glory for ourselves. Thus, given that God is jealous for glory, we had better live properly in light of His sufficiency so that He does indeed get all the glory.

To be sufficient is to be self-sustaining, self-adequate, and to have all power and strength. We can safely say that God is all of these things because He needs no one, and He is fully able to carry out His will and desires as He wishes. No one can thwart His plans, for He is God. There is none other. The grace of God enters into the picture in that He so loves His children, we who have received Jesus as our Savior, that He desires to involve us in His plans in the world. Thus, we have the invitation and opportunity to be co-laborers with the God of the universe, but how we understand the meaning of co-laborer makes all the difference.

In John 15:5, Jesus says, "I am the vine, you are the branches; he who abides in Me and I in him, he bears much fruit, for apart from Me you can do nothing." Christ gives us a picture of our oneness with Him. It is a picture in which He is the vine, the source, the strength, and the anchor, and we are the branches, fully dependent upon Him for life and for power and strength to do anything of spiritual value. Thus, to be a co-laborer with Christ is to recognize and believe that we are fully dependent upon the grace and resources of Christ to do ministry. It is coming to understand and appreciate that we can't do anything of spiritual value of ourselves. To do things without yielding to Christ is to come up with dead works (Hebrews 9:14), spiritually speaking, rather than true fruit of the Spirit. This is why fruit that is of the Lord is called the fruit of the Spirit (Galatians 5:22-23), not the fruit of the Spirit and of ourselves. True spiritual effectiveness is accomplished when we let Jesus empower us by His strength. Our strength is pitiful, but His is totally dominant and sufficient. We are insufficient and unable, but He is sufficient and able. As Jesus said in Matthew 19:26, "With people this is impossible, but with God all things are possible." Aside from Christ in us, we have no chance to see the kingdom advance, truth defeat lies, and people be set free from captivity to sin and the devil. Take away Christ and the most talented among us are rendered useless. This is why Christ is not impressed with natural abilities, but He desires faith (Hebrews 11:6). Simple faith in His power and in the power of His Word is what He desires. That way, He, not us, gets the glory. Of course, He is faithful to reward us for our cooperation in His work, but let us not forget that, if it wasn't for His indwelling power, our labor would be of no value to Him. So to be a co-laborer with Christ is to be one who walks by faith and fully submits and surrenders to the will and leading of the Spirit of God. It is to be clay that doesn't resist the Potter (Isaiah 64:8) and a vessel that doesn't attempt to steal the glory from the treasure of Jesus Whom it holds (2 Corinthians 4:7).

Christ's sufficiency means, by implication, that we are insufficient of ourselves. Indeed the Scripture says this outright in 2 Corinthians 3:5 which says, "Not that we are adequate in ourselves to consider anything as coming from ourselves, but our adequacy is from God." There is a powerful, powerful truth here. Without Christ we are inadequate. We lack wisdom (Colossians 2:3), we have no strength (Philippians 4:13), and we can't accomplish ministry (Zechariah 4:6), just to name a few of our insufficiencies. However, with Christ indwelling us and as we by faith surrender to Him in humility and obedience, trembling at His Word (Isaiah 66:2), we become sufficient to do eternally effective ministry. So the saints of God go from an incompetent, defeated army which fools itself into thinking it is advancing the kingdom, and it becomes one that is truly spiritually powerful and fully able because of Christ in them.

The frightening thing is that we can be saved and have Christ in us and still not take advantage of His power if we trust in our own ability. Do we merely need God to help us as if we are combining our strength with His? Is His power a mere supplement to our efforts rather than the entire package? Proverbs 3:5-6 says to trust in the Lord with all of our hearts, meaning that we are not to trust in ourselves at all. It says not to lean on our own understanding, meaning that we are to fully rely upon the wisdom of God. It says that we are to acknowledge God in all things, meaning that He gets the credit and not us. Only when we fully believe that we are dependent beings for anything and everything can Jesus become our all in all, strengthening us despite our human weakness so that His power can be perfected in our weakness (2 Corinthians 12:9-10) and so that His glory can be seen (2 Corinthians 4:7).

Instead of wandering about as fools in a flurry of vain self-effort, we should trust God to make our paths straight as we walk by faith in obedience and humility (Proverbs 3:6). But it all starts with a healthy, righteous, and humble belief in the insufficiency of man apart from Christ and a belief in the sufficiency of Christ which alone can make redeemed man effective for ministry (2 Timothy 3:16-17).

#48

LESSONS IN PERSEVERANCE

The Bible gives us some excellent counsel (as we would expect) as to how we can persevere when difficulty and temptation come. God's desire is that we would run the race of faith fervently, diligently, and to the finish, so let's look at an instance in Moses' life to glean some direction as to how we can better persevere in our own lives.

Exodus 7:9-13 says,

> "So Moses said to Joshua, 'Choose men for us and go out, fight against Amalek. Tomorrow I will station myself on the top of the hill with the staff of God in my hand.' Joshua did as Moses told him, and fought against Amalek; and Moses, Aaron, and Hur went up to the top of the hill. So it came about when Moses held his hand up, that Israel prevailed, and when he let his hand down, Amalek prevailed. But Moses' hands were heavy. Then they took a stone and put it under him, and he sat on it; and Aaron and Hur supported his hands, one on one side and one on the other. Thus his hands were steady until the sun set. So Joshua overwhelmed Amalek and his people with the edge of the sword."

For whatever reason, Moses understood from the Lord that as long as he held his staff above his head, the Israelites would prevail in victory over the Amalekites. But if Moses' strength would give out, causing the staff to fall below his head, then the Amalekites would suddenly prevail. Clearly, Moses had a challenge before him, one which would require an incredible amount of endurance. It is no easy task to keep our arms raised over our heads even for a matter of minutes, let alone for hours upon hours and with the weight of a staff. But Moses finished the task, and there is much to learn from just how he was able to finish.

There are those who tell us that in times of adversity we are to believe in ourselves and to just try harder, dig deeper, and somehow, by mustering some extra something from within, keep on keeping on. But the fact of the matter is that the victory in spiritual perseverance and in staying strong spiritually is not found within ourselves, as if we ourselves are strong. The flesh (Matthew 26:41), that is, our humanness, is weak, but Christ in us is strong. It is through Him, not through our own human willpower, that we are able to please Him and do His will (Philippians 4:13). This lesson of finding our strength and winning the victory through Christ was evident in this battle with the Amalekites. God was trying to make it clear to Israel that He was the only hope of their winning. Otherwise, what would a man holding a staff over his head have to do with winning a battle fought with brute strength and manmade weapons? The point that God needed to make to Israel and to us is that it is by His strength that spiritual victories are won. Without His provision, protection, blessing, and favor, we have no hope of advancing the gospel or growing in faith. Faith in Christ and His Word is the means to victory. So, as Israel was instructed through this very visible object lesson, perseverance is only possible by the strength which God supplies.

Sometimes in order for us to learn this lesson of dependence upon the Lord, God must remove all of the things which we thought made us strong so that we see our weakness and watch His strength be perfected in and through our weakness (2 Corinthians 12:9-10). There will be times when our strength will fail us, and no amount of digging deeper into ourselves will be able to get us through the predicament we face. Severe illness, crisis, disability, and near death experiences all remind us of our frailty and feeble nature. These circumstances are valuable in that they cause us to call out to God for strength which we come to recognize that we don't have and strength which we come to see that only He can supply. Why trust in our strength when we have God on our side Whose strength is without deficiency or limit?

There are times in which Christ will use others to supply His strength to us. Sometimes we will sense God giving us strength to do His will that we know is not of ourselves. Other times God might work through human agents to encourage us onward. Such was the case in this victory over the Amalekites. Moses didn't have the strength in and of himself to keep his hands raised through the duration of the battle, so God supplied the strength he needed through the wisdom of others who brought him a rock to sit upon and who then held up each of his hands. We need other believers who will be there for us to support us when we grow weak and in our times of need. *There is no glory in trying to win a battle on our own in situations where God has given others to help us win.*

Isaiah 40:29 says, "He gives strength to the weary, and to him who lacks might He increases power." But the key is that we wait upon God (Isaiah 40:31), seeking His strength in time of weakness rather than relying upon our own feeble power. As David says, "My flesh and my heart may fail, but God is the strength of my heart and my portion forever" (Psalm 73:26). There will be times when we lack strength to continue on, but we must believe God to be our strength. He will enable us to continue on in righteousness and to do the good works which He has appointed for us (Ephesians 2:10). He may supply others to help us, but one way or another He will give us the strength we need to do His will His way. When we feel like giving in or giving up, God's strength will enable us to persevere.

#49

NEVER ALONE AGAIN

Sometimes in life believers will find themselves with intense feelings of loneliness. Perhaps a person is recently widowed. Maybe a house full of children is suddenly empty as the children move away to start their own lives. Perhaps a spouse abandons the other or emotionally checks out on the relationship. Maybe none of the other kids at school accept a lone individual who becomes an outcast. Then again, maybe society looks down on a certain person because of race, age, past experiences, etc. The world can be a lonely place. Life brings with it its share of betrayals, griefs, and losses. Friends move away or friends just change and go their own way. God may choose to help us with our loneliness by providing brothers and sisters to encourage us. He does promise to meet our needs (Philippians 4:19), and He will never allow us to be tempted without also providing a way of escape (1 Corinthians 10:13). But even if there is no one there to keep us company and we feel like we are on an island all by ourselves, still there is hope. Even if we were isolated in a solitary prison cell because of our faith in Christ, we could have companionship. Even if the masses misjudge us and abandon us, we can still have a Friend who is closer than a brother. Whether an orphan, a widow, alone in a nursing home, or alone in a crowd of admirers, true friendship is possible through our Savior Jesus Christ. At all times and in all places and situations, He will be there for His children. Such is our privilege as children of God. How and why is this possible?

As Christ died on the cross for us because of His great love for us, He suffered in a way that was likely far greater than any of the bodily abuse and mutilation that He had to endure: His own Father forsook Him (Matthew 27:46). The word for forsaken means abandoned, left alone, left helpless, left behind, and deserted. This is a picture of total and utter aloneness. Because the sins of the world were placed upon Christ (Isaiah 53:6), God the Father could no longer look upon His Son. He had to let Him go and let Him die. Such was His good and perfect plan because He would soon raise Him from the dead in victory, having conquered sin and death so that we could be free in Him. But for the time being, Jesus suffered in a way that we cannot even begin to fathom. This was God in the flesh, and His own Father, Whom He was One with, deserted Him. There cannot be a greater feeling of being alone than Jesus felt on the cross as He was dying. This is just one of the ways in which we have a Savior Who can sympathize with what we have to face and endure (Hebrews 4:15). He knew what it was like to be alone. The disciples scattered as the Shepherd was struck (Mark 14:27). Rome had no love for Him. The Jews hated Him. He was rejected across the board, and then to top it off, He had to be rejected by the Father Himself. There is no greater loneliness than this. Indeed, our Savior understands when we feel alone.

Perhaps this is why He is so adamant that we remember that we are never left alone. In Hebrews 13:5, we read, "I WILL NEVER DESERT YOU, NOR WILL I EVER FORSAKE YOU." He was left and forsaken so that God would never have to leave us. Once saved, we would always be His, and nothing and no one could ever snatch us out of His hand (John 10:28-29). Not only this, but God is not afar off. He, even the Father Himself, let alone Christ and the Spirit, has made His abode within our hearts (John 14:23). God, Who cannot be confined and Who fills all things, has decided that those who put their faith in Christ will be His dwelling place. So God is never far away or somewhere out there for the child of God. He is always near, here, and in our hearts. We are never alone, and never will we be abandoned. The Shepherd will never leave His sheep. As Psalm 23:4 says, "Even though I walk through the valley of the shadow of death, I fear no evil, for You are with me; Your rod and Your staff, they comfort me." Jesus has all authority, and it is

His decree that He will be in us and always with us. Praise God for His constant friendship and perfect companionship!

If we feel alone even though we have God in our hearts, we need to draw near to Him because He promises to then draw near to us (James 4:8). If God seems far away, maybe it is because the devil is tricking us into thinking that way. Maybe we have let our feelings begin to inform our minds that God is absent, when, in fact, our feelings are leading us astray. We need to think through why we might be feeling apart from God because God never leaves us. Thus, if He feels distant, it is our move to draw near. We should take some time to praise Him, to pray to Him, to hear Him as we read His Word, and to call out to Him. If we have sin, we need to deal with it because God won't hear our prayers otherwise (Psalm 66:18).

Let us not be duped by the devil into thinking that God has abandoned us or given up on us. He doesn't do that. Jonah ran from God, but even a child can understand that he could never get away from God. David said that there was no place He could run where God wasn't already there. Not even darkness could hide him from God (Psalm 139:7-12). God is always there, and He is in our hearts as believers. We need to take comfort in His nearness, believing Him to be close and cultivating our relationship and friendship with Him. Psalm 73:28 says, "But as for me, the nearness of God is my good; I have made the Lord GOD my refuge, that I may tell of all Your works." It is by faith that we are to choose to believe that God is near and that He is our refuge. His nearness is our good, and it is the only real and ultimate solution to loneliness.

#50

COUNT YOUR BLESSINGS

Life comes at us fast. Some times good things happen, and other times we face an onslaught of difficulty after difficulty. When the waves of strife drive our faces into the dirt, we must not give up, lose heart, or stop trusting God. But lest "trusting God" becomes a mere cliché for us, God has ordained things for us to do to keep our minds fixed upon Him. It is a willful act that we must do to think upon Him and remember Who He is and what He has done. As Paul says in Colossians 3:2, "Set your mind on the things above, not on the things that are on earth." We are vulnerable to getting overwhelmed by the nonsense of this world, and it is imperative that we remember some things, particularly, that which is true about the many blessings which we have in Christ.

Surely, we can think of instances of answered prayer, of God's provision, of God's graces, of God's good and perfect gifts to us, and of the mercy of God. We have the memories of past acts of God on our behalf, and we have the promise of our future inheritance in Christ to look forward to. In the meantime, we have the Word of God to remind us of the good heart of God. We should benefit from all three. Many times in Israel's history, after a wonderful work of God, the Israelites would dedicate a song or build an altar in memory of what God had done. They were to tell their children of the mighty acts of God lest future generations would forget His faithfulness. We, too, need to look back and remember what God has done for us. There is hope in remembering where we were and seeing how God in all wisdom delivered us from ourselves or from enemies. God is so gracious, and we cannot take His grace for granted. Rather, we should thank Him for His provision, trust Him in the present, and think on the great blessings coming to us in the coming kingdom.

Paul said in 1 Timothy 6:8, "If we have food and covering, with these we shall be content." Elsewhere, we read that he learned to be content in any circumstance (Philippians 4:11), and it was the constant presence of Christ which made his contentment possible (Hebrews 13:5). Paul didn't learn contentment overnight, but it was over time through a great deal of suffering. He learned not to overlook the basic, small provisions of God, but to be thankful for them. With mere food and covering, he could be content. Sometimes, God allows suffering to help us be mindful of all of the many smaller graces that He has given us in our lives. It is easy to overlook things and take them for granted. We should be thankful to God for them, as insignificant as they might seem. Just comparing our state to somebody who is in a worse state does not necessarily make us feel better. But if we thank God that we have the things that we realize that others might not be so fortunate to have, then our thanksgiving can change our perspective and bring us contentment. We need to maintain Paul's attitude of thankfulness for all things and in even the most dire and unfair of circumstances. We need to make a point of it to thank God for the blessings that He gives us each and everyday. One of the first steps into spiritual decay is to refuse to give God thanks after experiencing His goodness and seeing His power manifested on our behalf (Romans 1:21). If we fail to acknowledge Him, we can begin to feel proud and self-sufficient, which is a dangerous road to be on. Rather, we need to acknowledge God's provision in everything (Proverbs 3:5-6) so that we can stay on the straight and narrow path.

God has been faithful, and He always will be. Even when we lack faith, still He is faithful (2 Timothy 2:13). Great is His faithfulness, and His mercies are new every morning (Lamentations 3:23). Every day God's thoughts toward us are so numerous that they cannot even be counted (Psalm 139:17-18). So already we have more things to be thankful for than we can even name or count. We have "every spiritual blessing in the heavenly places in Christ" (Ephesians 1:3). Eternity in paradise is ours. When all else fails, God never fails, and His mercy, love, and kindness endure forever (Psalm 52:1). As Paul knew firsthand, even in a dark, dank prison cell, these blessings stand fast.

There is so much to be thankful for, and so many blessings to count. In fact, if only we could see all that God does, we would have more mercies than we could ever account for. Let us not let the missiles of the devil knock us down such that we forget that we have Christ and the many blessings of God. We should never lose hope, and we should always have reason to be thankful. So what are you waiting for? Start counting!

#51

TWELVE REASONS NOT TO SIN

The church at Corinth had a lot of sin issues that they needed to deal with, and Paul confronted them about these in the book of 1 Corinthians. As he drew near the end of his letter, he summed up his heart for them by saying, "Become sober-minded as you ought, and stop sinning; for some have no knowledge of God I speak this to your shame" (1 Corinthians 15:34). The Bible is clear that God doesn't want us to continue in sin supposing that grace might then also increase (Romans 6:1-2). Such is foolish thinking, for it is grace which sets us free from the power of sin and death. Rather than live in bondage, we can live free (Romans 6:6-7). Christ promises us a way of escape from every temptation (1 Corinthians 10:13), and we have all the resources we need to live godly in Christ (2 Peter 1:3). We will stumble (James 3:2), but we need not live like the world. Most certainly, we need not justify sin as if it is normal. Such is offensive toward God because He wants us to cease from sin (1 Peter 4:1). We are not perfect yet, but by the grace of God, we should be growing more like Christ each day, putting away sin and self and living out Christ.

This is far easier said than done, and in the heat of the battle, it is easy to forget why the battle is worth fighting and winning. Thus, we should think ahead of time as to why it is worth it to walk in holiness and believe God for purity. Here are twelve reasons for going God's way rather than the way of the devil:

158

First, we have the prospect of eternal rewards for our faithfulness (2 Corinthians 5:10). The more faithful we are while on earth, the more honor and rewards we will have in heaven. This should seriously motivate us given that we will be spending considerably more time in heaven than we will here.

Second, when we sin, we grieve the Holy Spirit (Ephesians 4:30). We wouldn't walk up to our best friend and slug him or her in the gut, but we do a similar thing to the Spirit of God when we sin. For some reason, offending God becomes impersonal when it should be very personal.

Third, God tells us to be holy (1 Peter 1:16), which He wouldn't do if it wasn't best for us.

Fourth, God might discipline us for doing wrong because He loves us (1 Corinthians 11:29-31). Discipline is meant to be a deterrent to wrong behavior, meaning that it is not intended to be fun. Thus, why invoke the loving discipline of our Lord?

Fifth, sinning makes a mockery of Christ's sacrifice (1 Peter 1:17-19, 1 Corinthians 6:20). As believers, when we sin it is akin to robbing a person (Christ) who just bailed us out of prison. It is just utterly ridiculous and insulting to our Savior Who paid it all for us to be holy. We need to be mindful of the sacrifice He gave lest we carelessly give into sin.

Sixth, we must walk in holiness so that we can truly love our brothers and sisters in Christ (1 Peter 1:22). Since love is a fruit of the Spirit, it is not going to flow forth from us as from the Spirit if we are grieving the Spirit at the same time by our sin. It is only when we are pure before God that we can be to others what they spiritually need us to be. Sin is not merely an individual matter, but it limits our ability to serve and encourage others.

Seventh, the world needs to see a godly testimony (1 Corinthians 15:34). A righteous testimony allows God to work through His church to show Himself to the world as He truly is. If we are not living holy, sanctified lives, the world will not see Jesus in us (Hebrews 12:14). What a tragedy that would be, given that hell is an awful, eternal reality.

Eighth, sin is devastating by its very nature (Romans 6:23, 1 Corinthians 5:5). God commands us not to sin because He knows it severs relationships, destroys societies, harms our bodies, and perverts our desires and our thinking.

Ninth, sin spiritually incapacitates us. We need to abide with Christ by walking in faith, dependence, and purity if we want His power to work through us to advance His kingdom. When we hide sin in our hearts, God won't even hear our prayers (Psalm 66:18). We need to be healed by confessing our sin to God and to those whom we have offended (James 5:16a).

Tenth, sin is counter to ultimate pleasure. Sin provides a passing, temporary pleasure which dulls the spiritual senses to absolute truth and ultimate reality. Since God is truth and the source of ultimate, enduring pleasure (Psalm 16:11), sin thus alienates us from that which can truly satisfy.

Eleventh, sin looks better than what it can actually deliver. Ecclesiastes 6:9 says, "What the eyes see is better than what the soul desires. This too is futility and a striving after wind."

Finally, twelfth, a guilty conscience is miserable. As believers, the Holy Spirit will convict us of sin such that we will experience internal agony over our sin (Psalm 32:3-4). This can rip us apart on the inside, and it is a miserable way to live. Of course, God forgives us if we repent, but why create such a situation in the first place?

We are not going to get it perfect this side of eternity, but we need to try for the sake of our Savior. As Philippians 2:12 says, "So then, my beloved, just as you have always obeyed, not as in my presence only, but now much more in my absence, work out your salvation with fear and trembling." May we walk by faith today and each day forward such that we let God sanctify our hearts according to His will and pleasure.

#52

JUSTIFIED BY FAITH

When it comes to our eternal destination, no element of Christian theology is more important than that surrounding what we believe about salvation. In fact, when it comes to preserving an accurate gospel message, Paul says in Galatians 1:8-9,

> "But even if we, or an angel from heaven, should preach to you a gospel contrary to what we have preached to you, he is to be accursed! As we have said before, so I say again now, if any man is preaching to you a gospel contrary to what you received, he is to be accursed!"

Paul says the same thing twice to emphasize that the gospel will be attacked. Its purity will be distorted, and Satan will devise many deceptions that look and sound like gospel truth but are in fact far from it. Other religions and cults have been developed by those who claimed to hear angelic revelations of "new truth." But these failed to receive Paul's teaching that the gospel is fully revealed in Jesus Christ in the Scriptures, and those who alter it or add or take away from it will be accursed (Revelation 22:18-19). This leads us to the fact that we can have great joy and security in knowing our eternal destination because we have a gospel that cannot, does not, and will not change. There is one way to be saved, and if we go the way God has ordained, we will be saved. If we don't, we won't. It is as simple as that, and the future of all mankind rests upon what each person does with the absolute truth of the infallible (2 Timothy 3:16), perfect (Psalm 19:7), and enduring gospel message (1 Peter 1:25).

Given the profound implications of the gospel, we had better be sure we understand what it is and be able to communicate it to others. One of the key words that the Scripture repeatedly uses in describing salvation is **justification** (e.g. Luke 18:14, Romans 3:24, Romans 5:1, Romans 5:9, 1 Corinthians 6:11). *To justify someone is to declare or reckon him or her innocent. It is a pronouncement that one has been declared free of guilt as he or she desired to be.* Galatians 2:16 says,

> "Nevertheless knowing that a man is not justified by the works of the Law but through faith in Christ Jesus, even we have believed in Christ Jesus, so that we may be justified by faith in Christ and not by the works of the Law; since by the works of the Law no flesh will be justified."

Here we see that the way to be justified and made righteous in God's sight, innocent of evil and free from guilt, is not by the works of the Law but through faith in Christ. Ephesians 2:8-9 makes it clear that man cannot save himself by doing good works because as Romans 3:23 states, all fall short of God's glorious, perfect standard. Man, left to his own sin-marred inability is hopeless and helpless. But, God sent His Son to die for the sins of the world so that those who would believe in Him should not perish but have eternal life (John 3:16). The world stands condemned in its evil deeds and sin nature, and Christ did not come to condemn it (for it is already condemned) but to save it (John 3:17). Yet we as humans must respond to the gracious gift of God and receive the gift. As John 1:12-13 says,

> "But as many as received Him, to them He gave the right to become children of God, even to those who believe in His name, who were born, not of blood nor of the will of the flesh nor of the will of man, but of God."

God's grace must move in a person's heart (and Christ does draw all men- John 12:32) at which point each individual must respond to the knowledge and revelation that he or she has been given by believing Christ is Who He said He was (God, Lord, Savior) and will do what He said He will do (save, forgive, grant eternal life).

The way to be justified is thus very simple: believe upon Jesus (Acts 16:31). John 6:29 says, "Jesus answered and said to them, 'This is the work of God, that you believe in Him whom He has sent.'" Salvation is a work of God in our hearts as we believe in Jesus Christ to be our Savior and to forgive us. This belief is not merely faith that Jesus existed or a detached intellectual belief that Jesus is God without surrendering our hearts to Him. After all, even the demons believe in God (James 2:19). We must believe Jesus died for our sins, and we must yield to Him in repentance, the outworking of faith (Luke 13:5, Mark 1:15). It is only through the name of Christ and the work of Christ on the cross on our behalf that we can be saved. Acts 4:12 says, "And there is salvation in no one else; for there is no other name under heaven that has been given among men by which we must be saved."

We will all have to face the judgment one day (Acts 17:31), and the question of utmost importance is whether or not we have been justified. Some trust in receiving saving grace through baptism or through the Lord's Supper. This is not what the Bible teaches. Some trust in membership in a church. This is in error. Some trust in their own "goodness," a sure way to fail. We must come to a place where we choose to believe in Jesus and to trust in His work to be our hope of salvation. He becomes our Savior and Lord, and He changes us from the inside out (2 Corinthians 5:17). We can't idly and passively receive righteousness, as if we are not to have any role in the process. Nor can we suppose that it is we ourselves who can earn righteousness. Grace is a gift of God through Christ, and it is received by faith. Faith is a decision of the heart, mind, and will to believe. It is active, real, and a choice to be made. "ABRAHAM BELIEVED GOD, AND IT WAS CREDITED TO HIM AS RIGHTEOUSNESS" (Romans 4:3). As Abraham was justified by believing God's Word to Him, we must believe God's Word to us, the fullness of which has been revealed through the Person and work of Christ.

We must each come to a place where we choose Christ so that we may live (Deuteronomy 30:19, Joshua 24:15). Lest Jesus say to us, "I never knew you; DEPART FROM ME," (Matthew 7:23) we must be sure we know Him by choosing Him as we put our faith in Him and receive His grace. There is no other way to be justified.

#53

GRACE THAT IS GREATER
THAN ALL MY SIN

The Bible gives us a great promise in 1 John 1:9 when it says, "If we confess our sins, He is faithful and righteous to forgive us our sins and to cleanse us from all unrighteousness." Although this verse is in the context of a sinner coming to salvation, it is also true that God forgives His children when they sin if only they would come to Him and, in an attitude of repentance, ask to be forgiven. God's grace is so great that it can cleanse the sinner from his sin so that he or she can become a child of God, and it is so great that even when we as the children of God stumble, we can be forgiven still.

In Matthew 18:21-22, we read, "Then Peter came and said to Him, 'Lord, how often shall my brother sin against me and I forgive him? Up to seven times?' Jesus said to him, 'I do not say to you, up to seven times, but up to seventy times seven.'" Peter was probably thinking that he was being generous. Rather than repay a person who had committed a sin against him with equal retribution, Peter suggested giving the brother some leeway, say, up to seven times. But the eighth time, forgiveness and grace would run out. But Christ challenged the rules of Peter's suggested economy of grace by saying that forgiveness is infinite for those who are truly seeking it. This is only possible because of the infinite grace of God which is made possible through the shed blood of

Christ on the cross. Because of Christ's forgiving power, we can always be made clean after we sin if we humbly seek it. Furthermore, those who sin against us need to be forgiven time after time as long as they are truly repentant.

It is not Biblical to suppose that a person could sin habitually and continually as a lifestyle and still be a believer (1 John 3:8-9), though it is possible to give in to the ways of the world so extensively that we make shipwreck of our faith (1 Timothy 1:18-20). We as believers do stumble (James 3:2), and if we are not careful, we could really veer off course. All of us have weaknesses that we may or may not be aware of. These the devil exploits, and, though we need not fall because of God's sufficient grace, sometimes we do because we rely upon our insufficient strength. Sometimes we fall badly. When our faith grows weak, and we, like Peter, deny our Lord in word or in life (Matthew 26:75), there is still a chance to repent and be forgiven of our sin. David was certainly a believer, a man after God's own heart. Yet he sinned by committing adultery, deceit, and murder. Then he refused to admit it for some time. Yet even he was forgiven by God when he repented, though he did have to face the consequences of his sin and the discipline of God. There is no place we can go that God's grace cannot reach, and there is no depth to which we can sink that God is no longer able to pull us out. His grace is greater than all of our sin, no matter how small or big we might view what we have done. Whether we are just starting to wander off course or if we are already sinking and drowning in our sin, grace can be received.

One of the devil's traps is to get us into thinking that there is no hope in that there is no possibility that we can be forgiven, healed, and restored. He will try to get us to feel consumed and entrapped by false guilt such that we do not feel worthy of God's forgiveness any longer. But since when were we ever worthy of grace? Grace is a gift. When we sin, the Spirit will convict us of sin such that a godly sorrow should result (2 Corinthians 7:11). He will not condemn our souls as if there is no hope, for there is no longer any condemnation for those who are in Christ Jesus (Romans 8:1). The Spirit's conviction is a work of love and grace. The devil's work is to condemn and make us feel as if God has abandoned us. We need to refuse to listen to the devil's wiles that

166

God's grace cannot come to us. God loves His children, and He desires us to call to Him in repentance. He will forgive because He is faithful and just. **Based upon the work His Son accomplished on the cross, if He is to maintain His holiness and righteousness, He must forgive those who humbly ask.** The grace of God is there for us to receive. It is pride that says that we don't need it or cannot have it. Let us not fall for such deceptions.

Grace is not an excuse to sin, and it dare not be abused, meaning that sin must be called sin and that it cannot be treated as if it is innocuous. Unrepentant believers need to be lovingly confronted and guided to freedom, and unbelievers need to be told that they need to repent. Yet let us also emphasize the remedy, for we have been given grace upon grace (John 1:16). It is how we live, how we are saved, how we are sanctified, and how we will be kept and glorified. We who are God's children are benefactors of grace, without which we would have nothing. So let us not refuse to be gracious to others who are humble and seek our forgiveness. Freely we have received, and freely we should give (Matthew 10:8). Let us also receive grace ourselves when we sin by repenting and confessing our sin to God. Why live filthy when Christ offers to make us clean and whole?

#54
WHY ORIGINAL SIN MATTERS

Unredeemed man has always been self-interested, and it has never been his natural bent to look after the weak and to give up his own rights for the benefits of others (unless, of course, there is some kick-back to fuel pride or one's own selfish agenda). Scripture is plain that man is born a sinner, saying in 1 Corinthians 15:22, "For as in Adam all die, so also in Christ all will be made alive." Isaiah 53:6 adds, "All of us like sheep have gone astray, each of us has turned to his own way; but the LORD has caused the iniquity of us all to fall on Him." All people sin and fall short of God's glory (Romans 3:23). Therefore, we all need salvation through the one and only Savior Jesus Christ.

To believe that man is basically good and that he possesses a decency at his core makes the remedy for sin meaningless. Man must first recognize his sin before he can be saved, so those who deny sin propagate a great deception about the natural bent of man's heart. Jeremiah 17:9 says, "The heart is more deceitful than all else and is desperately sick; who can understand it?" The Bible doesn't buy into the jargon about man being basically good but not perfect. The Bible speaks of utter deceit and extreme wickedness, a nature that is set against God and His ways of humility, love, selflessness, and faith in Christ. This reality of man's evil bent must be understood, believed, and proclaimed lest the gospel lose its worth and meaning and the death of Christ be made a mockery. Our sins were laid upon Christ so that we could receive His righteousness.

We don't merely need some polishing up on our exterior because of a good core and loving heart, but we need to be born again. We need our heart changed (Ezekiel 18:31), our mind transformed (Romans 12:1-2), and our spirits regenerated (Titus 3:5). Man's only hope is a total rewiring of his inner person, a work which only Christ can do.

A person must learn of his sin problem before the salvation answer makes any sense. This is why the doctrine of original sin is so important: without it, man has no need for a Savior and has no motive to call upon Christ (unless of course it is one of self-interest such as in getting richer, smarter, stronger, etc.). The gospel is not about self-help or furthering our own inherent self-worship (i.e. pride and self-reliance). The gospel is about denying ourselves and turning to Christ as Savior and Lord (Matthew 16:24). Original sin must be dealt with if a person is going to be born again, and only Christ has the cure. Yet we have the message.

It is our job, our mission, and our calling to tell the world that it is sick with sin and that it needs a Doctor. As Jesus said in Luke 5:31, "It is not those who are well who need a physician, but those who are sick." Telling the world it is spiritually sick with sin often doesn't go over too well, and it is not popular. But it can be done gently and lovingly as we lead people through the Scripture and let the Spirit speak to their hearts about where they have fallen short. For those who desire the truth, they will be cut to the heart and repent (Acts 2:37). Others will be cut to the heart and gnash their teeth in anger (Acts 7:54). Either way, the Word of God does what God says it will do, cutting to joints and marrow and rightly judging the thoughts and intentions of the heart (Hebrews 4:12). Our job is simply to share the truth of the gospel. Preaching with hate is destructive to the message of grace, but helping one to see the problem of sin which we all possess as we enter the world is an act of great love and care as it opens the door to the gift of salvation being necessary and making sense.

Those who proclaim the inherent goodness of man are greatly deceived, and they are unable (or unwilling) to see (or at least acknowledge) the true state of their own hearts. It is a great deception and delusion to not see that our own attempts at righteousness are as filthy rags before God

(Isaiah 64:6). We need to, like Isaiah, come to see our own need for grace and for cleansing (Isaiah 6:5).

There is bad news before the good news, so let us make sure that in sharing the good news of the gospel that we remember to deal with the reality of sin. Then, grace will be beautiful as God intended it to be. "Just as it is written, 'HOW BEAUTIFUL ARE THE FEET OF THOSE WHO BRING GOOD NEWS OF GOOD THINGS!'" (Romans 10:15). Praise God for the good and beautiful truth that, though we are born into sin, we can be saved from it!

#55

GOD USES YOUNG PEOPLE

Solomon shares part of his reason in writing the Proverbs in Proverbs 1:4, saying, "To give prudence to the naive, to the youth knowledge and discretion." Too often young people are given a free pass when it comes to expecting much from them. Solomon didn't take this view, however. He believed that they were able to be taught and trained in God's Word such that they could learn wisdom, prudence, knowledge, and discretion. These are marks of spiritual maturity and having walked with God over time. These are characteristics even many who are older physically and older in Christ even fail to possess. Solomon's point is not to underestimate the youth, for they are capable of having great wisdom and understanding, or at the very least, being pushed and led in that direction. It is not Biblical for young people to be relegated as rebellious, a nuisance, and uninterested in the things of God. It is not acceptable to simply entertain them and tickle their ears, doing just enough to make church a social hour to keep them out of trouble for a short time. Solomon sets a higher standard, and so should we. Our youth will be the leaders of our next generation, and how wonderful it would be to teach them prudence and discretion early on.

Joshua was the servant of Moses from his youth, and we know that Joshua came to be a great and godly leader (Numbers 11:28). Josiah inherited the kingdom of Judah at a mere eight years of age (2 Kings 22:1). When he was sixteen, he sought God and began to reform the

171

nation (2 Chronicles 34:3-7). How about David? He was but a youth when he challenged the giant Goliath and stood for Jehovah against an entire pagan nation and before his own nation's frightened king and army. In 1 Samuel 17:33, we read the words of the king of Israel to David: "Then Saul said to David, 'You are not able to go against this Philistine to fight with him; *for you are but a youth* while he has been a warrior from his youth'" (emphasis added). Indeed, the attitude that young people are "not able" was around even back then. Saul ignored David, Samuel (a righteous man of God) didn't expect God to choose him to be king (1 Samuel 16:1-12), and Goliath ridiculed him. 1 Samuel 17:44 says, "When the Philistine looked and saw David, he disdained him; *for he was but a youth*, and ruddy, with a handsome appearance" (emphasis added). Yet we know how the story unfolded. God worked through this young man's faith and courage as he fought for Jehovah and not for himself such that he slew Goliath and started to win the favor of the people. He would eventually take over as king in God's timing. What a powerful and vivid lesson as to the relevance and value of serving God in our youth! Had David not stood up against Goliath, much would be different in Israel's history. But he, a mere lad, took on the challenge before him because he believed that God had a purpose for him. He couldn't figure out why the rest of the grown men of the nation balked and cowered in fear. This was shameful to God, and David would have none of it. So he stepped up to the plate and did what the grownups were failing to do.

We must be willing to encourage our young people to search through the Scriptures and to be a taught the full counsel of God. We cannot bail out and think that they are not ready to study the Bible or too young for it to apply. The Bible is always relevant and powerful. Then, it is up to our young people to receive its message and step out in faith. Nobody pushed David into fighting Goliath. He did it because he feared God. Thus, those who want to grow must find a way to separate themselves from the surrounding nonsense, laziness, indifference, and rebellion and get into the Word and grow. It will take courage, and it may well be a lonely road. But it is right and worth it.

Paul wrote to Timothy in 1 Timothy 4:12, saying, "Let no one look down on your youthfulness, but rather in speech, conduct, love, faith and purity, show yourself an example of those who believe." The assumption was that people wouldn't respect Timothy because he was relatively young despite his knowledge of Scripture and ability to shepherd the flock. Paul understood that people judge not based upon wisdom but upon outward appearance. His admonition to Timothy was simply not to bend to the ridicule of others but to fulfill his calling by living out a godly life before them. All he could do was be a godly example of wisdom and discretion and pray that God would show people that age is not the limiting factor whereas faith is.

So the message to our youth is clear: *be and do what God expects you to be and do, even if no one else expects it from you and even if no one else is leading you in the right direction.* Take courage, be strong in the Lord, and study His Word. Be an example of a young person who knows God's Word and who possesses sound judgment in his or her decision making. It is possible and desirable. May we as adults do our part to encourage this development, growth, and service for the kingdom, and may God raise up young people who are willing to do His work.

#56

TRUST WITH ALL YOUR HEART

Proverbs 3:5-6 says, "Trust in the LORD with all your heart. And do not lean on your own understanding. In all your ways acknowledge Him, and He will make your paths straight."

Trust in the LORD with all your heart.

The command to trust means to put one's confidence in, to be bold, to feel secure, and to rest easy in the Lord. God desires that we put our full hope in Him, that we turn to Him for strength, and that we rest safely knowing that His heart toward us is good. He does allow distress into our lives, but difficulties are our chance to let God work through our hearts to praise Him through unshaken faith by His grace. If we want to grow in our trusting of God or come to trust Him more, our faith will have to be stretched in order for this to happen. We will have to be pushed beyond where we feel we have things under control and where we sense that we are able to keep ourselves safe by our own means and power. The fact of the matter is that we are not the Sovereign of the universe and that we are not in ultimate control over our lives and circumstances. God is, and He loves us. Therefore, rather than trusting in our own strength, we ought to fall down before Him and give our lives and our circumstances to Him. (Not coincidentally, another rendering for trust is to fall down.)

God doesn't want to merely come to our aid when things get beyond our control. The fact is that we are never sufficient of ourselves (2

Corinthians 3:5), and apart from Him we can do nothing (John 15:5). Thus, God wants us to trust Him fully all the time. To trust Him with our hearts means that we let Him rule our thoughts, dictate our decision making, sanctify our emotions, and refine our desires. We come to Him as one in total and desperate need, and we let Him have His way in our hearts. God wants full surrender, taking up our crosses, denying ourselves, and following Him (Matthew 16:24). The road to spiritual strength and growth is through trusting God as we come to embrace and accept by faith our own weakness and inability apart from Him. Through Him we can do all things (Philippians 4:13), but without Him, nothing of true spiritual worth or gain is possible (Matthew 19:26).

And do not lean on your own understanding.

It is so very tempting to lean upon our own strength rather than that which God provides. It is not by our might or power (Zechariah 4:6) but by God's Spirit that anything of true spiritual value is accomplished. If we begin to elevate our own knowledge, abilities, and intellect above the wisdom which God provides us in Christ (Colossians 2:3), we will be prone to fall and be deceived. God wants us to grow in knowledge and wisdom in Christ through His Word, but He doesn't want us putting our confidence in our own strength and abilities such that we begin to trust in ourselves more than in Him and in His Word. The knowledge we need to remember so that we can stay humble is that we must not lean upon or depend upon our own knowledge, discernment, and reasoning abilities. They will lead us astray. We will misread people, we will interpret and apply Scripture erroneously, and we will just fail to seek God's will rightly. If we want to walk in wisdom and humility, we must walk by faith (2 Corinthians 5:7), seeking the Spirit's enabling to understand God's Word, to obey, and to do God's will. Those who walk by faith are those who will have true sight to know and do God's plan for their lives. Those who rely upon their own brainpower will be easily led astray by the evil one. *Trusting in the Lord and not trusting in ourselves go hand in hand.* Trusting in ourselves leads to the glory and praise of self. If it is we who pull ourselves through life, then it is we who should be praised. There may be nothing more spiritually tragic and dangerous than pride as we rest in ourselves and put our trust in ourselves, even part way and even some of the time. May God rid us of this spiritual cancer of self-reliance and vain glory.

In all your ways acknowledge Him...

God desires rather that we be mindful of our need for Him such that we choose to trust Him and walk by faith. He wants us to acknowledge Him, to consider Him, and to give Him the glory due Him as we go through life. Life is not about performing for God as if we need to impress Him and gain His favor. That leads to pride. Life, true abundant, eternal life, is knowing Christ (John 17:3). It is an intimate walk with God whereby we let Him live out His life and intentions through us and in us. We remain open to the Spirit's conviction, guidance, and leading, and we obey by faith. God gets the glory for our choices because we don't live by the feeble power of our flesh to gain His approval, but we act by the strength which He provides so that He can be glorified even through these weak jars of clay that we are (2 Corinthians 4:7). If we have a right view of ourselves as weak but strong only because of Christ in us and through us, we cannot help but give God the glory, and pride can be kept at bay. Humility leads to the praise of God and rejoicing in Him because He is acknowledged as our strength, support, and security each day.

...and He will make your paths straight.

As we acknowledge and glorify God rather than be obsessed with ourselves and our performance for God, let alone with selfish ambition and sinful agendas, we can trust God to make our paths straight. This means that we don't have to become crooked, we can maximize our stay on earth, and we can be kept from needless harm. This doesn't mean that we will never walk through a valley of the shadow of death and that all of life will be happy mountain top experiences, but it means that we can remain in a place of ultimate joy and satisfaction because of intimacy with God and a clean, upright, guilt-free conscience. Sometimes the wicked will prosper and the righteous will suffer, but what cannot be taken away from the righteous is a heart and soul that is at peace and at rest because its deepest longing has been met in Christ.

There is simply no better place to be than in the arms of God, and there is no better way to walk than by a fearless faith. May God enable us to trust as we lean upon Him and not ourselves such that our lives result in praise and glory to Him along with the satisfaction and peace of an upright life and heart, one which has much to look forward to in eternity.

#57
GOD IS ON YOUR SIDE

Deuteronomy 3:22 says, "Do not fear them, for the LORD your God is the one fighting for you." Just after the king of Sihon and the king of Og were defeated by the Israelites, Moses instructed Joshua to have no fear when he led the people into the promised land. Just as God had given victory to the nation under Moses, so, too, He would give victory to Israel under Joshua if only Israel would trust and obey. We are not fighting literal kings and literal armies, though we do fight the spiritual forces of darkness (Ephesians 6:12). Our call is not to fear evil or cower before the devil. The devil can only do what God gives him permission to do. Even though he has rebelled against God to set up his own kingdom, he knows that he is not the supreme power. This is why, for example, he had to ask God for permission to afflict Job and his family (Job 1:12). God had a plan for Job to sanctify him and use him to teach countless others great lessons about suffering and the sovereignty of God. When we read the accounts of Job and of Israel as they entered the promised land, we should be moved to have confidence that the same God who delivered them from their foes is the same God who can deliver us from our foe, the devil, today. In Christ, we have the victory. No demon and no scheme of the enemy can defeat the child of God or force him or her into sin. Because of Christ in us, the enemy must flee when he is resisted (James 4:7).

Not only, however, do we not have to fear the forces of darkness, but we do not have to fear mere mortal man. People can be difficult. If you have ever been teased, bullied, or made fun of in school, you understand. If you have an annoying neighbor or co-worker, you understand. If you have ever been given a raw deal and have been taken advantage of by another person, perhaps even a professing believer, you understand. It is easy to become angry at the person and desire to take vengeful action. It is easy to take matters into our own hands and begin to fret and worry. Sure, there might be some things we can do to try to be at peace with others and to defend justice, but ultimately we must put our hope in God. The command from Moses to Joshua was "Do not fear them." Who is your "them" that you fear? Who is the "them" that frustrates you to no end? Who is the "them" that is a thorn in your flesh? God's call to Joshua and to us as well is not to lose hope or give in to sinful measures simply because of the schemes and ways of evil man. What is man, after all (Psalm 144:3)? We serve a powerful God Who goes by the name of Jehovah Jireh, the God Who Provides. There is nothing He can't do. When we are pressed against the wall by our enemies and have every human reason to fear, God can deliver. He is the One fighting for us. When a relationship is just going nowhere and is just plain difficult, God is the One fighting for His children. When we are attacked, insulted, or mocked, God is the One fighting for our cause. Sometimes situations are easy to rectify, and other times it just seems as if the wicked are going to win because there is nothing we or anybody else can do to stop them. Sometimes the wicked do prosper (Psalm 73:3), and the righteous do suffer (Matthew 5:45). Our hope, however, is that God is just, justice will ultimately be served, God will avenge all wrongs (Romans 12:19), and He is on our side, taking up our cause. God is in our corner. May we always remember that, no matter what opposition or struggle we face. He is the One fighting for us. We are weak; He is strong. We are feeble; He is powerful. With us alone, the task is impossible. But with God, all things are possible (Matthew 19:26). What a mighty God we serve, and how wonderful it is that He fights with us and for us to accomplish His will in our lives. If God is for us, who can be against us (Romans 8:31)? In the end, righteousness always prevails because God gets the final say come eternity and judgment time.

Are you backed up against a wall? Or maybe you know someone else who seems to be in a sure bind of the enemy with no hope of escape. Why fear, when the Sovereign of the Universe, the One Who is in charge of it all, is on the case? God is always on call, always available, and always present. He is the One fighting for us. Political measures might fail. Personal influence might not get the job done. Money might not solve the problem. One's strength and resolve might not be enough, but God knew we would be in these strenuous kinds of situations all along. He wants us to see our helplessness so that He can be our Help, our Hope, our Deliverer, and our Provider. Whatever the situation and predicament, call to God and do not fear because He is the One fighting for you. And in this case, One is more than enough.

#58

All For Good

Romans 8:28 says, "And we know that God causes all things to work together for good to those who love God, to those who are called according to His purpose." As believers, God gives us a wonderful, hope-filled promise that He will cause all things to work for our good. Notice that things don't work for our good by themselves or just as a matter of chance. It is a privilege and benefit of knowing Christ that God works on our behalf to cause all things that come into our lives to work for our good.

Romans 8:29 continues by saying, "For those whom He foreknew, He also predestined *to become conformed to the image of His Son*, so that He would be the firstborn among many brethren" (italics mine). We can trust God that He is working all things in our lives for our sanctification. The Holy Spirit never rests when it comes to making us more like Christ, for such is God's will (1 Thessalonians 4:3). No matter what happens in our lives, God will cause things to work for our spiritual benefit. That is not to say that He does not work things also for our temporal benefit in terms of finances, health, etc., for we could all likely testify to a great many instances of God's provision and protection. God looks out for His children's welfare, both spiritually and practically, only allowing purposeful things into our lives which He will work for our good. But this verse is not a guarantee of perfect health, wealth, and prosperity of all kinds. The Bible explains that trials will be a part of this life

(John 16:33), so we should not expect everything to be smooth and easy. However, we can expect that God will use all things for our good. Even when things might not be pleasant circumstantially, God will be working for our sanctification, which is always a good thing.

God knows that the deepest longings and desires of our hearts are met in knowing Him and in enjoying Him forever. Thus, His purpose is to orchestrate all things in our lives so that we come to know Him better, to love Him more, and to reflect Jesus more accurately. As this becomes more of a reality in our lives, we will look forward to eternity more because we will be increasingly conformed to what we will be when Jesus returns when God finishes His sanctifying work in our lives and glorifies us to be forever with Him in heaven. *God knows that being like Jesus is the best thing that could happen to us and the thing that is required for us to experience the greatest joy and happiness. Thus, in His great love, He takes all things, even disappointments, attacks of the devil, and our own failures as means that can be used for our good as He uses them to make us like Christ.* Because of God's sovereign hand in the lives of His children, mockery and insult are ultimately for our gain. What others do that is an offense to us is ultimately for our profit. The evil which befalls us is actually transformed by God into a blessing. It is not that the righteous don't suffer or have travail in this life, but the promise is that God will use those things to bless us as He makes us more like Christ.

It is important to note that those who do not love God do not have the hope and promise that God is working behind the scenes to orchestrate all things for their good and sanctification. They don't even know God, for they have rejected the truth. They are left to fend for themselves and to try to maximize their pleasure in this world. They have no inheritance and no hope of eternal life with God in heaven. Thus, it makes no sense to tell an unbeliever that things will work out or get better. They may or they may not. Quoting Romans 8:28 to them wouldn't matter because it doesn't apply to them. This is the hopelessness and horror of life without God. We as believers, on the other hand, can have great hope and rest knowing that God is always working things for our benefit. Sometimes we might think we should take a certain job, move to a certain place, or get to know a certain person only to see God close a door as a means of protecting us or leading us to something much better. The unsaved person has no such backstop to their own short-sightedness and humanness. Christians have the benefit of a God Who knows everything and sees across time to be able to access every available resource in the universe to help us in the present. No one can thwart Him or interfere with His plans and purposes. Even our own infallibilities and failures can be used for our good. It doesn't even seem possible that through our failures God can make improvements and cause things to result in good, but that is exactly what He does. This is a potent, potent truth filled with hope for the child of God!

Next time we are blindsided by disappointment or difficulty, let us immediately recall this verse to mind. When we are wronged, let us remember that even this will work out for our good. What a God we serve that even that which we encounter that is not good He can make work for our good. Satan must be really discouraged by this verse, but we should find it highly encouraging.

#59

LIFE IS NOT FAIR BUT GOD IS

One of the most frustrating but necessary lessons that we each must learn in our Christian walks is that life is not fair but God is. In order to make sense of the very real prosperity and ease that the wicked can and do experience in this life, we must come to have an eternal perspective. Surely, we have all sensed frustration and maybe even grew bitter for a time when we saw someone get away with wrong. How irritating it is when justice is not served and the righteous suffer when in fact it should have been the wicked who were dealt the blow of justice. Yet, it is not always the case in this life and in this very fallen and imperfect world in which we live that justice is always served. Sometimes, life is not fair, and justice is not served. This is not how it should be, and it is not what a society should seek. However, unfairness and injustice does happen. The key for us as believers is how we respond to such situations. Of course, we should do our part to stand for truth and justice, but sometimes our calls, prayers, and petitions will go unheeded. Sometimes the wicked "get away with" their sin, at least in this life. So then what?

A very transparent portrayal of this internal struggle about holiness not necessarily leading to fairness and just retribution in this life is given in Psalm 73 by Asaph. Asaph knew the truth of God's Word as he said in verse 1: "Surely God is good to Israel, to those who are pure in heart!" This is truth that he has heard, written songs about, and thanked God for over and over again. He knows it is true, yet his experience is causing him to doubt God's Word. What he sees, feels, and observes doesn't necessarily correlate with his experience of witnessing the wicked prosper. After all, how could God be good if Israel suffers and the wicked nations triumph? How could God allow these things? Asaph had a heart for God, and it bothered him deeply that there seemed to be a lack of fairness in this world. In fact, this particular dilemma of the wicked prospering nearly caused him to begin vocalizing his doubt to others in Israel and thereby leading them into distrust of God also (v. 15). He says that his feet came close to stumbling (v. 2) because of his envy of the wicked (v. 3). This is so important: if we think that all on this earth must work out fairly while we are yet on this earth, we will be severely tempted to start envying the wicked to the extent that we might even start living as they live. Doubt leads to envy which leads to disobedience and to unfaithfulness. When Asaph thought merely temporally and not eternally, he grew greatly frustrated. He says in verse 12 and 13, "Behold, these are the wicked; and always at ease, they have increased in wealth. Surely in vain I have kept my heart pure and washed my hands in innocence." Asaph also speaks of suffering and even undergoing divine discipline of God (v. 14). Being a man of faith was tough, and it bothered him that all of God's refining work in his heart and life didn't lead to more material blessing and ease as the wicked experienced. His obedience before God felt like a wasted effort. When his focus was on evil people doing evil things rather than upon the God of justice and the God Who loves His people relentlessly, Asaph's heart sunk. He grew depressed, bitter, and angry (v. 21). But there was a turning point, an answer.

Asaph entered the sanctuary of God (v. 17). He may or may not have literally gone to the temple, but the point is that he came to rest in God's promises, God's sovereignty, and God's heart. God is good and just, and the only hope for Asaph and for us to be at peace despite the injustice all around us is to 1) do what we can to be and promote justice but more importantly 2) trust God to make all things just, fair, and right in the end. Romans 2:6 says that God "WILL RENDER TO EACH PERSON ACCORDING TO HIS DEEDS." Hebrews 9:27 says, "It is appointed for men to die once and after this comes judgment." We have got to remember that this life is incredibly short when contrasted with eternity.

In the end, all that we do here and now matters because God sees all and will render to each of us according to our deeds. Those who trust Christ for salvation will be rewarded on the basis of their faithfulness, while those who reject Christ will face the Great White Throne judgment where their evil deeds will condemn them to eternity in the lake of fire. Asaph's troubles and struggles with perceived unfairness and very real injustice in the short term were finally put to rest when he perceived the end of the wicked (v. 17). God will deal with them and hold them to account for all of their evil deeds because God is just. He is just to forgive those who seek redemption and just to punish those who reject it.

In the meantime, we have no reason to doubt, envy, or become embittered. We have our God, the God of justice, near to us, and such is our good (v. 28). Rather than envying the wicked, we need to tell them of all of the wonders of our good and just God (v. 28). Our hope is our eternal glory with Christ in heaven (v. 24), and to get all worked up about the ease of the wicked is just plain senseless given their ultimate end (v. 22). Let us not be ignorant but remember that the eternal judgment of God is altogether fair.

#60

THE ESSENCE OF REPENTANCE

There is a lot of confusion surrounding the concept of repentance in terms of what defines genuine repentance versus a mere regret over the consequences of poor choices. Scripture is clear, however, as to what leads us to repent, what repentance is, and how we can know if our repentance is, in fact, genuine.

After we have sinned, we are quickly made aware that we are guilty. The Holy Spirit will be active in convicting our hearts of sin and making us feel our guilt and shame acutely. But we can resist, grieve, and quench the Spirit's loving conviction in our hearts if we harden our wills against God. We can continue to hide sin in our hearts for great lengths of time despite the misery of a double-minded conscience. Even the threat of God's loving discipline may not be enough for us to want to change. What does move us to change with absolute certainty is God's kindness. As Romans 2:4 clearly states, "Or do you think lightly of the riches of His kindness and tolerance and patience, not knowing that the kindness of God leads you to repentance?" Believers will not face God's wrath, so His wrath will never be in play in terms of moving us to own up to our sin. The only thing that will move us to change is kindness. Even before we were saved, God showed us kindness by sending His own Son to the cross to die for our sins. As Romans 5:8 says, "But God demonstrates His own love toward us, in that while we were yet sinners, Christ died for us." God's kindness in salvation is key in moving souls to receive His grace, and His kindness in the lives of us as believers is key in leading us to repentance. That He is so patient with us despite the many times we ignore Him, spite Him, and reject Him can often be enough to move us to own up to our sin as it reminds us of His great love for us and just how much we love Him in return. Sometimes God will show us kindness in disciplining us by imposing some variety of consequences upon us, but even then, we will see that we had given Him no other choice. He will always act in our best interest, for our welfare, and for our preservation. God's feelings and heart toward us never change, and as our understanding of God's love and kindness deepens, the less we will want to sin and the quicker we will confess it when we do.

The other thing that moves us to repent is godly sorrow when confronted with the truth from Scripture. Scripture will cut us to the heart (Hebrews 4:12) and remind us of our sin. The internal guilt and agony becomes increasingly unbearable the more we sense God's love for us. Finally, at some point, we typically are overcome with genuine godly sorrow over what we have done. Godly sorrow is the first step in repentance as we finally acknowledge sin as God's sees our sin. We choose finally to see it as He does, grieving over its devastating effects and over how we have hurt God's heart. We are extremely saddened by having run from God and having made an allegiance with the devil. The depth of the depravity of our flesh so amazes us that we sorrow as we turn to God. If we have no sorrow over sin, it is hard to believe that we have truly repented. This is not just regret about being caught or a mere emotionalism or pouring out of tears. Repentance has not just any sorrow but a godly sorrow, one wrought in great grief over wronging Someone we love. It is a very personal sorrow.

This brings us to 2 Corinthians 7:8-11, which says,

> "For though I caused you sorrow by my letter, I do not regret it; though I did regret it--for I see that that letter caused you sorrow, though only for a while-- I now rejoice, not that you were made sorrowful, but that you were made sorrowful to the point of repentance; for you

were made sorrowful according to the will of God, so
that you might not suffer loss in anything through us. For
the sorrow that is according to the will of God produces
a repentance without regret, leading to salvation, but
the sorrow of the world produces death. For behold
what earnestness this very thing, this godly sorrow, has
produced in you: what vindication of yourselves, what
indignation, what fear, what longing, what zeal, what
avenging of wrong! In everything you demonstrated
yourselves to be innocent in the matter."

Godly sorrow according to the will and work of God in our hearts leads
to several fruits of repentance. Repentance has clear evidence of a
genuine change. Paul says that true repentance produces a "vindication
of yourselves." This involves us coming to our senses when we start
thinking and believing that we were really stupid in what we did and
that that is not who we really are or what we want to be. We begin
affirming truth after truth after truth about who we are in Christ and
rejecting the lies that Satan has put in our minds. It is a sort of defense
of who we are in Christ and who we want to be as we remind ourselves
of our true identity in Jesus. True repentance also produces indignation
as we get angry with ourselves for having giving into temptation and
not trusting God to escape. We get upset not just because we were
caught or now have consequences or a variety of inconveniences to
deal with but because we wronged God. True repentance also produces
fear as we realize just how close we were to really destroying our lives
or hurting someone else. Sin is dangerously deadly, and when we
come to our senses, we realize how foolish we were to be playing with
fire. True repentance produces a longing for being more like Christ,
a longing to get back in the saddle of doing God's work, and a desire
to push forward in obedience. Repentance has a corresponding zeal
for righteousness and the commands of Christ. Those who truly repent
don't just crawl ahead, but they start sprinting to avenge for lost time
and lost opportunities. They realize that Satan won that round, but they
want the next one. They want back in the fight to avenge the wrong and
advance the kingdom of God.

These fruits of repentance help us to know whether we have truly changed course in our lives or have just experienced a certain feeling without true godly sorrow. True repentance produces true change. We may fall again in the same way, and certainly we will fall again in some way. But when we do, we need to yield to the Spirit's conviction, receive the truth of Scripture, turn from our sins, and press on in righteousness. God's forgiveness is immediate because He is that kind. He is the kind of God that we want to obey and Who deserves our allegiance. Praise Him that He is patient with us and works to keep us on the right track.

#61

WORK AS WORSHIP

Sometimes we as believers separate the "sacred" from the "secular" in terms of jobs, careers, and callings. In other words, sometimes we tend to develop a thought process that sees only what pastors, counselors, and missionaries do as being ministry or service for the kingdom, whereas we might view the person who goes to work from 9 to 5 in the secular workplace as not also being a minister and servant of God. Sometimes it is easy to feel like we cannot worship God while we are delivering newspapers, changing diapers, selling real estate, answering phones, or on down the list. Whatever line of work we might be in, the fact of the matter is that God can be honored and the kingdom can be advanced as we do our secular jobs. Think about it for a moment. Many churches have one full time minister to shepherd hundreds of "lay persons" as we call them. Can only the pastor be serving God and the rest be mired in "lesser" service for the kingdom? This is a major thing to think about given that we will spend the vast majority of our lives working and not being at church, unless of course, we are called by God as a pastor or full-time Christian worker of some kind. For those who are in Christian ministry, work is obviously ministry, and this has its own challenges. For those who are not in full-time Christian work, we must not fall for the devil's wile that we cannot serve and worship God in what we do as well. We might not be preparing a sermon or feeding the hungry during business hours, but how we live our lives and how we do our work is our chance to worship God. We each must find joy in the places to which God has called us, and we all have a chance to bring God glory wherever we might be each and every day.

In Ecclesiastes 3:9, Solomon asks, "What profit is there to the worker from that in which he toils?" Are we to work simply for money for money's sake? If so, we will be disappointed. Solomon says in Ecclesiastes 5:10, "He who loves money will not be satisfied with money, nor he who loves abundance with its income. This too is vanity." Are we to work just so that we can eat and then eat again until eventually we die? Scripture is plain that this is a vain and unsatisfying way to live. Solomon says in Ecclesiastes 2:25, "For who can eat and who can have enjoyment without Him?" Only when God is factored into the equation can work take on its right and full purpose. God has ordained work for man. Even before sin entered the world, God gave Adam a garden to tend. (Genesis 2:15). *Thus, work plays a certain role in how we interact with God, and the only way to understand the purpose of work and to enjoy our work and the fruit of our labor is by also enjoying God as we work* (Psalm 16:11).

God seeks worshippers (John 4:23-24), and Scripture is plain that one of the major ways in which we worship God is by our work. Solomon says in Ecclesiastes 9:10, "Whatever your hand finds to do, do it with all your might." Colossians 3:17 says, "Whatever you do in word or deed, do all in the name of the Lord Jesus, giving thanks through Him to God the Father." Certainly, work would fall under the category of "whatever you do," regardless of whether it is church-oriented or not. God desires worshippers, and He has ordained work as a major way that we can worship Him. So how do we make sure we worship God in our work and as we work?

Obviously, doing our work in love and holiness is essential (John 13:34-35, Hebrews 12:14). Where possible, we should seek to share the gospel (Acts 1:8). Our factory, shop, or vehicle is our mission field. We must also guard our hearts so that we have a good attitude, one that doesn't complain (Philippians 2:14), one that is thankful (Colossians 3:15), and one that is willing to show respect for superiors (1 Peter 2:13-14). God doesn't need brownnosers, nor does He need slackers. God wants those who work with diligence (Romans 12:11) and for His favor, not merely as men-pleasers. Colossians 3:23-24 says, "Whatever you do, do your work heartily, as for the Lord rather than for men, knowing that from the Lord you will receive the reward of the inheritance. It is the Lord Christ whom you serve." There is no ambiguity from the Scripture that whatever we do, all kinds of work included, can be and ought to be worship of God, for it is He Whom we serve. He is our ultimate Boss, for it is He Who will give our ultimate evaluation and review. The best thing we can do is to live as sacrifices that please Him even as we work (Romans 12:1-2).

There is nothing wrong with praying for a new job or seeking a career change, but the admonition to worship is for the present, even if the job is less than desirable. Let us thank God for the work which He has given us rather than taking it for granted. Let us not think that God cannot use us even in the secular workplace. We are all missionaries (2 Corinthians 5:18), we are all God's workers (1 Corinthians 3:9), and we are all called as worshippers. We must remember that God is our Joy, our Life, our Hope, our Sustenance, our Provider, our Master, and our Judge. He gives meaning and purpose to work, and He enables us to have joy as we work, as we eat, as we rest, and as we go through our lives.

May God teach us and enable us to honor Him in and through our work, whatever our specific line of work might be. Next time we go to work, let us go to worship.

#62
SANCTIFICATION THROUGH SUFFERING

There is a serious misconception that is becoming increasingly widely held within Christian circles which teaches that, as believers, we have the right on this earth to have freedom from sickness, financial struggle, and, in fact, struggle and suffering of almost any kind and nature. This position and line of thinking is absolutely contrary to the Scripture.

Jesus taught that this life would have trial and tribulation, and He gave us hope that He has overcome the world (John 16:33). In other words, the believer can put his hope in eternity being free of all that ails this life, from pain, to hunger, to illness, etc. A true kingdom focus accepts that life on this earth is imperfect because the world is fallen (Romans 3:23, 8:22, Genesis 3:17), and such a mindset looks forward to the hope that is yet to come. *The problem with much of the teaching of today is that it is extremely focused on what God can do for us in this life rather than what we should be doing for God in light of the life to come.* Temporary blessing which comes to be defined as health, wealth, and prosperity comes to replace true spiritual blessings of holiness, freedom from sin, and the privilege of storing up treasure in heaven. This life is so short when compared to eternity, and eternity, not what rust and moths can destroy (Matthew 6:19-20), ought to be our single focus and driving hope (see 1 Peter 1:13).

The Biblical writers had no problem understanding that suffering was normal in this life. Jesus said that His followers would be persecuted for righteousness' sake (Mark 13:13). In fact, persecution itself is to be considered a blessing because it is an honor to suffer for the name of Christ (Matthew 5:10). Paul spoke in 1 Corinthians 4 of his present suffering being relatively insignificant when compared to eternity to come (see 1 Corinthians 4:16-18). He suffered greatly, being beaten, shipwrecked, stuck out in the cold, stoned, imprisoned, and eventually beheaded for Christ's sake (2 Corinthians 11:23-28). This man knew suffering. Even when he had the privilege of experiencing profound heavenly visions (2 Corinthians 12:1-6), God ordained and allowed a minister of Satan to torment and buffet him. God knew that Paul needed this to keep him humble so that he would not exalt himself (2 Corinthians 12:7). God has a plan and purpose in ordaining suffering for us in this life.

James 1:2-4 says, "Consider it all joy, my brethren, when you encounter various trials, knowing that the testing of your faith produces endurance. And let endurance have its perfect result, so that you may be perfect and complete, lacking in nothing." First off, we should note that Scripture does not say if we encounter trials but *when*. Trials will happen, so we ought not to be surprised when they do. As Peter said in 1 Peter 4:12, "Beloved, do not be surprised at the fiery ordeal among you, which comes upon you for your testing, as though some strange thing were happening to you." What is important is that we, like James, see a purpose in suffering. Suffering is meant to teach us endurance which results in making us perfect, complete, and lacking in nothing. God uses suffering to restore a right perspective in our hearts and minds about what this life is all about and what our eternal priorities are. Trials point us to our need for God and our innate human weakness. The result of God's testing is to sanctify us by making us more like Christ in faith and holiness. This is in direct contradiction to the erroneous teaching that says that enough faith will keep us from suffering. The Bible says that suffering builds our faith. In other words, *suffering is not a sign of weakness; rather, it helps us to see our weakness so that we can be strengthened through sanctification in Christ.* Suffering produces character, endurance, and hope such that we should exult in it. As Romans 5:3-5 says,

> "And not only this, but we also exult in our tribulations, knowing that tribulation brings about perseverance; and perseverance, proven character; and proven character, hope; and hope does not disappoint, because the love of God has been poured out within our hearts through the Holy Spirit who was given to us."

Trials are not evil, pain is not necessarily bad, and suffering can be for our good. In fact, those who suffer have a great opportunity by faith to be refined unto the likeness of Christ as their weaknesses and impurities come to the surface so that the Refiner can purify their souls. Furthermore, as we see God continue to provide and strengthen us to do His will even under great duress, our faith grows such that we are able to keep believing and keep obeying even better than before.

Suffering has its place and purpose here so that we would look forward to eternity and live in light of eternal priorities now. We might pray that, where necessary, God would allow suffering into our lives so that we can be refined to His glory. It is a tough prayer, but it is a safe prayer because God is good, faithful, and true. May our Lord make us more like Jesus, whatever it takes.

#63

GOD KNEW WHAT HE WAS DOING THE WHOLE TIME

Perhaps there has been a time in your life (probably more than one) in which you came to wonder why God led you to do something or to go somewhere. You were sure that God's hand was involved in directing you one way, and yet things only seemed to end up going poorly. Perhaps you encountered a lot of conflict and struggle and experienced a lack of smooth sailing, to say the least. If you can at all relate to this dilemma, the story of Joseph is highly applicable to you.

Joseph didn't do anything wrong to be the preferred child of his father, Jacob. That was Jacob's issue, yet it led to his brothers hating him. Joseph did nothing wrong for God his brothers to hate him for the dreams that God had given him about them bowing down to him. He didn't deserve to be thrown into a pit by his brothers only to be sold into slavery by the very ones who should have been looking out for him. Yet Joseph is such a remarkable story because he kept believing and persevering. He didn't give up, throw a pity party, or develop a seething, hateful, vengeful personality. He just kept being faithful, and he lived to please God. He sure didn't understand why this all happened as it happened, but he had faith nonetheless.

The interesting thing about Joseph was that, despite the many challenges and hardships that he encountered, his life was noticeably blessed by God. Scripture says repeatedly that God was with Joseph (Genesis 39:2, 21, 23), which resulted in blessing, favor, prosperity, and success. Joseph became a blessing to Potiphar while he was a servant in his house (Genesis 39:4-6). While Joseph was in prison, he was given charge over all the prisoners because the chief jailer trusted him (Genesis 39:22-23). Eventually, he would interpret Pharaoh's dreams and be appointed second in command over all of Egypt (Genesis 41:43). God never abandoned Joseph, but He had a purpose in all of the things that He allowed into Joseph's life. He knew things that Joseph didn't know about the future, particularly that a famine would occur which could wipe his entire family out. By God orchestrating his steps into Egypt and into a position of great power, God would use Joseph to spare his family and provide them food in Egypt. The entire future of the nation of Israel was at stake, and through Joseph, it was preserved.

God could have used someone else to deliver Jacob and his family, or He could have spared the land from experiencing a severe famine. But that is not what God did; rather, He chose to work things out in such a way that all would be in awe of His providence. The very evil that his brothers committed turned out to be used by God for their own survival. As Joseph said to his brothers, "As for you, you meant evil against me, but God meant it for good in order to bring about this present result, to preserve many people alive" (Genesis 50:20). This is such a wonderful picture of God's grace and sovereignty. **We might not know what God is doing in our lives much of the time, but God knows what He is doing all of the time.** It took many, many years before Joseph had an answer to some of the why questions which he likely had in the back of his mind. In this instance, God allowed Joseph to see some of the reasons why such awful things happened to him as he was blessed to be the savior of his family and the nation of Israel. God does sometimes let us see glimpses of why He does what He does, but He owes us no explanation this side of eternity. In eternity, we will praise Him for His wonderful plan and purposes, and the right thing to do now is to praise and thank Him because He is good, kind, and in complete control, even if we are confused about what He is doing.

People might intend evil for us, and Satan will try to attack us. But what is sure is that God is ultimately working behind the scenes for His children such that all is intended for a blessing and for our good and even for the good of others as we remain faithful to God. Joseph didn't let the unfair treatment that he received cause him to wallow and give up. It is a good thing, too, that he kept believing, or the consequences of his rebellion could have bled over into the survival of his family. Every life matters, and every decision matters. Joseph remained obedient to God, and God blessed Him and watched out for him every step of the way. God was sovereign over his circumstances, and he recognized that and trusted God in that, as difficult as that was. He realized that he was not the maker of his own destiny in terms of where he would live and what he would end up doing; however, he controlled what he could control, which was his faithfulness.

No matter where God takes us, He has a plan and a purpose for our good and for the good of others. Even evil things that happen to us can be used of God to work for good on our behalf. Joseph saw that God knew what He was doing the whole time, and Joseph's God is our God. He knows what He is doing, and we must trust Him. His mercies will be there every step of the way. Let us be faithful and obedient as we wait and watch for the good that only God can do.

#64
HOW TO BE A GODLY FATHER

Many men desire to be good fathers, but the criterion that really counts is whether or not they are godly fathers. Here are four Biblical principles that, by God's grace, will lay a sound foundation in helping fathers become godly fathers.

First, godly fathers are first godly men. It doesn't work for fathers to bail out and say to their children, "Do as I say, not as I do" (Matthew 23:3). Children must be able to see an example of Christ in their fathers. Paul says to his spiritual children in 1 Corinthians 11:1, "Be imitators of me, just as I also am of Christ." Until men by faith follow in the example of Christ themselves, they cannot be godly examples for their own children. Those who imitate Christ in thoughts, attitudes, and actions are those who have the right and Biblical ability to properly train and disciple their own children.

Second, godly fathers love their children unconditionally. Unconditionally is a significant word. It implies that love is not merited or earned and that the father's treatment of his children is not dictated by what they can offer him in return. Some fathers want to see their children work their way into their favor or accomplish something which will make the father appear more successful. In other words, their focus is upon themselves and upon what they can gain rather than upon unconditional love for their children. I think of the father of the prodigal son who stood waiting and watching for his son to return to him (Luke 15:20). When he finally did return, the father didn't judge the son or force him to earn back his favor, love, and approval. He simply embraced him and threw a celebratory party for his son (Luke 15:21-24). He could do this because his love for his son wasn't based upon what his son could do for him but simply and strictly upon the fact that he was his son. He never disowned his son for leaving in a pattern of rebellion, but he waited, hoped, and longed for his lost son's return. Godly fathers don't make their children earn their approval, and they don't use their children's behavior as a condition for their love. That doesn't mean that they don't discipline, but it does mean that they never disown. Such is the nature of unconditional love.

Third, godly fathers train their children how to love and honor God. The willingness and ability to train in righteousness is the call of every godly father. Proverbs 22:6 says, "Train up a child in the way he should go, Even when he is old he will not depart from it." Ephesians 6:4 echoes the Proverbs passage, saying, "Fathers, do not provoke your children to anger, but bring them up in the discipline and instruction of the Lord." It is not good enough just to make children go to church, say their prayers, and learn Bible verses. Those things ought to be part of the training process; however, we don't come to know Jesus or grow in Him by having external practices forced upon us. Fathers need to teach their children Scriptural truths as they model their own love for the Lord. Kids aren't stupid. In fact, they are a lot smarter than most parents give them credit for. They can tell when religious rituals are empty or hypocritical, and even though the child might come to know the Bible inside and out, he or she will likely develop a hatred or bitterness towards Christianity if the only Christianity the child knows is vain and ugly. Training in righteousness requires learning the Scripture (2 Timothy 3:16-17), but how that Scripture is applied must correlate with true righteousness. Otherwise, the child will be left spending years trying to reconcile the Bible with his own experience. But let us not forget the role of discipline in the training process. Even our heavenly father disciplines those sons whom He loves (Hebrews 12:6), and the fact that a father is willing to discipline his children demonstrates love. Young children need to know their boundaries as it makes them feel secure. As kids grow older, they must see that they don't run the home and that

Biblical principles will be followed in the home. Discipline reinforces these realities through imposing consequences. But it must be evident to the children when they are being disciplined that the father's love for them has not changed. Discipline is never aligned with wrath because it is kindness that leads to repentance (Romans 2:4). Discipline is simply another expression of love (Deuteronomy 8:1-6, Hebrews 12:6).

Fourth, a godly father seeks to give his children good gifts such that his children are blessed through him. Of course, love, discipline, and the training of the Lord in righteousness are blessings of eternal value, but godly fathers go beyond just spiritual gifts to seeking to give good gifts of all kinds. Our heavenly Father is the ultimate example of this. James 1:7 says, "Every good thing given and every perfect gift is from above, coming down from the Father of lights, with whom there is no variation or shifting shadow." Our Father is the giver of every good and perfect gift because He knows when, how, and what to give us. He knows what we desire and ask for because He knows and cares for what we really want and need (Psalm 37:4, Philippians 4:19). He is the Father of lights that don't vary or shift because He is pure, consistent, and devoted to His children. He can constantly be believed and relied upon to offer His children that which is kindest, wisest, and best. He is not a deified Santa Claus that spoils children and is subject to their every whim. Spoiling is not the purpose of giving good and perfect gifts. Rather, the purpose of such provisions and blessings is the security that God cares about us perfectly and intimately. Knowing that He knows what we need and that He cares about what we want and hope for is so important in our relationship with Him. In the same way, earthly fathers should seek to be in tune with what their children hope for, desire, and need such that they can wisely meet and address those needs and wants. A father's wisdom is a blessing and security to his children as they can trust what he does for them and gives to them.

May God raise up more such men.

#65

HOW TO BE A GODLY MOTHER

Christian mothers must never underestimate their calling. It is an extremely difficult, challenging, and tiring calling, but its rewards are in proportion to the tasks. God has given principles in His Word to guide mothers as they navigate through the challenges of raising children.

#1 Godly mothers relish their young children and tenderly nurture them.

As 1 Thessalonians 2:7 says, "But we proved to be gentle among you, as a nursing mother tenderly cares for her own children." There is great comfort, rest, and security in a mother's embrace. Isaiah 66:13 says, "As one whom his mother comforts, so I will comfort you." Psalm 131:2 adds, "Like a weaned child rests against his mother, my soul is like a weaned child within me." Men can be nurturing, but there is just something unique about the tender embrace of a mother to her child. Children can sense the difference, and they crave a mother's gentle touch and love. Women should not run from bearing and nurturing children, thinking that there is something supposedly more important or significant for them to do. Even Hannah who dedicated her son Samuel to serve the Lord still took him home to care for him until he was weaned (1 Samuel 1:22-24). God honors mothers who invest in their children, and mothers should adore and treasure the moments that they have with young ones. As Luke 2:19 says, "But Mary treasured all these things, pondering them in her heart." Children are only young for a short time, and the mother should be there to enjoy her God-given children.

#2 Godly mothers recognize that children are a great gift and reward and thus view and treat them as such.

Eve said in Genesis 4:1, "I have gotten a manchild with the help of the LORD." Every time a woman becomes pregnant, it is because God is involved in creating a life (1 Samuel 1:5,19, Psalm 113:9). This is another reason why life is precious and why children are precious to God. It is imperative that mothers recognize the value of children and that they are indeed a gift from God. Psalm 127:3 says, "Behold, children are a gift of the LORD, the fruit of the womb is a reward." If a mother views her children as a punishment, inconvenience, or the like, she needs to change her perspective quickly lest she treat her children as such. Godly mothers value their children as rewards from God and are thus motivated to do all that they can to nurture, care, and train their children rightly.

#3 Godly mothers instruct their children in God's truths.

Proverbs 1:8 says, "Hear, my son, your father's instruction and do not forsake your mother's teaching." Proverbs 6:20 adds, "My son, observe the commandment of your father and do not forsake the teaching of your mother." King Lemuel in Proverbs 31:1 said that it was his mother who taught him about how to recognize a godly woman who would be a godly mother for his children. Timothy's godly heritage was a result of his mother and her mother before her (2 Timothy 1:5). Mothers must never underestimate the role that they play in teaching their children about God, about His Word, and about salvation. From as early on as possible, God is to be central in a mother's instruction. Even in the case of an unsaved or absentee father, mothers can still reach their children by faith (1 Corinthians 7:14). Teaching children the Bible is a huge calling with eternal ramifications, and godly mothers are honored to take up the challenge.

#4 Godly mothers are willing and faithful to discipline their children.

Proverbs 29:15 says, "The rod and reproof give wisdom, but a child who gets his own way brings shame to his mother." Mothers who enjoy or tolerate their children disrespecting and disobeying them are not operating as God would have them. They should be ashamed of themselves, and they must become willing and faithful to discipline.

#5 Godly mothers do not pick favorites among their own children.

Proverbs 28:21 says, "To show partiality is not good, because for a piece of bread a man will transgress." Not only is picking favorites not Christ-like behavior (James 2:1), but it can lead to children sinning as they grow jealous, establish rivalries, and become deceptive and manipulative. Unconditional love for children and fairness in discipline is essential to being a godly mother.

Regardless of a mother's marriage or work situation, God is faithful to honor the faith and obedience of mothers who do whatever they can by faith to follow His principles in raising godly children. Some mothers will have all day with their children, while other mothers will need to work for various reasons. In either case, mothers can follow Biblical principles and be godly mothers. As Galatians 6:10 says, "So then, while we have opportunity, let us do good to all people, and especially to those who are of the household of the faith." Mothers, as you have opportunity to be with your kids, to love them, to nurture them, and to care for them, perhaps even to provide for them, do it with all your heart unto the Lord (Colossians 3:23). God will remember and honor your faithfulness. As Galatians 6:9 says, "Let us not lose heart in doing good, for in due time we will reap if we do not grow weary." Motherhood is certainly wearying, but mothers must stand fast in their calling. As they are faithful in their work at home (Titus 2:4-5), God will be honored, and He promises to honor those who honor Him (1 Samuel 2:30, Proverbs 31:28).

#66

EVERY WORD COUNTS

If the Word of God is food, which the Bible says it is (Deuteronomy 8:3), then the church must feast upon it in order to be healthy. But in order to feast upon the Word, the church must first believe the Word. If the church fails to believe the Word, then they won't choose to eat it, they won't understand it, and they won't live and apply it. Thus, when the church begins to pick and choose what parts of the Bible it wants to accept, it will inevitably become malnourished, weak, defeated, and deceived. It makes no sense for us to cut out fruits and vegetables from our diets because we don't like them or because we don't like how they taste. Our feelings and experiences don't mean that fruits and vegetables are truly bad for us; indeed, they are necessary to maintain good health. In the same way, we have no right before God to tell Him which parts of His "meal" we are willing to accept and which parts we are not. None of us are allergic to God's Word, so we have no excuse but to read and accept all of it. God has not served us a bad meal, but it is a meal that He knows will be good for us, even if it tastes bitter going down as it reveals truths about our hearts that we might not like. Truth must trump feelings, the Word must overrule experiences, and God's Word must not be merely tolerated but that which makes us tremble as we are humbled and submit to it (Isaiah 66:2).

The Bible is not something that we are to bend to our own agendas or treat as a smorgasbord where we choose a part here that makes us feel good while we ignore the rest. It is interesting that people tend not to discount verses that pose little threat, but they have difficulty accepting the ones that fly in the face of what they prefer or which contradict the way in which they have chosen to live. All of a sudden, they have trouble accepting a certain passage. As they stubbornly reject portions of Scripture that they deem unnecessary or erroneous, they essentially instruct God to rewrite His letter to man, a very arrogant thing to do because it lifts our minds up as being smarter and wiser than God's. How dare we tell God that His Word is not up to our standards or that it doesn't fit in with our priorities!

It is important that we note that God is extremely dogmatic about His Word being true through and through. *First, He says that His Word is tested.* Proverbs 30:5 says, "Every word of God is tested; He is a shield to those who take refuge in Him." God's Word is fool-proof, meaning that those who reject it prove themselves to be fools. *Second, He says that man needs every Word that God has spoken in order to live.* Jesus responds to the devil's temptation in Matthew 4:4 by quoting Deuteronomy 8:3, saying, "It is written, 'MAN SHALL NOT LIVE ON BREAD ALONE, BUT ON EVERY WORD THAT PROCEEDS OUT OF THE MOUTH OF GOD.'" Man is a spiritual being as well as a physical being, and the soul needs food even as the body needs food, and even more importantly so. To ignore some words and to not eat every word is to become famished and spiritually weak. Every word counts because every word is food and from God. *Thirdly, God takes His revelation to man very seriously such that He warns those who tamper with God's Word that they could prove themselves to be unsaved and thus miss out on eternal life.* Revelation 22:18-19 says,

> "I testify to everyone who hears the words of the prophecy
> of this book: if anyone adds to them, God will add to him
> the plagues which are written in this book; and if anyone
> takes away from the words of the book of this prophecy,
> God will take away his part from the tree of life and from
> the holy city, which are written in this book."

This might seem harsh, but it is what God says because God knows that the church is built upon truth and called to communicate truth (1

Timothy 3:15). If truth is cut or compromised, the whole pillar falls and the way for evil is opened wide. Paul affirmed the seriousness of accepting God's Word and not altering its meaning when he says in Galatians 1:8-9,

> "But even if we, or an angel from heaven, should preach to you a gospel contrary to what we have preached to you, he is to be accursed! As we have said before, so I say again now, if any man is preaching to you a gospel contrary to what you received, he is to be accursed!"

The meaning of "accursed" is to be devoted to destruction with no hope of redemption. Indeed, it is serious business to alter the meaning of God's Word, to change the gospel to be more palatable, and to redefine sound doctrine. What God has given must be preserved, guarded, kept, and preached without altering the text and without compromising the entirety and integrity of the Scripture.

Man may teach God's Word incorrectly and incur judgment, *but man cannot ever change it*. Matthew 5:18 says, "For truly I say to you, until heaven and earth pass away, not the smallest letter or stroke shall pass from the Law until all is accomplished." And as Peter says in 1 Peter 1:25, "'BUT THE WORD OF THE LORD ENDURES FOREVER.' And this is the word which was preached to you." God's Word will never fail, and God will preserve it. Its eternal truths are always true, no matter what man might try to say about them. Man does not stand in judgment over God's Word, though he might think he does and even try to do so, but God's Word will always stand in judgment over him. As Psalm 119:160 says, "The sum of Your word is truth, and every one of Your righteous ordinances is everlasting."

Our calling before God is to be faithful to believe every Word of Scripture. If we don't receive it all, we will miss out on much that God wants to teach us, and we will fail to be able to be used as God would prefer to use us. Let us take in God's Word cover to cover, and let us value God's Word as highly and as seriously as God does.

#67

SELF-CONTROL IN ALL THINGS

In ancient Greece, every year before and after the Olympic games were held, the Isthmian games took place in the city of Corinth. Those who won would receive a wreath made out of pine. No doubt those who participated in these games trained rigidly as the athletes of our day do for the Olympics. It takes strict discipline, sound eating habits, rigid training programs, a burning desire to win, and a persevering commitment to the task to prepare for an athletic event of this caliber. Those who compete at this level run to win, and in order to win, they must discipline their bodies. Self-control is a key component for victory.

In 1 Corinthians 9:24-27, Paul alludes to these athletic competitions when he says,

> "Do you not know that those who run in a race all run, but only one receives the prize? Run in such a way that you may win. Everyone who competes in the games exercises self-control in all things. They then do it to receive a perishable wreath, but we an imperishable. Therefore I run in such a way, as not without aim; I box in such a way, as not beating the air; but I discipline my body and make it my slave, so that, after I have preached to others, I myself will not be disqualified."

Paul says that it makes no sense for a boxer to punch the air. His goal is to train so that he can land his punches, knock down his opponent, and win the match. In the same way, it makes no sense for a runner to deviate from the course and go for a stroll through the country. His mission is to stay on track within the boundaries and cross the finish line before everyone else. Winning will require self-control in all things, from the training and preparation to the execution and performance on race day. Spiritually it makes no sense to view life as haphazard or to approach it carelessly. God has called us all to run a race, and we are in it to win it, or at least we should be. Paul viewed his commission to share the gospel as even more intense and serious than the training of a world-class athlete. He knew that a race only has one winner, and he lived the Christian life as if he wanted to get the most rewards possible for the sake of Christ.

What helps make an athlete successful is the same thing that contributed to Paul's spiritual discipline- self-control. Paul speaks of disciplining his body to the point of making it his slave. The word that is translated as self-control could also be rendered temperance, which implies mastering fleshly passions and sensuous lusts. Just as an athlete has to discipline his mind, will, emotions, and body in order to perform at the highest level, a Christian must discipline his thoughts, behaviors, attitudes, and actions in order to bear abundant spiritual fruit. Self-control means that we don't make any provision for the flesh and its lusts (Romans 13:14). We refuse do anything to aid and abet self. Rather, we yield to God by faith Who by His Spirit will enable us to live as new creations in Christ rather than as those who are enslaved to sin. We have been set free from being slaves to sin (Romans 6:6), and self-control is thus the process of continuing to reckon by faith that we are indeed free such that we choose not to indulge the flesh. If we want to run to win, we must be committed to making our spirits strong by studying God's Word, by meditating upon it, by praying, by serving, and by doing all that Christ has commanded us.

Life will riddle us with encumbrances, and Satan will fire temptations at us more often than we would like. Self-indulgence gives into a little sin here and there, and self-righteousness abstains from sin for the purpose of glorifying self. Self-control, on the other hand, remains disciplined by faith to think rightly and obey no matter what we might feel like at the time. When this fruit of the Spirit is manifested in our lives as believers, we will be able to resist temptation, persevere under fire, and finish the race of life strongly.

Paul was adamant about being self-controlled so that he would not be disqualified in his Christian testimony. He wanted to continue to be filled by the Spirit, to be used of God, and to be a benefit to others as he preached the gospel to them and taught them the Word of God. Giving into sin saps the power of God and wrecks our ability to serve God as we should. We need to be faithful lest we wreck our testimony and lead others astray.

The eternal rewards that we have waiting for us as we live faithfully for Christ's sake are far greater and longer-lasting than the pine wreaths given to the Isthmian winners. Therefore, let us run to win, pressing on so that we might receive the eternal prize (Philippians 3:14).

#68

WILLING TO BE REAL

There is a severe malady that has affected much of the church today. The funny thing is that the church is almost proud of its error, glorying in its shame. This is very sad. This spiritual illness affects both those inside of the church and those outside. What is missing is authenticity, being real, and being discerningly transparent and vulnerable. Because the church has degraded into a place where we must look like we have it all together, like we have no doubts, like we have no struggles, and where we must perform rather than be, we have lost much. Churches go on to lament a lack of community and true fellowship and hope that merely instituting another program will fix the situation and make love happen. It doesn't work that way. The church needs to recover an aspect of love and compassion that it once knew and which compelled those outside of the church to watch and wonder and even long for being part of such loving community and fellowship (Acts 2:42-47). The church needs to be real.

We have gotten so good at role-playing, acting, and mask-wearing when we are "at church" that it makes it very hard to know someone for who they really are. How can a friendship or any kind of relationship even in Christ's church happen or develop when one person is being dishonest about who they are, where they are at, and what they need? Sadly, this dishonesty about a person's true state of being is encouraged when the church lacks compassion, sympathy, empathy, and the desire to meet needs (c.f. Hebrews 4:15). For some reason, too many churches fail to actively seek out needs in their own body of believers, let alone in the community. Needs aren't bad; they are normal (Philippians 4:19). Part of the church's life and ministry is to meet needs, physical, financial, emotional, and most importantly spiritual. But how can that happen unless it actively seeks needs out and unless it cultivates an environment of acceptance and compassion which invites needs to be expressed and shared? Too often admitting needs is associated with lacking faith or being disorganized or lazy. The reality is that needs are part of life, and the church is there to help one another out.

Many churches are proficient at the 20 seconds or less "shake the hand of the person next to you" attempt at fellowship which amounts to nothing more than a mere "good morning" or "how are you?" Those rituals of pseudo-relationship are dangerous because they make us as churches feel like we have achieved love and care when really we have achieved nothing more than a handshake and a smile, if either are even genuine. There is nothing wrong with a welcoming handshake, a "how are you this morning," or a genuine smile, but we can't suppose that this defines having arrived at community akin to that which the early church possessed and experienced.

So what makes an authentic, Christ-like community? *When people who recognize their own imperfection are willing to let Christ shine through them such that they love another person in his or her imperfection, something powerful and wonderful takes place. It is called Christian fellowship in its truest, purest, and warmest sense. It is not contrived, forced, or fake. It is genuine, authentic, and real. Needs can be shared without being judged, doubts can be voiced and be gently answered, and something that cries "you are safe" is present in such a community.* Only when people feel safe will they be willing to share struggles or seek help that the church is called to provide. In too many churches the feeling of safety is nowhere to be found because there is such pressure to conform to various external things that identify that particular church or denomination. In other churches, people are just too busy doing church things to have time to care about a visitor or even one of their own. Yet in other churches, the churches purposefully ignore the visitor and just let him or her observe. The whole point about a church community is to be there for one another, to communicate, to care, and to serve each other. This can't happen if we hide from one another, if we avoid one another, or if we are too busy for each other. Churches must learn that it is normal and acceptable for its people to have needs and for them to be able to seek out help for whatever they might be struggling with. If everybody acts like everything is fine even when it is not, how can compassion be shown? Kindness leads to repentance (Romans 2:4), not judgmentalism, church activity, church membership, or any other externality associated with church. Church is a living organism made up of God's people and indwelt by God Himself. We, not the association, locality, or building, are the church. How loving we are is how loving the church will be. We can be the difference; we need to be the difference.

Let us pray for churches to have leaders who aren't too busy building ministries to minister to people. Let us hope for church people to care and not perform. The community that the early church had in Acts 2 is possible for us today, but it starts with being willing to be real.

#69

PREREQUISITES FOR ANSWERED PRAYER

The Bible gives five components of prayer that we must heed and obey if we want God to hear and answer our prayers.

1. Faith

Mark 11:22-24 says,

> "And Jesus answered saying to them, 'Have faith in God. Truly I say to you, whoever says to this mountain, "Be taken up and cast into the sea," and does not doubt in his heart, but believes that what he says is going to happen, it will be granted him. Therefore I say to you, all things for which you pray and ask, believe that you have received them, and they will be granted you.'"

The principle here is that we must have faith that we have received what we have asked of God in order to receive it. There is no room for doubt (see James 1:5-8). This is not some power of positive thinking ploy, nor is it an excuse for commanding God to do what we want. The message is that when we are fully in line with the Spirit's leading, we will know that what we are praying is indeed God's will. When that is the case, we will believe that God has heard and will answer our prayer. If there is any doubt, we should question whether or not we are praying for the right thing because when we are praying for the right thing, we will have faith that we will receive what we have asked for.

2. Persistence

Luke 11:5-10 says,

> "Then He said to them, 'Suppose one of you has a friend, and goes to him at midnight and says to him, "Friend, lend me three loaves; for a friend of mine has come to me from a journey, and I have nothing to set before him"; and from inside he answers and says, "Do not bother me; the door has already been shut and my children and I are in bed; I cannot get up and give you anything." I tell you, even though he will not get up and give him anything because he is his friend, yet because of his persistence he will get up and give him as much as he needs. So I say to you, ask, and it will be given to you; seek, and you will find; knock, and it will be opened to you. For everyone who asks, receives; and he who seeks, finds; and to him who knocks, it will be opened.'"

The clear lesson in this story is that God honors persistence in prayer. God doesn't always give us what we ask for right away. Sometimes He tests our faith by allowing us to have to continually and consistently seek God in prayer. Persistence demonstrates faith, and as God puts us in such positions, our motives can be purified and refined so that we can see what is really going on in our hearts. If we want to see answers to our prayers, we need to tarry in prayer, not just one time, but over and over again, not losing heart all the while.

3. Without Ceasing

1 Thessalonians 5:17 gives us another qualification for answered prayer. It says that we must "pray without ceasing." Since Jesus Himself wasn't literally praying constantly but only at certain times, it would be unwise to conclude that we should spend our entire lives in a prayer closet. Prayer wasn't a compartmentalized aspect of His life as if He could only pray at a certain time of the day for a certain length of time for certain

things. As the Spirit led Him through His life and ministry, prayer was part of His being and life. As issues came up, as He struggled with things internally, as time permitted, and as needs arose, He prayed. We need to come to the place where prayer is reflexive because we view it as an essential component of healthy Christian living. Though it will likely mean that we will pray more often and for longer durations, just praying for longer intervals does not fulfill the heart of this admonition. Praying without ceasing ultimately stems from a spiritual viewpoint that truly believes that prayer moves mountains and changes things in the world, especially our own hearts. It is a perspective where prayer is an utter need, a deep desire, and a means for hope and refreshment.

4. Righteousness

James 5:16 says, "The effective prayer of a righteous man can accomplish much." The principle which this passage exposes is that prayer is hindered by the presence of unconfessed sin. If we regard iniquity in our hearts, God says that He cannot hear our prayers (Psalm 66:18). Those who are living a double life by walking in darkness and in light are not going to have effective prayer lives. On the other hand, those who are submissive to God, to His commands, and to the leading of the Spirit will be burdened with Spirit-led prayer and given wisdom to know what to say (Romans 8:26-27). If we want to discern the will of God and pray rightly, we must first confess our sin to God and to those whom we have sinned against.

5. According to God's Will

1 John 5:14-15 reminds us that we must pray according to God's will if we want to see our prayers answered. It says, "And this is the confidence that we have before Him, that, if we ask anything according to His will, He hears us. And if we know that He hears us in whatever we ask, we know that we have the requests which we have asked from Him." To pray according to God's will is to pray according to what God wants done. This is something the Spirit of God will enable us to do (see Romans 8:26-27) if we are humble and willing to listen and be changed according to the Scripture.

God delights in giving us the chance to commune with Him through prayer and to move mountains just by faith if only we would ask. Prayer is powerful, and we must not underestimate its worth. Answered prayer is possible and the desire of God, but we must do it God's way by His Spirit and according to His Word and guiding principles therein. May God make us effective and powerful for kingdom purposes as we pray.

#70

DEVELOPING DISCERNMENT

In a day and age where false teaching abounds more and more, discernment is something that God's people need more than ever. Now this idea of things going from bad to worse in terms of the propagation of lies and half-truths is not mere rhetoric but Scripture. 2 Timothy 3:13 says, "But evil men and impostors will proceed from bad to worse, deceiving and being deceived." The reality is that evil men (and women) and impostors abound. They deceive the masses because they look like the real deal, but, of course, they are fakes. Even they themselves are deceived such that they might even think they are on the side of truth and glory when in reality they are doing the work of the devil himself. Deception is a very sticky trap because, once deceived, people can be blind to the fact that they are even bound by the devil and doing the work of evil. Yet this is reality. Today, more than ever before, deceptions abound along with those doing the deceiving and being deceived themselves. Tomorrow will be worse than today and so on and so forth. This is the truth from Scripture that deceptions will increase in number, in power, in subtlety, and in severity. Sadly, too many believers don't recognize just how pervasive the threat is and how prevalent it is. Deceptions are everywhere. We must grow mature in our faith such that we can recognize truth from error and grow in our ability to discern.

When "discernment" shows up in the Scripture, the words from which it is translated invoke the idea of wisdom, understanding, insight, and reasoning (e.g. 1 Kings 4:29, Proverbs 2:3, Daniel 2:14, Philippians 1:9). It incorporates the ability to identify lies, the skill of being able to rightly divide the Scriptures (2 Timothy 2:15), and the spiritual sensitivity to be alert to the work of the enemy. As our right understanding of Scripture grows, our discernment can be honed and sharpened. This is not just Bible knowledge, facts, and trivia, but it is a work of God in our hearts as we humble ourselves to be taught His Word. Diligence in studying the Scripture is fundamental to being discerning. Many people trump the Scripture for their own ideas and self-proclaimed authority, and we must always remember that the Scripture is the sole and final authority for truth and life. There are those who know the Bible well but who are still deceived. So we must not think that mere intellectual growth in Bible knowledge will keep us from succumbing to the devil's wiles. Faith is our shield against his missiles of deceit and temptation (Ephesians 6:16), and God will give wisdom to His children who are humble enough to recognize that they need it. As 1 Corinthians 10:12 says, "Therefore let him who thinks he stands take heed that he does not fall."

We must keep learning the Bible, for the more we know it, the more we can be set free and be equipped so that we can avoid being deceived (Hosea 4:6). Yet, this very important truth must be processed along with the idea that we cannot rely upon our own minds to be the sole means to substantiate our ability to discern, lest we fall. Our hope in having wisdom, discernment, and understanding is never the intellect alone. It is never the ability to read people alone. It is never prior experience alone. God can and does teach us through our minds and through our experiences, but we must remember that the way to increase in wisdom is simply to ask for it. God will take care of the rest of it as we walk by faith and in obedience.

James 1:5 says, "But if any of you lacks wisdom, let him ask of God, who gives to all generously and without reproach, and it will be given to him." Solomon, the wisest man ever to live, also asked of God for wisdom, and God bestowed it upon him (1 Kings 4:29). Wisdom is given to us by God as we ask Him in faith. It is not self-generated, but it is a gift of God. God's grace then infuses our study of Scripture so that we grow in wisdom. The Spirit's prompting in our hearts becomes fined tuned so that we are alert when we need to be alert. Discernment is God's gracious gift to those who seek it by faith. Those who really want discernment will then do as the Bereans did when they daily searched the Scriptures to see if what they were being taught was indeed true (Acts 17:11). Those who seek to grow in discernment won't believe somebody just because he or she has written a best selling book, has built a national ministry, has a theology degree, or is a good communicator. They will believe a person only when he or she teaches the truth of the Scripture. To get better and better at this (and none of us have arrived or are totally immune to the deceptions around us) we must be students of the Book, students who do not gloat in our understanding but rather students who continue to ask God for wisdom. God does not want those who think that they have arrived but rather those who understand that they have not. We must recognize our human weakness, fallibility, and vulnerability such that we humbly ask God for wisdom. He will give it to those who ask in faith (James 1:5) and who are humble, teachable, contrite, and trembling before His Word (Isaiah 66:2).

Colossians 2:3 says, "In [Christ] are hidden all the treasures of wisdom and knowledge." Therefore, we can never afford to neglect turning to God for wisdom and discernment. He will train us and teach us, but we must be continually willing to learn, willing to admit when we were wrong, willing to be humbled, and willing to keep seeking. As deceptions increase, so must our ability to discern them. May God increase our discernment so that we can see as He sees, looking beyond the lies and loving only the truth.

#71

FIVE DISTINGUISHING MARKS
OF THE CHRISTIAN

We can make a difference, but we must do it God's way. Something changes inside of us when we are born again (2 Corinthians 5:17). We become children of God, called by His name (John 1:12). What was old passes away, and a new creation comes to be. This inward change is of the utmost importance, but what is not so often emphasized in Christian circles is the reality that our outward behavior ought also to change in response to our decision to follow Christ. There ought to be fruit bringing evidence of a change, for it is by our fruit that we are known (Matthew 7:20).

It is rather remarkable that the greatest and most common rebuttal to an invitation to come to church or to become a Christian is that Christians are hypocrites. Now we all do stumble at times, sometimes more severely than others, but if we grant that we are no different than the world, what could possibly interest the unsaved about true Biblical Christianity? Christians are to be fundamentally different (2 Corinthians 6:17). The key is that our difference should be spiritually palpable such that it is convicting, an aroma of life to life for those who believe and of death to those who don't (2 Corinthians 2:15-16). In other words, it is who we are on the outside because of a new inward reality that can open doors so that we can declare the gospel which is the power of God unto salvation

(Romans 1:16). Sadly, the reputation of Christians and churches is very poor, but we can be the difference by faith. God's Word never changes, so we can still be salt and light. People can still get saved, and how we live can be a means to God creating an open door for the gospel. As Colossians 4:5 says, "Conduct yourselves with wisdom toward outsiders, making the most of the opportunity." Too many preachers and believers make concession to the helplessness of the hypocrisy of Christians, and, in so doing, snuff out the light that the church ought to be shining. There is to be a difference, and the unsaved should see it, sense it, and know it. This is God's plan and design, and thus we must take how we live as believers seriously for the sake of the lost. We must make no mistake that the unbeliever is watching us in judgment. God has wired unbelievers such that they do watch us whether or not they even realize it. The proof is in the Scriptures that follow.

Here are five major ways given in the New Testament that a person can identify a believer. (Now, of course there are more if we start going through the fruit of the Spirit (Galatians 5:22-23), for example, but these five are more than enough to start etching the importance of how we live upon our hearts.) First, believers can be identified by their *love*. John 13:34-35 says, "A new commandment I give to you, that you love one another, even as I have loved you, that you also love one another. By this all men will know that you are My disciples, if you have love for one another." All men, believers and unbelievers, will be able to identify a true follower of Christ by their love for other believers and for unbelievers. Love is a distinguishing mark of the Christian. When we fail to love, we confuse the world and encourage them to stay blinded and enslaved to the evil one. When we practice love, light shines into darkness, whether they fully understand it or not and whether they receive it or not. 1 John 4:7-8 makes it clear that love is of God and that those who love are those who are born of God. The world cannot love as God loves because they don't know God. Only believers can have a true, selfless care for one another that the world doesn't offer or even care to consider. The world looks for how things will benefit themselves, while Christlike love distinguishes Christians because it looks not for personal benefit but for the benefit of others (Philippians 2:4-5).

Unity is another Biblical characteristic by which believers are distinguished from the world in which they live. Jesus prays in John 17:21 regarding His disciples and all who would come after them through their testimony, "that they may all be one; even as You, Father, are in Me and I in You, that they also may be in Us, so that the world may believe that You sent Me." If true Christian unity is seen among believers, then the world might believe that the Father sent the Son to earth. In an age where people believe almost anything, Christian unity cuts to the core of the matter, giving the greatest evidence that Jesus really did come to earth and die for the sins of the world. The world knows that people are evil, untrustworthy, and difficult to get along with. When believers actually get along with one another, this is strong evidence for the legitimacy of the Christian faith.

Holiness, which represents the summation of all Christian virtues, is clearly God's design for the believer in practical day to day living. Hebrews 12:14 tells us that no one will see God without holiness on the part of the believer. Our conduct must be righteous, or unbelievers will struggle to see how we are any different and why they should believe in the Jesus we claim to follow in word but not in deed. True faith has works that follow (James 2:17).

Matthew 5:16 tells us that if we do *good works* for others that some people just might come to glorify God because they see the Light of Christ in us. There are all sorts of kind things that we can do for others, ranging from holding a door open for someone to feeding the hungry. We cannot solve all of the world's problems ourselves in one fell swoop, but we can be part of the change that the world needs by meeting a need and doing something kind for someone. People know that it is not natural for someone to go out of their way to do something nice for another human being, so they do take note when Christians do something that is otherwise out of the ordinary.

Fifthly, 1 Peter 3:15 says that people will ask about why we have so much *hope*, presuming, of course, that they can see that we are hopeful people. Is there something supernatural (Christ) sustaining us that the world must have no natural explanation for? If there is and if it is visible and tangible, we should anticipate that God will open a door for us to share about the reason for our hope.

Let us pray that love, unity, good works, holiness, and hope would so saturate our lives that others would take notice. May God give us grace to answer boldly as we speak of Christ (Colossians 4:6), the reason for our new and very different life.

#72

GOD'S SOVEREIGN TIMETABLE

Waiting is a tough task, yet patience (i.e. longsuffering) is a desired fruit of the Spirit (Galatians 5:22-23). So, in other words, God's purpose is to allow situations to come about in our lives which will require us to wait. As we walk by faith and by the Spirit, He will enable us to have patience and thereby glorify Him in our waiting. This, of course, is easier said than done. We don't always get what we desire right away. God is not a fast food operator; He is honored when we persist in prayer and keep believing even when we have not yet received what we have asked. *Waiting, plain and simple, is part of the Christian life.*

Abraham had quite an ordeal of waiting that he endured, too. God promised him a child when he was 75 years old through whom all the nations of the world would be blessed (Genesis 12:1-4). Yet he was 100 years old (Genesis 21:5) when Sarah, his wife, finally conceived. Not only is this miraculous, given their ages, but Abraham waited *25 years* for the promise of God to be fulfilled. That is a long time! Let's remember this in our waiting and tarrying in prayer. Abraham was willing to wait and continue to believe God's promises to him (albeit imperfectly and with some stumbling), and in so doing, God credited Abraham with righteousness (Genesis 15:6). Faith is what pleased God in Abraham's time, and it is what pleases God in our time (Hebrews 11:6).

God's timetable is something only He has complete control over. He is sovereign, and therefore all times and events are in His hands. God's timing is purposeful and right and good. He is not cruel and unjust to ask us to wait, for He remembers our faithfulness and will reward us for it (Colossians 3:23-24).

Genesis 15:16 is a fascinating verse, and it comes in the context of God reiterating His promise to Abraham to give his descendants the land of Canaan. It says, speaking of the Hebrew people, "But in the fourth generation they shall return here, for the iniquity of the Amorites is not yet complete." God made a promise to Abraham that his descendants would one day return from captivity and have this land to themselves. The pagan nations currently living there would be driven out, but this wouldn't happen for a number of generations. Some time had to pass according to God's sovereign timetable. God says that the iniquity of the Amorites was not yet complete. In other words, God wasn't yet ready to pour out His just wrath upon this pagan nation. They hadn't committed all of the sins that God knew that they would commit and which would incur His wrath. He was being kind and patient, giving them fair opportunity to repent. A few hundred years later, they would be conquered at the hand of Israel, having not repented. So part of Israel's waiting in Egypt had to do with the Amorites not yet being ready to be destroyed. Events in a foreign, seemingly unrelated nation impacted the events in their own lives. This is important because it reminds us that God is over all, that all people matter, and that *our waiting may not be due to some lack of faith on our own part but rather due to the sovereign purposes of God.* Waiting is a God-ordained and God-designed part of the Christian experience which requires faith on our part and which is an opportunity to honor God and let Him shape and refine us.

Many factors, more than we can observe or count, go into the events in our lives and in the lives of those around us. God is sovereign over all of them, and always in all of them He will keep His promises. But sometimes we will have to wait as God gives us a chance to honor Him with patience, as our faith is tested, as we are pruned to grow and bear more fruit, and as certain other events must first happen. God is never late, so let us not rush God's plan and be early. The only perfect timing is to wait for the timing that is God's and His alone.

227

#73

NOTHING IS TOO DIFFICULT
FOR THE LORD

In Jeremiah 32, Jeremiah received instruction from the Lord to go and buy land within the boundaries of what had been the nation of Israel. Israel had been taken captive by Assyria, and now Judah was going to be absorbed into the Babylonian conquest. As the city of Jerusalem was being put under siege by Nebuchadnezzar, king of Babylon, Jeremiah was in prison in the king's house. Doom for the nation was soon to be realized, but the fact that God told Jeremiah to buy land in the conquered land of Israel was a sign of great hope. It meant that God would bring them back to this place after a time in captivity. God would again be merciful and compassionate despite the hardness of the hearts of the people of Israel. Jeremiah exclaimed with praise to God in verse 17, "Ah Lord GOD! Behold, You have made the heavens and the earth by Your great power and by Your outstretched arm! Nothing is too difficult for You." Jeremiah was reminded that the God Who made the entire world is the same God Who was working on his behalf. This all-powerful God cared about a meager human being, Jeremiah, and his nation. God could still bring this nation back and give them yet another chance. Indeed, nothing is too difficult for the Lord.

This trust, hope, and confidence that Jeremiah had that nothing is too difficult for the Lord is to be contrasted with the lack of faith that David had. David, in a time of peace and prosperity for the kingdom of Israel, chose to take matters into his own hands. God had given him so much, yet he lusted for his neighbor's wife, committed adultery with her, and killed her husband to cover it up. There was something that he wanted that God had not given him. In his mind, there was a desire that God had failed to meet, and he went ahead and met it unbiblically, greatly angering the Lord. When Nathan confronted David in 2 Samuel 12, he said in verses 7-8,

> "You are the man! Thus says the LORD God of Israel, 'It is I who anointed you king over Israel and it is I who delivered you from the hand of Saul. 'I also gave you your master's house and your master's wives into your care, and I gave you the house of Israel and Judah; *and if that had been too little, I would have added to you many more things like these!*'" (emphasis added).

Whereas Jeremiah had exclaimed in faith that nothing is too difficult for God, David, on the other hand, communicated to God through his faithless, rebellious actions that God was unable to satisfy his longings. The point that God made to David through the prophet Nathan is that He had been abundantly generous and gracious toward David, and that if that were not enough, more could be given still. David failed to have faith and call to God to provide, and that is where he went wrong. He needed to believe that nothing is too difficult for God. After all, this is the same David who witnessed God give him the kingdom and the same David who watched God work through him to kill the giant Goliath. David had seen much in the way of God's power, and yet he decided to deal with his feelings in an immoral fashion. Surely, God could have found a way to deal with David's struggle, but David didn't give God a chance. Too often we are more like David and less like Jeremiah because we take matters into our own hands as we doubt God and stop believing that He is able. We must remember that God is not the bad guy, He is not malicious, and He does not withhold things from us to torment us. He is not like that. He is good, benevolent, and kind. He delights in giving good and perfect gifts to His children (Matthew 7:11, James 1:17). In fact, only God can give perfect gifts as David learned the hard way (2 Samuel 12:10-15). So we are blessed that, since we need God to give us what is good and perfect, that He actually promises to do just that! The key is whether or not we will keep believing God and obey even when what faith says does not match what our sight says. We must walk by faith not by sight (2 Corinthians 5:7), remembering that nothing is too difficult for the Lord.

It is important to note that God never said that He would have given David more things. He says "if that had been too little," He would have gladly given more. It might have been that David had many good and perfect things to enjoy right in front of him, but he grew discontent with them or failed to enjoy them as he should have. He might have had more than he needed, but he may just have failed to recognize just what great things he already had. We do this sometimes, too, failing to enjoy the good things of God already given to us because we are constantly thinking about the next thing that we "need." We can freely enjoy the good things that we have because we can trust God that if there are other things that we need, He will add them to us also (Philippians 4:19).

Nothing is too difficult for the Lord, and He delights in giving good things to His children. If what He has given us is too little, He will gladly add more if only we would wait upon Him and trust Him for His good and perfect gifts. When we believe God and turn our needs over to Him (1 Peter 5:7), great rest, joy, and peace can be ours in Him. Nothing is too difficult for the Lord.

#74

THE DESIRES OF YOUR HEART

Psalm 37:4 gives a promise that can often strike us as too good to be true when it says, "Delight yourself in the LORD; And He will give you the desires of your heart." But it is Scripture, it is given by the inspiration of the Holy Spirit, and it is God's personal promise to each of His children. One of Satan's greatest and most frequently used lies to believers and unbelievers alike is that God is a cosmic killjoy. In other words, his assertion is that God does not want to give us what we want, and by implication, He will not give us what we want. Therefore, in order for us to get what we want, we would need to go and get it by ourselves, by our own means, by our own power, and by our own ways. Of course, anytime we do this we will come to regret it as we recognize that God's ways are the best ways and that He tells us not to sin because He doesn't want us to hurt ourselves or anybody else. Psalm 37:5 gives a complementary truth to verse 4 saying, "Commit your way to the LORD, Trust also in Him, and He will do it." The idea is that God wants us to trust Him by committing the entirety of our lives, desires, and hopes to His care and perfect timing, planning, and giving. He doesn't want us to do things our own way, walking by sight and human wisdom but rather by faith and the wisdom which only He can supply. As we trust Him, we can be sure that God will do what is good, right, and pure. When difficult things are allowed into our lives, we can be sure that God will cause all things to work for our good because we are His children whom He loves (Romans 8:28). God does not have evil plans for His people but plans for hope and a future inheritance (Jeremiah 29:11). Our God is deserving of our trust and surrender because He is good, and as David says in Psalm 23:6, "Surely goodness and lovingkindness will follow me all the days of my life."

The context of Psalm 37 emphasizes over and over again that the wicked who seem to prosper will in the end be destroyed, while the righteous who suffer for the sake of righteousness will in the end prosper and find fullness of joy. This is because their faith is in God Who cannot fail, Who does not disappoint, and Who always keeps His promises. So our hope is in our unfailing and unchanging God. Circumstances are fleeting and changeable, and people can disappoint. But God never fails, and His mercies are new every day. Thus, it only makes sense to delight and take joy in Him for Who He is and for what He has done. In His presence is fullness of joy (Psalm 16:11). It is not Satan who gives endless pleasures, but it is God at Whose right hand are pleasures forever (Psalm 16:11). God is the good guy, not the villain. Satan wants us to think that he is the giver of life and all that is good. Granted, when we are thinking sinfully and selfishly, his sinful methods do provide a temporary good feeling. However, they are enslaving, and he will gladly suck all of the remaining life, hope, and joy out of us. Only when we do things by faith God's way can we experience true freedom. Willing enslavement to God is the only road to freedom and joy. The key is that we must believe that God is not a vicious taskmaster but that He is the giver of every good and perfect gift (James 1:7). Satan has never given a good or perfect gift, only evil and perverted gifts. Satan desires our destruction, but God wants to give us the desires of our hearts. So the essential thing for us is that we do not doubt God's heart toward us but rather believe that He is perfectly and flawlessly good to us always and forever. Once we get that, it is easy and desirable to commit our ways to Him believing that He will do what is good and best for us, which, of course, He will.

The funny thing as we seek the fulfillment of our deepest desires is that sometimes our desires are twisted and confused. We think we want one thing, and we might be totally sure about it. Yet God might not answer our prayers for that thing, person, experience, job, etc. knowing not only that it is not best for us but that we wouldn't even want it if we got it. He knows what will disappoint us, and He knows what will satisfy us. God prefers to satisfy us, and so He wants to give us that which is the desire of our hearts. From our perspective, however, this may well mean waiting and disappointment until we come to see the goodness of God in our spiritual "rear view mirror." It is not always easy to see God's provision, goodness, and mercy as we forge ahead in life, but it always follows us such that, in retrospect, it becomes all the more clear. The key is that we must not forget in the present that God is good and faithful. He does give us our deepest heart desires, but we must always delight fully in Him lest we fail to see His goodness and fail to enjoy His gifts.

God knows better than we do what we want and need, and we must be willing to keep taking joy in Him and in His will as we wait for Him to meet our desires and provide. He will show us what steps to take and what we need to do to be ready to receive His gifts. But it is only as we let Him shape and change our thoughts, ambitions, desires, and wills that we can truly arrive at the desires of our hearts. When we are totally submitted to God, we will find that His will is no longer a hardship or something to be angry and bitter about but rather a perfect blessing and gift beyond all that we could ask or imagine (Ephesians 3:20). **May God strip us of the things that we think we want so that we can enjoy the things that He wants to give us because they are the things that we will find that we really wanted all along.**

#75

THE LUST FOR MONEY

Proverbs 23:4 says, "Do not toil to acquire wealth; be discerning enough to desist." The principle here is not that it is wrong to have money or even a lot of it. The principle is that there are those who live their entire lives ruled by and driven by the notion of having more money so that they can one day be rich in their own opinion and perhaps also in the opinions of others. There is a clear lack of contentment, whereas the Bible teaches that godliness with contentment is great gain (1 Timothy 6:6). To spend an entire lifetime toiling after finally striking it rich for the sake of riches itself is a great loss. Being content with what God gives us and working diligently and faithfully as we have opportunity for His glory and in balance is great gain. There is nothing wrong with being poor and then working hard and becoming wealthy. The issue is not how much money is in the bank; it is the state of the heart of the individual. Some people work hard and eventually earn a lot of money. They are able to do it in a godly fashion and still maintain a healthy balance in life, and more importantly, a devotion to the kingdom of God first and foremost. Money, for them, is not a god or the primary driving mechanism in their lives. It is one of the "all these things" that Scripture says in Matthew 6:33 that ends up being added to them as they have sought after the kingdom of God first and foremost. They then can recognize their blessing as being from God, and they recognize their responsibility before God to look after those who are less fortunate.

People end up losing a lot of money and creating a lot of hardship by falling into various schemes which promise to make them a lot of money and fast. Others compromise on their moral principles in order to advance in a business or climb a corporate ladder all because money becomes their god. We must heed the Scripture and recognize that we need to be discerning enough to stop chasing money lest it harm our walk with Christ. God is ultimately in charge of how much money we have, and our job is simply to be responsible stewards of our talents and training so that we make the most of what God has given us. Some will make a janitor's salary, while others will make a doctor's salary. Both are one hundred percent pleasing to God if both live in contentment and godliness and in accordance with God's gifting, provision, and direction for their lives. God does care about our deepest longings, and the key is that we align our desires with His. Then we will find joy in whatever we are doing, and we can trust Him to put us just where He wants us. We might be rich or poor, but either way, we can be satisfied and joyful.

Let us not fall prey to the popular trick of the devil that money and more of it is the answer. The gospel is not about making us rich, and God's job is not to give us the world. In fact, Jesus said that we will have trouble in this world and that we are to look forward to the life to come (John 16:33). The emphasis in Scripture is on being rich in the life to come (Matthew 6:20, Luke 12:21), not in the here and now. Worldly wealth is neither right nor wrong; neither is it a sign of God's blessing or the lack thereof. Many who have toiled to acquire wealth by spending their hard-earned money on gambling tickets see the misery of throwing money to the wind. Even those who win often end up in more misery than when they started. They come to realize that money only exposes what was in their hearts all along, whether irresponsibility, the greed for more, a lack of contentment, selfishness, or a fleshly desire to earn God's approval by "doing something for God" with the winnings. God is not interested in money that is gained by those who operate sinfully. He has all the money in the world. There is nothing that exists that He does not own (Psalm 50:10), and those who love Him can trust Him that He will give them what they need without them having to sacrifice their morality to acquire wealth. There is great peace in this perspective, whereas there is great suffering and internal turmoil if not also external turmoil in the lives of those who become slaves to the next dollar.

As believers, we don't need to live a sad existence based only upon money. What if the stock market crashes? Will we jump off of buildings like many did in the last crash? They toiled for money only to enjoy it for a short time and then see it all vanish. Their heart was in money, and when money was gone, they assumed they had nothing to live for. It is so sad, but it exposed them for who they were on the inside. The victory over the deceitfulness of wealth (Mark 4:19) is a heart attitude that recognizes that money doesn't satisfy or provide the security that only God can. Money is paper that can burn, rot, and decay. We would do well to enjoy what God gives us, even simple things like food and drink (Ecclesiastes 9:7), rather than toiling for wealth. God is what the heart seeks (Psalm 16:11), and only a heart ruled by God can be trusted to wisely steward money.

Money is a great measuring stick of the state of our hearts, so let us make sure that it is not taking any of the authority that is to be God's alone or robbing us of our joy. Do not toil to acquire wealth, but recognize that life is more than money. Life is about knowing, loving, and worshipping God. May God give us undivided hearts, not compromised by greed and enslaved only to doing His will.

#76
EVIDENCES OF A HUMBLE HEART

James 4:6 says, "GOD IS OPPOSED TO THE PROUD, BUT GIVES GRACE TO THE HUMBLE." The proud set themselves in opposition to God, glorifying in themselves rather than in Him. It is not a smart thing to be opposed to God, so we would do well to think through Biblically what it is to be humble so that we can continue operating as God would have us.

1. The humble heart understands dependence upon God.

John 15:5 makes it clear that apart from Jesus we cannot accomplish anything of eternal value. It is impossible to do God's will and to store up treasure in heaven if we think that we are fully able without God. The humble rightly understand their insufficiency and powerlessness apart from Christ.

2. The humble heart trembles before God's Word.

Isaiah 66:2 says, "But to this one I will look, to him who is humble and contrite of spirit, and who trembles at My word." God not only delights in those who tremble before His Word, but He promises to look to them to use them mightily for the purposes of the kingdom. Those with humble hearts don't read God's Word carelessly but rather with hearts that are tender to what God's Word might have to say to them to convict them or teach them. They take God's Word seriously and the act of hearing it with great reverence. There is a love and value for what God says that clearly sets apart the humble from the proud.

3.   The humble heart is willing to own up to sin.

Isaiah modeled this in Isaiah 6:5 when he cried out to God in acknowledgement of his uncleanness. In light of God's holiness, he realized that his sin would destroy him. He wanted God's cleansing, and God forgave him and commissioned him for service. If we want to be used of God, we need to first be humble, a significant part of which involves dealing with any sin in our hearts promptly, readily, and rightly.

4.   The humble heart is willing to acknowledge human weakness so that Christ can show Himself to be strong.

Paul rightly understood that God's power is perfected in our weakness and that it is in our weakness that He can be strong (2 Corinthians 12:9-10). God allowed Paul to suffer so that he would not be tempted to exalt himself (2 Corinthians 12:7). He knew that Paul could fall prey to pride given all of the wondrous things he had seen and experienced. So God ordained suffering for him to remind him that he was but a very weak human being who needed God for everything. We need to remember our weakness if we want to let Christ be strong through us.

5.   The humble heart has the fruit of obedience.

The Israelites cried out to God in Judges 10:15-16, "The sons of Israel said to the LORD, "We have sinned, do to us whatever seems good to You; only please deliver us this day. So they put away the foreign gods from among them and served the LORD; and He could bear the misery of Israel no longer." As long as Israel held on to their worship of fake, foreign deities, they were opposed to God. God in His great love for them allowed them to suffer at the hands of foreign peoples. If their gods were so powerful, they only needed to trust in them. So God taught them a valuable lesson about Who has true power, and the people repented and put their gods away from them. Truly humble hearts that truly repent and turn to God will no longer be opposed by God. When we draw near to God, immediately He will draw near to us. He only wants us to be humble enough to call sin "sin" and to deal with it by repenting and seeking the forgiveness that He is fully ready and prepared to offer. The humble heart is an obedient heart.

6. The humble heart values the welfare of others ahead of its own.

Philippians 2:3-4 says, "Do nothing from selfishness or empty conceit, but with humility of mind regard one another as more important than yourselves; do not merely look out for your own personal interests, but also for the interests of others." The humble of heart are cognizant of the needs of others, and they are willing to sacrifice so that others can be ministered to.

7. The humble heart accepts the role of servant.

Jesus said in Mark 9:35, "If anyone wants to be first, he shall be last of all and servant of all." The way to greatness in the life to come is by being a servant in the present. Jesus demonstrated this to the utmost in that His purpose in coming was not to make the most people like Him, to gain the most popularity, or to gain a position of great earthly power. His mission was to lay down His life for His sheep (John 10:11-15). He came not to be served, but to serve (Mark 10:45). Now He is exalted in heaven with great power, but in this life He was a servant. We would do well to realize the importance of being a servant in this life if we want to be great in the next.

Humility may not be a characteristic that the world exalts in, but they don't understand God's ways. 1 Peter 5:6 says, "Therefore humble yourselves under the mighty hand of God, that He may exalt you at the proper time." There are no shortcuts to true exaltation, something only God can bestow. What is sure is that those who are humble in heart will, at the proper time, be exalted. If we want to truly be exalted we need to truly be humble, saying with our Savior the ultimate expression of humility, "Lord, not my will but Yours be done" (Luke 22:42).

#77

The Advantage of Having the Holy Spirit

What an incredible opportunity and experience the disciples had, getting the chance to walk and talk with Jesus, God in the flesh in their very presence. They could look into His eyes, touch His hands, and in the case of the disciple John, even recline his head upon Jesus' chest (John 13:23). Jesus had called His disciples friends (John 15:15). They had spent several years together, learning and studying under this Master Teacher. But as the death of Christ neared, He spoke to them about having to leave them. He understood that this would bring them sorrow (John 16:6), but they needed to know something very important. It would be to their *advantage* that He would leave them. He says in John 16:7, "But I tell you the truth, it is to your advantage that I go away; for if I do not go away, the Helper will not come to you; but if I go, I will send Him to you." The Helper is the Holy Spirit, the Spirit of truth, as He is referred to in verse 13. This third Person of the Trinity is of no less value to the disciples than Jesus having come in the flesh. In fact, according to Jesus, it is an advantage for the disciples for Jesus to leave and for the Helper to come. This is a potent realization that is highly relevant for us today because, though we don't get to walk and talk with a physical, tangible Jesus, we most certainly have the Helper within our hearts if we have trusted Christ by faith.

It could be tempting at times to wish for a physical Jesus to be here with us given that we might think it would help us to feel closer to God, to be more adequately comforted, or to gain better insight and understanding into spiritual things. However, Jesus makes it abundantly clear that we have an advantage because we have the Holy Spirit. We don't get to walk and talk with physical, tangible Jesus; rather, we get something profoundly more intimate than that. He lives within our hearts through the Person of the Holy Spirit. We get Jesus as close as we could possibly get Him, with all the accompanying spiritual power and authority to do His will.

Think of the disciples. They seemed very confused and at a loss throughout their time with Christ to the point where Christ at times seemed to wonder if they were ever going to catch on (though of course He knew they would) (Matthew 15:16, Matthew 16:5-12). Yet Christ knew that it would be the Holy Spirit Who would guide them into all truth (John 16:13). Jesus taught them and taught them and taught them more still, yet it would be the Spirit Who would come after His departure that would really begin to help them understand. This Helper, God the Spirit, immediately and radically transformed the uneducated disciples into powerful preachers, healers, evangelists, and bold, bold witnesses (Acts 2). People who observed them could tell (now that the Spirit had come to indwell them) that they had been with Christ (Acts 4:13). So, too, by way of the Spirit's work in our hearts and lives, the world will be able to see that we know Jesus and that we have "walked and talked" with Him through reading the pages of Scripture.

Lest we doubt just how much of an advantage we have in having the Spirit of God in our hearts, let us consider the many ministries that He accomplishes in and through us:

- He regenerates us so that we can be born again and be made new creations in Christ (John 3:5-6, 2 Corinthians 5:17).

- He renews us so that we can be washed clean and made into a proper dwelling place (Titus 3:5).

- He justifies us so that we can be declared righteous before God in Christ (1 Corinthians 6:11).

- He spiritually baptizes us into the body of Christ and the family of God (1 Corinthians 12:13).

- He indwells our hearts (Romans 8:11).

- He empowers us to do the work of the ministry, something we could never accomplish without Him (Acts 1:8, Zechariah 4:6).

- He teaches us about God as we study His Word, giving us understanding that we would otherwise be unable to ascertain (1 Corinthians 2:13).

- He sanctifies us so that we can be continually and progressively shaped into the image of Christ (Romans 15:16, 2 Thessalonians 2:13, 1 Peter 1:2)

- He leads us, giving us direction in this life (Romans 8:14).

- He guides us into all truth (John 16:13).

- He convicts us of sin in our hearts (John 16:8).

- He fills us, giving us strength and power to do the will of God (Ephesians 5:18).

- He intercedes for us, helping us to pray (Romans 8:26).

- He testifies to our spirits that we are indeed saved (Romans 8:16).

- He helps us, being there to aid us and comfort us (John 16:7).

- He helps us remember the Bible (John 14:26).

- He seals us, guaranteeing our future inheritance in heaven as property of the King (Ephesians 4:30).

- He helps us know what to say (Mark 13:11).

- He gives us joy (Luke 10:21).

- He frees us from enslavement to sin and legalism, showing us a new grace-filled way to live (Romans 8:2).

- He fills us with Christlike love for others (Romans 15:30).

- He gifts us so that we can advance the kingdom of God (1 Corinthians 12:7).

- He unifies us with other believers (Ephesians 4:3).

- He testifies for the truth in us and through us. (1 John 5:6).

What the Spirit does in and through us is no small matter; in fact, it encompasses the whole of our lives in Christ. We are not supposed to be able to do anything without Him, and He is there to help us in all things. Having Him in our hearts is a great advantage, so let us take full advantage of it.

#78

WHERE ELSE COULD WE GO?
A REMINDER FOR DISAPPOINTING TIMES

In John 6, Jesus taught at length about His having come from heaven and being the only way to the Father. He used the illustration that people would need to eat His flesh and drink His blood in order to enter heaven. Many found the teaching difficult, and, as a result, they abandoned Christ. Of course, those who had ears to hear would have recognized that Jesus was simply saying to believe in Him, that He was the giver of life, and that His truth had to be spiritually ingested and applied at the deepest heart level. This would require an allegiance to His teachings, a faith that was willing to follow Him wherever He led, and an abandonment of the approval of the world. These were difficult things, and despite the wondrous miracles that Christ had worked in their presence, many refused to follow any longer. John 6:66-69 says,

> "As a result of this many of His disciples withdrew and were not walking with Him anymore. So Jesus said to the twelve, 'You do not want to go away also, do you?' Simon Peter answered Him, 'Lord, to whom shall we go? You have words of eternal life. We have believed and have come to know that You are the Holy One of God.'"

At least the twelve still believed. They rightly recognized that there was nowhere else to go. This Man was the truth, and He was God. He was the Messiah that the Jews had been waiting for. There was no point in leaving Him or trying to find some other "messiah." They even recognized that their lives were caught up in something more important and significant than what they had previously known. This was the call and purpose of God for them, to know and follow Jesus Christ. Where else could they go?

There are many things that are spiritually easier than serving God. Many of those who followed Christ and then left Him left not because the teachings were intellectually difficult but because they didn't want to follow this Jesus anymore. They didn't recognize Him as God, or if they did, they weren't impressed enough to abandon their old ways of living and follow Him. He wasn't worth their time, their ears, their money, their interest, or their investment. They had other things to do, other people to meet, and other places to see. The twelve who stayed with Christ acknowledged that they had nowhere else to go. They found God, and there was nothing else that could compare. But for many others, that is, the vast majority, their sin and their worldly enterprises were far more interesting than seeking God's will for their lives and living lives that bowed to the authority of Jesus Christ.

If we are deceived by sin, we might decide that Jesus isn't worth following or that perhaps we can follow both Him and something else. But we cannot serve two masters. If we are discouraged by all that God has ordained for our lives, we might consider another path. But if we truly have come to know Jesus for Who He really is and if we really believe in Him, we will know in our spirits that there is nowhere else to go. Then once we cease from our unbelief and stubbornness we will remember that He cares and that He does not disappoint. Scripture is clear in 1 Peter 2:6, "For this is contained in Scripture: 'BEHOLD, I LAY IN ZION A CHOICE STONE, A PRECIOUS CORNER stone, AND HE WHO BELIEVES IN HIM WILL NOT BE DISAPPOINTED.'" Those who make Christ the cornerstone of their lives can be assured that they will not be ultimately disappointed. Even in the temporal world, they can trust all things to work for their own spiritual benefit (Romans 8:28-

29). But it takes a persistent and consistent viewing of the world by faith rather than by sight in order to keep from succumbing to disappointment and the consideration that maybe the devil has something better than this to offer. God does not disappoint.

Paul said in 2 Corinthians 4:8-9, "We are afflicted in every way, but not crushed; perplexed, but not despairing; persecuted, but not forsaken; struck down, but not destroyed." This man's life got so much more brutal, trying, and difficult when He chose to follow Christ. But he was convinced that Jesus was God, and despite the fact that he was frequently near death for the sake of the gospel, he didn't despair of following Christ. If his perspective had been that surrendering to Christ on the Damascus Road meant that Jesus would make his life easier, wealthier, and more humanly successful, he would have been gravely disappointed. But that wasn't his view from the beginning of his conversion. Christ sought him, Paul believed, and Paul understood that it was about faithfulness and a supreme allegiance to Christ. He knew full well that heaven was a place of honor and reward, but earth would be a battleground with much suffering for the sake of the gospel. Yet nothing made him disappointed in his Lord because Jesus was his joy even in suffering, and especially in suffering (Philippians 3:10).

The difficulty of each of our lives varies, and Paul's was definitely on the high end. But he didn't grow disappointed or angry with God. He, like the twelve disciples, who would also suffer greatly, recognized that there was nowhere else to go. Jesus was the Christ, and His message was their calling. Since Jesus would always be God and the gospel would never change, disappointment could never happen if their perspective was right.

So just because things don't go like we think they will does not give us reason to be disappointed. Just because God allows suffering to continue doesn't give us grounds to succumb to despair. Jesus is still God, God is still on the throne, and we still have kingdom work to do. One day, we will see what we have now only believed, and it is guaranteed, that when we see Jesus in heaven, we will not be disappointed for having left what the world has to offer so that we could follow Him.

#79

RENEW YOUR STRENGTH

A verse that is often misquoted and misapplied is Psalm 46:10. We hear "Be still, and know that I am God" and think that God just wants us to tune out, calm down of our own accord, or be silent. Others imply some mind-numbing mystical experience which is not at all what God wants in this passage or anywhere in Scripture. What God is really getting at in Psalm 46:10 is better received and understood when it is more accurately translated, "Cease striving, and know that I am God." Striving implies a feverish toiling on our own power to fix a problem or situation. Panic and anxiety enter into our being when we realize that our efforts are like running faster and faster on a treadmill. The belt can go around that machine at whatever speed we run, and we get nowhere fast. Solving problems by our own intellectual acumen, willpower, and skill never works. God hates pride, but He gives grace to the humble. The humble are the ones which bow the knee to God (1 Peter 5:5), cast their cares upon Him (1 Peter 5:7), and trust Him with the result. We are to pray because prayer is an acknowledgement that it is God Who must fix our situation rather than we ourselves. Perhaps He might choose to fix it in and through us as we act as instruments of His working, but there is a landmark difference in letting God work in and through us as He desires versus problem-solving our own way and on our own power. When we feel this internal striving and fumbling around, we need to pause and simply stop. The Spirit's exhortation to us is "Cease!"

We need to stop the fussing and the pride trip and just let God lead and provide. Not letting the Spirit lead in our hearts creates friction and takes more energy and effort on our part because we have to resist God. We are not to resist the Spirit (Acts 7:51), grieve the Spirit (Ephesians 4:30), or quench the Spirit (1 Thessalonians 5:19). We must yield to the Spirit by letting Him lead (Romans 8:14). This is a willful act of obedience whereby we let God take our burdens, our stress, and our pain. We must call to Him in earnest telling Him that we need help, that we are out of ideas, that we need guidance, and that we need provision. He knows even before we ask what we need. Sadly, too often He knows that we need to learn the lesson of our inability before we can be reminded of His ability. The whole of Psalm 46:10 says, "Cease striving and know that I am God; I will be exalted among the nations, I will be exalted in the earth." When we act in our own power, our success would be our own exaltation and boast, rather than God's. When we yield to God, He alone gets the glory which is how it ought to be.

Striving on our own power will drain our spiritually energy and life faster than we can imagine. However, if we cease striving in our own power, we can have our strength renewed. Isaiah 40:31 says, "Yet those who wait for the Lord will gain new strength; They will mount up with wings like eagles, They will run and not get tired, They will walk and not become weary." The way to be truly rejuvenated, refreshed, reenergized, and restrengthened is to wait upon God, trusting in Him for deliverance rather than in something of our own fleshly concocting. Waiting upon God does not mean just sitting idly by passing the time, but it is from the Hebrew word "Qavah," meaning to "wait, hope, look for, or expect." Waiting on God is an active, exciting, dramatic, and hopeful faith experience. Just as we eagerly await the return of Christ when we can finally escape this body of death and be with Jesus, we are eagerly to long for, look for, and hope for His deliverance and ministry in this life. Wherever we are, God is there to comfort. We don't know what form His deliverance or provision will take, but that is not the issue as far as our joy, peace, and sustenance is concerned. The issue is the state of our hearts. *It is those who choose by faith to wait upon God, longing, hoping, and expecting, who will run and not grow tired and walk and not become weary.*

There will likely be multiple times in our Christian lives where we will feel like serving God is too difficult, too trying, or too frustrating. We might encounter obstacle after obstacle in ministry, and we might want to give up. We might have tried to stop a certain sin in our lives only to fail more times than we would like. We might have tried to reach out to a person, but our message of hope and love just isn't getting through. These types of life experiences are severely draining. Strength is not just how much we can bench-press, but it has much more to do with an internal spiritual stamina that gets its drive and energy from trusting in, hoping in, and waiting upon God. Difficult experiences drain our strength, and rather than strive in our own vain self-effort, we need to call to God and lean upon Him in eager expectation. Even young men and youths, who of all people should have the most energy, strength, and stamina, grow tired and weary (Isaiah 40:30). Even they will need to have their strength renewed. No matter what age we are or where we are at in life, we will inevitably come to a place where we find ourselves feeling drained in life. Our only hope to be able to continue on and grow in strength is to wait upon God. As God promises in v. 29, "He gives strength to the weary, and to him who lacks might He increases power."

We must not abandon hope, quit battling temptation, or stop serving God. When we are spiritually out of fuel, God will lift us up and empower us to do His will as long as we keep hoping in and trusting in His provision. As Paul said in Philippians 4:13, "I can do all things through Him who strengthens me."

If we want to mount up with wings like eagles and feel what it is to spiritually fly with joy and peace and strength from God, we must cease striving in our own strength, cast our cares upon God, and hopefully and expectantly wait upon Him. He will keep His Word, and our strength will be renewed.

#80

SEARCH MY HEART, O GOD

David prays a very admirable prayer in Psalm 139:23-24 saying, "Search me, O God, and know my heart; Try me and know my anxious thoughts; And see if there be any hurtful way in me, And lead me in the everlasting way." David is quick to understand and admit that he is prone (as we all are) to hidden sins (see Psalm 19:12), errors of heart of which we are not yet aware. Once we become aware of them, we need to deal with them, and it is David who sets an example of being proactive in this process. Rather than waiting for sin to happen and the consequences to result, David asks God to show him where his faults might lie. If he can be made aware of them before they hurt him or others, why wouldn't he prefer to be changed ahead of time? This is exactly what a person with a tender heart toward God ought to do. He ought to ask God to search his heart so that he can be made aware of anything that needs to be dealt with. The wonderful thing is that David has already acknowledged in verse one of this same chapter that God has already searched him and known him. God already knows the errors in David's heart and makeup. It is once David realizes just how much God knows about him and how much God thinks about him that David comes to welcome God's searching out of his heart so that he can benefit from the knowledge which God possesses about him. It is a privilege as a child of God to have the mind of Christ (1 Corinthians 2:16), part of which, is to be made aware of our weaknesses and sin.

God has given us as the body of Christ a specific time to be introspective, though His desire is that we should deal with sin as quickly as possible all the time. The Lord's Supper is a fixed time to meditate upon the work of Christ on the cross, a large part of which involves doing what David did in asking God to search and know his heart. When we partake in communion, we ought to ask God to try us and see if there are any wicked ways within us. If there are, we ought not to partake until we repent or make an issue right with a brother or sister whom we might have sinned against. This is the sanctifying part of this ordinance instituted by Christ. It is a time to reflect upon the blood of Christ shed for us and the body of Christ broken for us such that we remember who we are in Christ to the extent that we want to honor Him fully with our lives. Paul is adamant in 1 Corinthians 11:29 that we be introspective about sin and "judge the body rightly." Verses 28-30 say the following: "But a man must examine himself, and in so doing he is to eat of the bread and drink of the cup. For he who eats and drinks, eats and drinks judgment to himself if he does not judge the body rightly. For this reason many among you are weak and sick, and a number sleep." When we let sin go unchecked in our lives, it can bring decay to our bodies (Psalm 32:3), and it certainly brings decay to our souls (Galatians 5:9). God doesn't take lightly to blatant blasphemy and hypocrisy during such a solemn occasion. The highest honor we can give Christ Who died for us is to die to self and live for Him. As children of God, the greatest insult we can cast upon our Savior is to refuse the sanctifying power and forgiving grace for which He died so that we could freely receive. When we hide sin in our hearts, we insult Christ by refusing His forgiveness, thereby blaspheming His redemptive work. It is not that we lose our salvation when we harden our hearts, but we certainly grieve the heart of God greatly. It delights God's heart when we purify ourselves as He is pure during the time of communion or at any other time (1 John 3:3). May we not forget the importance of introspection and self-examination when partaking of the Lord's Table.

One of the best ways to keep walking in the straight and narrow way is to be regularly introspective. This involves being sensitive to the Holy Spirit's conviction, being humble in reading the Word, and praying proactively for God to reveal character flaws that need to be rectified and sanctified. May we take it upon ourselves to pray as David did that God would search us and know us so that we could be sanctified and changed.

#81

WHY FELLOWSHIP MATTERS

The Bible clearly teaches the sufficiency of Christ (John 16:13, Philippians 4:13) and the sufficiency of His Word (John 17:17) such that even a believer isolated on a remote island (such as the apostle John) could still be comforted, encouraged, and enabled to grow in Christ. However, the Scripture does not in anyway advocate "lone ranger" Christianity. God's desire is quite the opposite, in fact. His plan and purpose for building His kingdom is a corporate purpose (Ephesians 4:1-16). Granted, it is accomplished by individual believers who are held accountable before God for their individual roles of stewardship. However, God's desire is that believers team up as the body of Christ to do His work.

The idea and essence of the church implies a sharing of lives, resources, encouragement, comfort, etc. Acts 2:44-47 says,

> "And all those who had believed were together and had all things in common; and they began selling their property and possessions and were sharing them with all, as anyone might have need. Day by day continuing with one mind in the temple, and breaking bread from house to house, they were taking their meals together with gladness and sincerity of heart, praising God and having

favor with all the people and the Lord was adding to their
number day by day those who were being saved."

The church had true fellowship, being a spiritual family whose head
was Christ (Ephesians 4:15). As they studied the Word together, prayed
together, and shared meals together, not neglecting the needs of any
brother or sister, they enjoyed God's plan of fellowship. This kept their
focus right, their passion for the Lord fervent, and their growth in Christ
stimulated. Hebrews 10:24-25 says, "And let us consider how to stimulate
one another to love and good deeds, not forsaking our own assembling
together, as is the habit of some, but encouraging one another; and all
the more as you see the day drawing near." This passage correlates
assembling together with other believers with stimulating or provoking
one another to love and good deeds. Some believers were neglecting
corporate worship, perhaps even choosing to isolate themselves from
other believers in general. This was not a healthy trend, and God's
instructions were to get together, study the Word, pray, and encourage
one another so that love would not grow cold and good works would be
accomplished so that the glory of God could be seen (Matthew 5:16).
Without true Christian fellowship, we are prone to coast along in our
walk, we might miss out on opportunities to serve, and we are left to go
without the unbiased instruction of Spirit-led preaching to our hearts.
The absence of true, Biblical fellowship makes the Christian life much
more difficult.

It should be emphasized that fellowship is exclusively Christian. It is
not something the world can possess or know. They might have their
clubs, societies, groups, fraternities, gangs, or associations, but they
cannot experience fellowship. This is because the world does not know
the love of Christ, without which there can be no fellowship. They are
still in darkness, and only those in the Light can have fellowship with
others in the Light (1 John 1:7). Only with Christ is true love (John
13:34-35) and true unity (John 17:21) possible.

Yet even in the church fellowship that could be enjoyed with true believers
can be undermined. We still need to work by faith on some things to
keep fellowship as it ought to be. First, there needs to be authenticity.
Authenticity is being real, genuine, not deceiving, not wearing a mask

to church, and being open and vulnerable as wisdom and discernment allow. When people pretend, go through the motions, and hide their true selves and desires, dangerous and dark deceptions can emerge. This undermines fellowship and its benefits. Second, there needs to be a spirit of grace. There should be no judgmentalism, partiality, merit-based love, or a refusal to forgive a truly repentant brother or sister. "Holier than thou" thinking makes people feel unsafe to seek the help, counsel, and encouragement that they need, thus undermining fellowship. Third, there needs to be a corporate uncompromising pursuit of the truth. It is important to grow to "attain to the unity of the faith" rather than to be "carried about by every wind of doctrine" (Ephesians 4:13-14). Doctrine has a unifying effect on the church, and the church must be willing to continue to be guided by the Spirit into all truth in order for unity to increase. This relentless pursuit of truth is utterly essential to vibrant fellowship.

Let us not forget that we are the body of Christ, with each of us having a part to play (1 Corinthians 12:14-27). It is only when these individual parts work in concert with one another that the church maximizes its testimony and effectiveness. Fellowship is critical to each believer's growth and to the church's overall mission in the world. May God give us people to enjoy fellowship with, and may He deepen and purify fellowship in His churches. It is something we as believers desperately need and something the world desperately needs to see.

#82

JESUS' TREASURE PRINCIPLE
OF THE HEART

In God's mind, the heart is the central issue (1 Timothy 1:15, 2 Timothy 2:22, Matthew 5:8). He is not interested in externalities, showmanship, performance, or smiles falsely pasted on our faces. He cares about who we really are on the inside, and therefore, so should we (1 Samuel 16:7). When we come to Christ, He gives us new hearts that can and do desire the things of God (Ezekiel 18:31, 36:26, 2 Corinthians 5:17), though our hearts can be corrupted and definitely need continued sanctification (2 Corinthians 7:1, James 4:8). But we ought to consider the state of our hearts because it will affect everything we think, do, and say.

The heart is the seat of desires and affections and the true measure of a person. Do we have Christ living in our hearts and are we letting Christ have full control of all that we desire and possess affection for? These are the key questions. Jesus gives a treasure principle as a means to assess the true state of our hearts. He says in Matthew 6:21, "For where your treasure is, there your heart will be also." There is a direct correlation between what we treasure and the state of our hearts. How do we know what we treasure? Frankly, we probably do have a pretty good idea of what we really get excited about and really desire, but in case we have deceived ourselves, here are some criteria. *First, what we treasure is what we spend a lot of time thinking about.* Mary, after experiencing the birth of Christ and the miraculous events associated with it, treasured those things, pondering them in her heart (Luke 2:19). The events were so wonderful that she just couldn't stop thinking about them. Her heart was filled with joy and delight in what God had done, and she was thrilled to keep thinking about it. *Second, what we treasure will be born out in what we do and what we say.* Jesus said in Luke 6:45, "The good man out of the good treasure of his heart brings forth what is good; and the evil man out of the evil treasure brings forth what is evil; for his mouth speaks from that which fills his heart." The state of our heart affects the actions we will take and the words we will speak. **We can suppress our actions or words for a time with extreme willpower, but ultimately the heart will win out because it is who we really are.** God's desire for us is that we would not be springs that yield both fresh and bitter water. Such things ought not to be (James 3:10-11). What we say and what we do, as with what we think, should be driven by the leading of the Holy Spirit Who must transform our hearts so that we are no longer conformed to the ways of the world (Romans 12:1-2). It is only He Who can give us self-control which can provide more consistency and persistency in our Christian lives. Sanctification is a process (Philippians 2:12-13), but as we submit to our Lord, it will be accomplished.

Proverbs 4:23 says, "Keep thy heart with all diligence; for out of it are the issues of life" (KJV). So if the heart affects our thoughts, attitudes, actions, and words, it is crucial that we take care that it is not corrupted or deceived. The Bible says we can accomplish that by keeping it with all diligence. The idea here is to watch over, guard, and blockade the heart from any corrupting influence. The imagery created by the original words used in the text are of a guard posted at a prison cell standing watch over a prisoner so that everything remained secure and as it should be. There would be no escape and no unlawful entry. Nothing would get in to that cell unless the guard gave his approval and consent. This is what the Bible wants us to do with our hearts, guarding them fervently and vigilantly, not letting anything in that could corrupt us and take us down.

The battle for the heart is very much related to the battle for the mind. 2 Corinthians 10:5 says that we are to take every thought captive to the obedience of Christ. This involves thinking only on what is true, honorable, right, pure, lovely, of good repute, excellent, and worthy of praise (Philippians 4:8). Our mind is to dwell on these things, for in so doing, we will help shape our heart's affections.

Staying pure and guarding our hearts involves following the directive of Psalm 119:11 when it says, "Your word I have treasured in my heart, that I may not sin against You." When God's Word becomes the treasure of our hearts and good and right things become the subject of our thoughts, we will be able to walk in purity before God. But if our thoughts are compromised as we take in unholy things, we will quickly begin to treasure evil things. This sin of the mind and heart can quickly carry over into sin of word or deed. Colossians 3:17 says, "Whatever you do in word or deed, do all in the name of the Lord Jesus, giving thanks through Him to God the Father." Doing something in the name of the Father and giving thanks to Him implies that Christ is our treasure. Without God as the treasure of our hearts, we cannot give thanks properly, and we will not be able to do His will in word or in deed.

We need to ask ourselves what it is that we treasure, and we need to make sure that it is God and His will (Matthew 13:44). If we treasure other things as much as God or more than God, we will be in trouble, and our words and actions will bear that out. God must be our chief delight, and His priorities must rule in our hearts. We must never underestimate the connection between what we treasure and who we really are. May God change us where we need to change, and even if we don't want to change, may He change our hearts still. May He be always that which is our greatest treasure of all.

#83

BE CAREFUL TO REMEMBER

In 1 Samuel 7:12, we read, "Then Samuel took a stone and set it between Mizpah and Shen, and named it Ebenezer, saying, 'Thus far the LORD has helped us.'" Samuel rightly understood that the victory of the Israelites over the Philistines was a result of the work of God on their behalf. It was God who thundered and enabled the defeat of the Philistines (v. 10). In a very simple and symbolic gesture, Samuel picked up a rock, set it at a particular geographic location, and named it "Thus far God has helped us" as a remembrance of what God had done for Israel on that day. Hitherto the Lord had helped Israel, and it was imperative that Israel would remember God's help going forward. How easy it is for us to forget the goodness and provision of God and to even forget specific and highly memorable events in our lives when we are sure that God has worked on our behalf! The Ebenezer stone is an Old Testament example of a symbolic event that would help Israel recall to mind the faithfulness and power of God. Perhaps someday a child would stumble upon that Ebenezer rock and wonder why it was there. The story could then be told of how God delivered Israel from the Philistines as a means to bolster the child's faith in God. Remembrance can and does spur increased faith and faithfulness.

One of Satan's schemes is to distract us and allow us to forget how God has been faithful to us in the past. Perhaps Satan will, with God's permission (Job 1), bring tragedy into our lives to trick us into forgetting the mercy of God as we become distracted by present difficulties. Or, perhaps, he will exploit the goodness of God manifested in our lives by distracting us from worshipping the true Source of the goodness. Whatever his methodology, his desired result is that we forget God and His faithfulness to us. God, on the other hand, wants us to remember (Deuteronomy 8:2, 18). Here is God's warning to Israel for when they would enter Canaan and finally experience the fruition of the promise of God to Abraham:

> "When you have eaten and are satisfied, you shall bless the LORD your God for the good land which He has given you. Beware that you do not forget the LORD your God by not keeping His commandments and His ordinances and His statutes which I am commanding you today; otherwise, when you have eaten and are satisfied, and have built good houses and lived in them, and when your herds and your flocks multiply, and your silver and gold multiply, and all that you have multiplies, then your heart will become proud and you will forget the LORD your God who brought you out from the land of Egypt, out of the house of slavery" (Deuteronomy 8:11-14).

The lesson here is that there is a direct correlation between the heart becoming proud and forgetting God which inevitably leads to a less than faithful lifestyle. When times are bad, we can get caught up in the overwhelming circumstances and emotions, dwelling on ourselves rather than God, which is a twisted form of pride. When times are good, the many things around us to enjoy can become our undoing if we forget our God Who is the best and most valuable resource that we have. Our enemy is shrewd, and we must remember that we are vulnerable in both good times and in bad. We are prone to forget the deliverance of God and how He has worked in our lives specifically in times past. This is why Samuel's example of setting up a rock and naming it "Ebenezer" matters. Samuel made a point to remember and to help himself and the Israelites remember a specific instance of God's faithfulness. As they would go on with their lives, it would be valuable to recall to remembrance this instance of God's faithfulness because it would remind them of the very nature of God, Who is faithful.

Now we don't necessarily need to go and find a rock or other object and name it. It is not the exact methodology that needs to be applied as much as the intentionality behind the methodology. In other words, it is not the physical memory tool that matters nearly as much as the exercise and effort to recall God's faithfulness on our behalf in the past. No matter what the events are around us or how we feel, we need to recall to mind Scripture about God's love and faithfulness. And it is also helpful and edifying to remember when we were in confusing, difficult places before and how God caused all things to work for our good. We need to remember, for example, when we were pulled out of a pit of despair, had our eyes and hearts opened to the truth, were saved from an addiction, were delivered from temptation, were spared a negative relationship, were miraculously provided for, were granted new strength, were given what we prayed for, etc. We each have a story to tell of how God has worked in our lives, and we, of all people, need to recall those provisions and works of God in our lives. God is real, He is at work always around us and in us, and He cares. He cares that we would remember His goodness such that we would choose to believe and be faithful in the present.

We may not have named a stone "Ebenezer" in honor of God's deliverance, but surely we have our own stories to recall to mind of His faithfulness, provision, mercy, love, and power. When we feel like giving up or giving in or if we begin to feel nothing at all in regard to our Lord, let us be faithful to recall to remembrance the faithfulness of our God. May God enable us to be intentional about remembering and to beware lest we forget.

#84

SEEK AND YOU WILL FIND

Jesus said in Matthew 7:7, "Ask, and it will be given to you; seek, and you will find; knock, and it will be opened to you." There is a huge theme that runs through Scripture about the culpability, responsibility, and accountability of man to seek the truth (Romans 2:6, 10:9-10). God doesn't force someone into salvation or to do the right thing. Of course, He is sovereign over all things, including salvation (Romans 8:30), but He gives each and every person the chance to choose for themselves their own eternal destinies (Joshua 24:15). Even beyond the choice of receiving or rejecting Christ, we make decisions all the time every day. Some people spurn the truth in their decision-making, not caring about God's wisdom and direction. Others desperately want to know what the right thing is to do, and they earnestly plead for the wisdom of God. So there are two kinds of people according to the Scripture, the humble and the proud, the pliable and the stubborn, the teachable and the unteachable, the wicked and the righteous, and the seeker and the scoffer. All of these terms and categories are interrelated because the true seeker is the one who will become the righteous because he is also humble, teachable, and pliable. Of course, it is God's gracious calling to people that enables us to even want to seek the truth given that nobody seeks God of their own natural accord (Romans 3:11). However, in this grace-drawing process as God calls all people to repentance and to knowing and loving Him (Luke 19:10, 2 Peter 3:9), we all have a choice to make that God is not going to force upon us. He is not to blame for our scoffing or mocking the truth. Only we bear that responsibility, culpability, and accountability.

The idea of seeking in a Biblical sense is a healthy thing, something even commanded of God for both unbelievers and believers to do (Matthew 7:7). We are responsible before God to seek the truth in salvation and in sanctification according to God's Word. This Biblical seeking is not a fleshly process of self-discovery or self-enlightenment. It is not a careless, disconnected trial and error based on a "comfortability" factor. For the unbeliever, Biblical seeking is a humble, driven, willful searching out to find the God Who made the universe and to know Him by His Word. Once a person is saved, Biblical seeking is a humble, driven, willful searching through the Scriptures to know and love God deeper and with increasing wisdom and maturity. Yet let us remember that there is nothing about the salvation process or spiritual growth process that can be manipulated or sped up by the works and ingenuity of man. Only God draws a person, and only hearing the Word of God can bring faith to the seeker of truth (Romans 10:17). Once saved, only the grace of God through the ministry of the Holy Spirit in our hearts enables us to choose by faith to continue to seek God through the truth of His Word. So God is gracious, and, at the same time, we are responsible to keep seeking.

Jeremiah 33:3 says, "Call to Me and I will answer you, and I will tell you great and mighty things, which you do not know.'" We get to a point of staleness in our Christian lives when we are content with what we know about God and His Word. The reality is that we will never exhaust the wisdom and knowledge of God. There is so much that God wants to teach us about Himself and His ways, and He asks us to call out to Him so that He will tell us great and mighty things. He even promises to answer that prayer because it is indeed the will of God! This is a prayer that we all should take a moment to pray. God wants us to spend our lives searching out truth by way of His Word. Of the faithful Berean Christians, we read in Acts 17:11, "Now these were more noble-minded than those in Thessalonica, for they received the word with great eagerness, examining the Scriptures daily to see whether these things were so." God called these Christians noble because they received the Word with eagerness of mind. They wanted to grow, they wanted to keep learning, and above all, they wanted to know the truth from the lies. Many teachings float around in churches, Christian bookstores, Christian websites, etc., and the only way to know who is telling the truth is to go to the Scriptures and by faith search them out. We can trust the Holy Spirit to do as He has promised to do and guide us into all truth (John 16:13). God delights in His children seeking Him out and asking Him to learn more, to gain wisdom, and to grow to maturity.

Biblical seeking is not done callously or half-heartedly. Jeremiah 29:13 says, "You will seek Me and find Me when you search for Me with all your heart." The key in asking God to help us grow in Christ is to ask with all of our hearts. Hearts that truly want to know the truth and who ask accordingly will find it.

So let us seek God with all of our hearts, continuing to grow in truth by the Spirit Whose job it is to lead us into all truth. May God give us the desire to know great and mighty things about Him through His Word, and may He use us to teach the truth to true truth seekers.

#85

THE NAME OF JESUS

For the Christian, the name of Jesus is certainly valued. We pray in His name, we recognize Him as part of the Trinity, and we know that He was the sacrifice for sin. But the question to ponder is whether or not we as a church are continuing to value Him as highly as we ought to. Or, to put it another way, do we value the name of Jesus in the same manner and to the same degree that the early church valued it?

Acts 5:40-42 says,

> "They took his advice; and after calling the apostles in, they *flogged them and ordered them not to speak in the name of Jesus*, and then released them. So they went on their way from the presence of the Council, *rejoicing that they had been considered worthy to suffer shame for His name*. And every day, in the temple and from house to house, *they kept right on teaching and preaching Jesus as the Christ*" (italics mine).

The apostles were boldly preaching the name of Jesus and the gospel of salvation through Him, He being the true Messiah, the Christ, Who had come to deliver Israel and all who would believe from their sins. But there was a huge backlash from the Jews who had refused to accept Jesus because they didn't like His version of the Messiah. It was too convicting, too radical, and too undermining of their lifestyle, self-righteousness, and earthly privileges. The apostles knew Jesus was the true Son of God and that salvation through any other name was impossible. As Acts 4:12 says, "And there is salvation in no one else; for there is no other name under heaven that has been given among men by which we must be saved." Despite horrific beatings, they kept on preaching the name of Christ, even rejoicing that God found them worthy to suffer shame for His name. They didn't bail out and start talking about a more generic-sounding God rather than Jesus and finding common ground with the Jews who believed in Jehovah. Their message remained Jesus the Christ and preaching, healing, praising, praying, serving, singing, and so on in His name. There is something of utmost importance in the name of Jesus, and the apostles knew that and didn't back down from declaring Jesus, Jesus, Jesus.

It was an angel who told Mary and Joseph to name the child in her womb Jesus because He would save His people from their sins (Matthew 1:21). Jesus is Savior. Indeed, even the literal name of Jesus means "Jehovah is salvation" indicating Jesus' primary purpose of salvation and clearly implying the divinity and deity of Jesus. That He was called Christ emphasizes that He was indeed the Messiah, the promised one of God sent to redeem Israel and to one day free them to live under His peaceful rule (Micah 5:5). But before He comes back to rule, He had to first come in the form of a man to die for our sins (Philippians 2:5-7). It was His submission to the plan of salvation deemed necessary by the Father that enabled Him to be given by God the name which is above every name. At some point, every knee will have to bow before Him and every mouth will have to declare Him as Lord (Philippians 2:8-11). Those who bow to Jesus and confess Him as Lord and Savior while they are yet alive will live in heaven, while those who do it before the Great White Throne Judgment, whether in a recognition that is too late or in a bitter, non-submissive manner will end up in hell. The name of Jesus is the watershed issue in salvation. Luke 2:34-35 says, "And Simeon blessed them and said to Mary His mother, 'Behold, this Child is appointed for the fall and rise of many in Israel, and for a sign to be opposed-- and a sword will pierce even your own soul-- to the end that thoughts from many hearts may be revealed.'" What a person decides about Jesus reveals the true state of his or her heart before God. Some will "rise" into heaven, while others will "fall" into hell. It is not what a person does with a generic "Higher Power," but it is all about Jesus. This is what Scripture teaches in Hebrews 1:1-2, "God, after He spoke long ago to the fathers in the prophets in many portions and in many ways, *in these last days has spoken to us in His Son, whom He appointed heir of all things, through whom also He made the world*" (italics mine). Jesus is the final and definitive means of salvation because He is the culmination of God's revelation to us as given by the New Testament Scripture. Why doesn't a generic Creator God or Higher Power suffice? Because, as this passage clearly states, it was through Jesus that Jehovah God created the world. Jesus has been there from the beginning, being both God and the Son of God. So today, given that we have the New Testament account, we cannot really know Jehovah unless we know Jesus. This is why the apostles couldn't stop preaching in His name. They knew that the gospel wasn't the gospel without Jesus and His work on the cross (Colossians 1:4, 13-14).

If we read the New Testament long enough, we will recognize that everything is by Him, through Him, for Him, in Him, unto Him, because of Him, etc (Romans 11:36). Jesus is indeed the foundation of the church and the keeper of it. He deserves the highest place in our hearts and in our worship. May we never devalue His name, and may we only exalt it today as we will in heaven, saying, "Worthy is the Lamb that was slain to receive power and riches and wisdom and might and honor and glory and blessing" (Revelation 5:12). Worthy is His Name.

#86

PEARLS BEFORE SWINE

After speaking about not judging our neighbor before dealing with the sin in our own hearts lest we become hypocrites, Jesus speaks a very important principle that often gets overlooked. He says in Matthew 7:6, "Do not give what is holy to dogs, and do not throw your pearls before swine, or they will trample them under their feet, and turn and tear you to pieces." Let's take this piece by piece.

First, He says that we are not to give what is holy to dogs. What is holy is anything that is set apart, pure, undefiled, and Christlike rather than worldly. We know God is holy as is His Word, but we are supposed to tell the world, even "dogs," about Christ. So Jesus can't be saying not to share the gospel. So what else could be holy? The answer is the child of God. Positionally God sees those who have trusted in Christ for salvation as holy (Ephesians 2:1-8). Conditionally, we are works in progress until we die (Philippians 2:12); however, since Christ is in us, the world can see His holiness in and through us (2 Corinthians 4:6-7). In fact, they should see this if we want to have any chance at credibly sharing the gospel (Hebrews 12:14). So the idea Jesus is after here is that we don't disrespect ourselves such that we allow ourselves to be given over to destructive, evil entities. There are many who would manipulate us, deceive us, teach us false information, and just suck the very life right out of us (Revelation 22:15). There are people who are encouragers, and there are those who take our energy and hope away.

Paul affirms this reality in Philippians 3:2 saying, "Beware of the dogs, beware of the evil workers, beware of the false circumcision." We are not to disrespect ourselves who are the very vessels of Christ by letting others walk all over us, abuse us, or lead us astray. We should not give what is holy to the dogs because we are not dogs but rather children of God. We should love those in the world, but we should not be like it, of it, or darkened and defeated by it. We must maintain our holiness, preach the gospel, stand for truth, and yet all the while we must not let ourselves get weakened, defeated, and confused by errors of practice and thought. We must not let others manipulate or control our emotions, thoughts, or behavior, whether purposefully or not. Only Christ should control us because He is the ultimate example of holiness (2 Corinthians 5:14). Only He is to be our Master.

Yet there is another meaning to this exhortation from our Savior as well. He says that we are not to throw our pearls before swine. Swine eat the leftovers, not the delicacies, and they are content with doing so because they are pigs. That is what pigs do. Dogs eat the crumbs from the table and even things worse, and pigs aren't much better. In fact, pigs love rolling in mud, refuse, and the like. They are stinky, filthy animals. So why would a person give a shiny, valuable jewel to such an animal? It doesn't make any sense, but obviously we must be prone to such foolishness or our Lord wouldn't have had to tell us otherwise. When would we do such a thing? Well, sometimes Christians get burned by their own desire to be "loving," "caring," and "nice." The fact of the matter is that Jesus was much more than just a nice guy who was always there for everybody all the time. The reality is that He had a mission, an agenda, a clear-cut purpose and focus, and a schedule crafted by the will of God. He didn't stop to heal every single person or to cast out every single demon. Sometimes He left the crowds to pray. Sometimes He went on to another village or town. He knew His time was short and that there were things He needed to do. By implication, there were things that He couldn't do, things to which He had to think and say "no." There will likely come a time when we will choose to sacrifice our own well being and even the well being of others who need us in order to "minister" to a person in need. The fact of the matter is that, though we are called to serve and be sacrificial, we are not to give pearls to swine.

For example, consider the Christian pastor or counselor who advises a professing brother or sister in the Lord over and over again, yet the person never changes. At what point should he stop and recognize that the person is hard of heart, enjoying the life of the swine? There are limits that we must be willing to seek. Sometimes Satan sets people in our paths in order to destroy us because he knows that we will sacrifice the things we should be doing in order to minister to the "needy" and "weak" one. We must be discerning enough to know when to say when and how to concretely place limits upon people. *Swine don't deserve pearls of wisdom because all they will do with the wise counsel is roll around with it in the mud.* We should always pray for people, and there is never a reason to give up hope. However, there is a time to let a person be and let God deal with him or her alone. There are many true seekers who need our help, so we need to beware of the impostors, the swine who at first don't seem to be so.

We must learn discernment and who is truly humble, teachable, and willing to learn and change. *Why is this so important? Because the swine do more than just ruin pearls; their purpose is to ruin us.* The swine to whom we keep giving our precious pearls of energy, time, wisdom, and sacrifice are not really interested in the pearls as they profess to be but in, as Jesus says, turning and tearing us to pieces. They were never interested in the truth or in turning from sin but rather in destroying us and feasting upon us. As we function in the church long enough, we will encounter these people. We must be careful and watch out for the swine because our very spiritual, physical, emotional, and financial well-beings are at stake.

We have been sent out as sheep among wolves. We will be hunted and preyed upon, for such are the devil's methods (1 Peter 5:8). By God's grace, we can be shrewd as serpents and innocent as doves (Matthew 10:16) such that we can discern the right paths to take and avoid falling into destructive traps and fruitless pursuits. May God protect us, give us discernment, and lead us to those who truly need some pearls of God's wisdom.

#87

THE LORD IS MY SHEPHERD

If you have grown up in the church, you are probably familiar with the terms clergy and laity. Clergy is generally considered to be anyone who is ordained or doing the work of the ministry, usually full-time in nature. The laity is made up of the "lay people" who are not formally trained in the ministry and who typically do not serve full time. Now why does this matter and why bring it up? Man-made terminology that is not in the Bible can lead to dangerous distortions of the Bible. The terms clergy and laity come across as having a condescending tone to those who are not seen as members of the clergy. Furthermore, it can create a perception among the ordinary folks like the rest of us that we could never understand the Bible to the same extent that an ordained person could. These misimpressions could allow pride to seep in to the "powers that be" and for complacency and blind submission to take over among the non-clergy.

The New Testament is clear that all believers are part of the royal priesthood (1 Peter 2:9). We are all brothers and sisters in Christ on the same level (Romans 8:17). The Bible doesn't use the terms clergy and laity at all; rather, it views the entirety of the church as one body with our head being Christ (Ephesians 4:15). Thus, we need to be careful how we view our leaders, and they need to be careful how they view themselves. If each has a proper understanding of the role they play and Who is the real Head of Operations, then the church can be at peace and avoid abuses of power or other maladies and destructive forms of church government. God has given pastors and elders to lead His church because they meet the Biblical qualifications for ministry, being able to teach the Bible and possessing impeccable character (1 Timothy 3, Titus 1). These deserve honor and respect (1 Timothy 5:17), but they are not to exploit the influence that comes from being in a position of leadership.

Matthew 23:1-12 is a rebuke from Christ to the religious leaders of the day. Let us reflect upon it and draw some conclusions for how leaders should operate and how followers should follow. Scripture says,

> "Then Jesus spoke to the crowds and to His disciples, saying: 'The scribes and the Pharisees have seated themselves in the chair of Moses; therefore all that they tell you, do and observe, but do not do according to their deeds; for they say things and do not do them. They tie up heavy burdens and lay them on men's shoulders, but they themselves are unwilling to move them with so much as a finger. But they do all their deeds to be noticed by men; for they broaden their phylacteries and lengthen the tassels of their garments. They love the place of honor at banquets and the chief seats in the synagogues, and respectful greetings in the market places, and being called Rabbi by men. But do not be called Rabbi; for One is your Teacher, and you are all brothers. Do not call anyone on earth your father; for One is your Father, He who is in heaven. Do not be called leaders; for One is your Leader, that is, Christ. But the greatest among you shall be your servant. Whoever exalts himself shall be humbled; and whoever humbles himself shall be exalted.'"

Jesus plainly and directly rebuked the Pharisees for not living out what they taught and for desiring to be seen for what they supposedly did religiously. They looked the part, played the part, and even had the titles and power to be the part, but they weren't what they ought to have been. They had influence and power, and they misused it and abused it. They longed to be called Rabbi because they loved hearing the title before their names and because they loved the authority it implied over the people. They loved being called father whereas they ought only to have considered themselves as brothers. They were leaders and in so doing they did not sin; however, *their sin was that they loved being called leaders*. Those in positions of authority, pastors, elders, etc., must not love being called whatever title they love being called. Leading, shepherding, and teaching the church is not about a power trip or feeling above the other sheep. Even pastors are sheep themselves, brothers and joint heirs with the rest of the children of God. It is easy for there to become an abuse of power when church leaders love their titles and their power and positions. Jesus is the head of the church, not them (Colossians 1:18). They are merely called of our Master Servant to be lead servants, so to speak. The true leader is the one who understands that his call is to serve others. This humility leads to true exaltation from the only One Who can rightly give it.

In the church, we are all members of the same body, some having more prominent positions and callings than others. But none is superior, none is inferior, and none is to be neglected (1 Corinthians 12). This theology when properly understood and applied makes church government a lot less threatening, complex, and dysfunctional. After all, it is the Word of God that stands in judgment over all (1 Peter 1:25).

The question for those in leadership is this: Do you delight in being called Reverend, Doctor, Teacher, Bishop, Pastor, Elder, etc.? Is there a love for the title? There ought not to be. God is not impressed with titles earned, bestowed, or granted by men. True "ordination" is a blessing only God can give (Genesis 39:21). The rest of the sheep need to remember to keep studying the Word to make sure that the lead sheep is headed in the proper direction. The only way to know that for sure is if he is following the Shepherd.

Whether we are the lead sheep or the caboose, when we can say with David, a mighty leader of old, "The Lord is my Shepherd," we will be in a good place.

#88

THE REAL MEANING OF
WALKING BY FAITH

2 Corinthians 5:7 gives a reminder and exhortation that believers are to "walk by faith, not by sight." "Walk" speaks of how we live our lives, conduct ourselves, behave, and use the time and opportunities that God has ordained for us. Walking "by sight" speaks of choosing to live based upon how things naturally appear, feel, and seem at first glance. Those who walk by sight rely upon fleshly instincts and temporal pleasures to make decisions. They are concerned with the present rather than the eternal and with blending in with the world rather than with keeping the commands of Christ. Walking by sight is selfish, shallow, and according to the Scripture, a totally insensible way to live. Walking by faith, on the other hand, makes sense if we understand what faith is and the profound glory of what it accomplishes and gives back to us in return.

Hebrews 11:1-2 gives the definition of faith, saying, "Now faith is the assurance of things hoped for, the conviction of things not seen." *Faith is being absolutely convinced and assured that what we hope for and believe in according to the promises of God in the Scripture is indeed going to come to pass.* Faith is more than just empty hoping or thinking positively. It is an assurance and confidence that pierces to the depth of our souls that what God has said is true because God is for real and His promises are sure. As Hebrews 11:6 says, "And without faith it is impossible to please Him, for he who comes to God must believe that He is and that He is a rewarder of those who seek Him." Even though in this life God and heaven are unseen, those who believe God and His Word still choose to adjust their lives in light of eternal priorities. They choose not to walk by what is only visible to them now but rather based upon an unwavering belief of what they will see later. They are confident in their coming reward and in God's ability and faithfulness to keep His Word.

Those who walk by faith are keenly aware of the temporal nature of this life and world, and their focus and hope is fixed upon heaven. Hebrews 11:10 says of Abraham who operated by faith, "For he was looking for the city which has foundations, whose architect and builder is God." This city is an eternal city guaranteed by the promises of God to those who believe. Sarah, Abraham, Noah, and other men and women of faith from times past had to, like us, wait until after they died to see the fullness of God's promise to them. Although it is true that they did see God's faithfulness throughout their lives, they had to wait until heaven to see that they were wise and correct to follow God, to obey His leading, to stand for truth, and to deal with the ridicule that comes from doing so. Hebrews 11:13-14 continues, "All these died in faith, without receiving the promises, but having seen them and having welcomed them from a distance, and having confessed that they were strangers and exiles on the earth. For those who say such things make it clear that they are seeking a country of their own." For believers, our true country is heaven where we are eternal citizens. We cannot forget this because nations come and go, societies rise and fall, cultures ebb and flow, but God's promises stand forever. What we only believe in from a distance and what others mock and ignore is to be our anchoring hope. Though we are strangers now, we can be confident that we will go home one day soon. It is imperative if we want to walk by faith rather than by sight that we desire a better country, namely heaven (Hebrews 11:16).

Walking by faith requires a willingness to suffer now, knowing that there will be no suffering later. Moses left Egypt, "choosing rather to endure ill-treatment with the people of God than to enjoy the passing pleasures of sin, considering the reproach of Christ greater riches than the treasures of Egypt; for he was looking to the reward" (Hebrews

275

11:25-26). Sin is the easy way out, but the pleasure it offers is short-lived. It only breeds further and deeper pain and death. Moses chose to join up with his people, Israel, despite the difficulty and the cost of doing so, having to flee and later being mocked and persecuted. Yet he could do this by faith because he was looking to the reward. *The reward Christ offers is so much better than any earthly pleasure, and suffering for His sake is more fulfilling than any earthly treasure* (Hebrews 11:35-38). We must remember this if we are to walk by faith in this life.

Walking by faith isn't only marked by suffering and sacrifice, however. It is also marked by service for the Lord. Hebrews 11:33-34 speaks of the many things that the saints of old were able to accomplish, from winning wars to shutting the mouths of lions to performing acts of righteousness, because they walked by faith. The fact of the matter is that of ourselves we can do nothing of eternal value. Only by faith can we accomplish true spiritual victories through and in Christ. It is those who are willing to suffer and sacrifice and to believe and obey who will be used powerfully by God to do the work of the kingdom, advancing the truth, being ministers of light and love, and proclaiming the gospel to a world desperately in need.

If we want to truly be those who make a difference in ways that are eternal and not merely temporal, we must do as these faithful saints of old did and choose to walk by faith.

#89

WHEN FAITH IS TESTED

Sometimes when difficult things come into our lives, we wonder why. Though we must be willing to trust and obey even if we don't know why or aren't given that answer for some time, we do need to distinguish between tempting and testing. Satan tempts; God tests. *Tempting is for our failure and destruction; testing is in order to make our faith stronger.* Testing reveals to us where we are in terms of our faith as God already knows whether or not we will pass a given test. It is as we go through the fire of testing and trial that we can be strengthened, sanctified, and purified (James 1:2-4). We are never to say or think when tempting comes that God is behind it. Scripture expressly denounces this in James 1:13 which says, "Let no one say when he is tempted, 'I am being tempted by God'; for God cannot be tempted by evil, and He Himself does not tempt anyone." God does allow Satan to tempt us, but we can take hope that we will not be tempted beyond what we can handle and escape from by faith (1 Corinthians 10:13). Even in temptation, God is there to deliver us if we listen and obey.

When God tests us, He wants us to succeed. He wants us to see that our faith is real and that it has been refined by fire. 1 Peter 1:6-7 says,

> "In this you greatly rejoice, even though now for a little while, if necessary, you have been distressed by various trials, so that the proof of your faith, being more precious

than gold which is perishable, even though tested by fire, may be found to result in praise and glory and honor at the revelation of Jesus Christ."

We see from this passage that God only tests us as is necessary. In other words, God doesn't put us through a refining process for no reason. He is not malicious or desiring to see us suffer through trial. Just as a goldsmith only puts the metal into the fire in order to get rid of impurities, so is the way of our Lord. God will test us so that we can see where we need to improve. We can be sure that God crafts each test specifically to show us individually and personally what our defects and impurities are so that we can be sanctified and changed. *Testing is thus something to hope in rather than to dread. But we must be willing to go through the fire if we want to come out more like Christ than we were before.*

God put Abraham through quite a test in Genesis 22. God had promised Abraham descendants through Isaac that would be as numerous as the sand on the seashore. Yet, out of the blue it seemed, God commanded Abraham to do something that totally contradicted His promised blessing to him. He was to take his son Isaac and offer him up to God as a sacrifice. Now God is not honored by sacrificing children or human beings in any way, shape, or form. Yet He commanded Abraham to do this. Certainly Abraham must have been initially baffled at this directive, wondering why. But Abraham had great faith, and so he obeyed God, even going as far as binding up his son and taking the knife up in readiness to slaughter his only son (Genesis 22:9-10). We learn what Abraham was really thinking in Hebrews 11:17-19 which says,

> "By faith Abraham, when he was tested, offered up Isaac, and he who had received the promises was offering up his only begotten son; it was he to whom it was said, 'IN ISAAC YOUR DESCENDANTS SHALL BE CALLED.' *He considered that God is able to raise people even from the dead,* from which he also received him back as a type" (italics mine).

Abraham was willing to slaughter Isaac because he was so confident that God knew what He was doing and that God would keep His promise to him even if it meant bringing Isaac back from the dead. That is amazing faith. Abraham's faith was evident, and God told Abraham to stop and provided instead a ram to sacrifice. Of course, God never intended for Isaac to be killed. This was merely a test of Abraham's heart. *Which did he love more: the promised son from God or the God Who had promised his son?* This was the question for Abraham, and Abraham passed the test, demonstrating that He loved and trusted God even more than the blessings of God themselves (Genesis 22:12). Abraham called the place "The Lord will provide," and God went on to reiterate His promised blessing to Abraham (Genesis 22:16-18).

The result of God's kind testing is to reveal just how much we believe His Word and promises to us. God is powerfully glorified by those who do continue to believe even when things don't make sense and perhaps even appear to be contradictory, as in Abraham's case. We do not need to fear the tests that God brings to us; rather, we need only to trust Him to bring us through them. God is good, faithful, and true, and we can rest assured that we will end up better than we were before. God causes all things to work for our good, even if for a short time, it doesn't make sense, it hurts, or it is difficult. We will be the better for it, so, as James so accurately stated (James 1:2-4), *we can consider it all joy.*

#90

The Man Who Went
Against the Grain

According to the Bible the vast majority is wrong about salvation, about God, about Christ, and about His Word. The way to destruction is wide, but the path to life is narrow (Matthew 7:13-14). Even though we know we are right, nearly the entire religious, societal, scholastic, political, and philosophical establishment tells us that we are wrong. In some places this stand against the grain can cost believers their lives, or at least their freedom. 2 Chronicles 18 and its parallel account in 1 Kings 22 of Micaiah the prophet has much to say in terms of taking a stand for Christ.

Micaiah was a man of God, a true prophet in a land where the rest of the prophets had sold out to the pagan enterprises of King Ahab of Israel. All of the king's prophets were deceived and telling the king only what he wanted to hear. Yet an incident unfolded where Ahab was forced to summon Micaiah one last time and to be irked again by his condemning and negative prophesies concerning him. This incident was of Ahab's own concocting. He had wooed good king Jehoshaphat of Judah into joining him in battle against the king of Aram (2 Chronicles 18:1-3). But before Jehoshaphat was ready to go and fight, he wanted to seek the Word of the Lord (v. 4). Ahab brought in his own prophets, all four hundred of them, who in perfect collusion and conformity, told Ahab that Israel would win and succeed in battle (v. 5). Jehoshaphat wasn't convinced by these pagan impostors (v. 6), and Ahab was forced to call upon the last man of God in the land, Micaiah (v. 7).

So Micaiah was summoned before Ahab in the presence of all of the 400 evil prophets. But before Micaiah was to enter before the king, the messenger who was sent to bring him in told him the following in 2 Chronicles 18:12: "Behold, the words of the prophets are uniformly favorable to the king. So please let your word be like one of them and speak favorably." This messenger knew the kind of man Micaiah was and his track record with the king. He knew Micaiah would likely say something bad about Ahab, and, though his motives are not given, either he didn't want to see the party stop or Micaiah get hurt, or both. But it is not for the man of God to look out for his own welfare or to concern himself with the happiness of those to whom God has brought judgment. Micaiah responded to the messenger by saying, "As the LORD lives, what my God says, that I will speak" (v. 13). This is the heartcry of the true follower of Christ. We are not to be concerned with the results of our preaching, only that we preach the Word of God. It doesn't matter if our opinion stands alone or if we, like Micaiah, are outnumbered 400 to 1. We must be so confident in the authority of the Bible that we choose to cling to it and preach it even in a hostile environment. Satan may try to convince us that we must be wrong given that there are so few who stand by our side, but God's Word renders the only verdict that counts. Others might call us "arrogant" for believing that we know the truth while they are wrong, but we must stand firm. If we believe God's Word and obey it, we can expect to be in the minority and to have persecution. Being a spokesperson for the Lord has never been a popularity contest or a glamour job. Just ask Jesus Himself. The crowds left him, and only the twelve stuck with Him (John 6:66-68). But He did the will of Him Who sent Him (John 4:34), and that was the only thing that mattered.

Micaiah told Ahab the truth that Israel would be defeated and that Ahab would be killed in battle (v. 16, 19). One of the evil prophets struck Micaiah across the cheek for having the audacity to claim that he was being deceived (v. 23). Ahab also reacted angrily to the prophecy and commanded that Micaiah be thrown into prison with minimal food and water (v. 26). Yet Micaiah didn't back down or regret his decision to speak the truth. He wanted the people to remember what he said and to listen, for he was confident that the future events would prove him to have been the true prophet of God (v. 27).

Ahab tried to thwart the prophecy from God by disguising himself in battle and setting up Jehoshaphat as a target (v. 29). But God protected Jehoshaphat (v. 31), while a "random" arrow pierced one of the joints of Ahab's armor, killing him (v. 33). God's Word always comes to pass, even if we try to thwart it. Nothing can change about God's Word, for it endures forever (1 Peter 1:25). This is why, in the long run, we will always be better off standing with God than with man. In the end, we will be honored, rewarded, and proven right. But in the meantime, we must be willing to believe, to speak boldly, to stand for truth, to obey, and to never compromise the Word of God. The call of the Christian is to do as Jesus did, obeying the will of God no matter the cost and no matter the loss, being mindful of the reward and gain to come. May God give us the strength, perseverance, and boldness to go against the grain, even if it requires us, like Micaiah, to stand alone.

#91
STABILIZING TRUTHS FOR
UNSTABLE TIMES

The history of man is one of instability and change far more than stability and peace. It has been the rise and fall of empires as stronger armies come in or a nation-state grows complacent and weakens from the inside. Even in the time of King David, it was routine for nations to go to war seasonally to secure their borders and their place in the world (2 Samuel 11:1). The evil, sinful heart of man that craves more power, more money, and more influence means that constant fear, intimidation, and instability is part and parcel to the world in which we live. Here are four Scriptural truths to keep in mind during times of upheaval so that we can remain spiritually stable, morally uncompromised, filled with joy, kept in peace, and brimming with hope.

#1 Those who remain focused on Christ and believe His promises will be guarded in perfect peace by Christ Himself.

"Thou wilt keep him in perfect peace, whose mind is stayed on thee: because he trusteth in thee." (Isaiah 26:3 KJV)

When things around us begin to destabilize, we can really lose focus if we are not careful. If we want to be at peace, we must keep our minds fixed upon Christ and His promises to us, believing them to the utmost.

283

If we look only to the threats around us, we will likely falter and become dismayed. We must recall the Word of God, the power of our Lord, and His good promises to us. He, Who is in complete control, is the only One Who can keep us at peace.

#2 Our hope is that we have entered the veil with Christ to be with Him forever in heaven, and this is our anchor of the soul, a sure and steadfast encouragement.

"So that by two unchangeable things in which it is impossible for God to lie, we who have taken refuge would have strong encouragement to take hold of the hope set before us. This hope we have as an anchor of the soul, a hope both sure and steadfast and one which enters within the veil." (Hebrews 6:18-19)

We as believers have a hope that transcends this life. God never promised that this life would be easy or that we would be kept from pain and hardship (John 16:33). Just ask Jesus about the cross, Job about loss, the Old Testament prophets about persecution, or the disciples about martyrdom. Our hope is not in a politician's charismatic but empty promises. Our hope is not that we will be rich one day and live a life of ease. Rather, our hope is that God loves us, will keep us, will provide for our needs, will comfort us in our affliction, and will never leave or forsake us. We can trust Him to give us calm during the storms of this world. Though the waves crash and threaten, we have an anchor, and the anchor holds. We will enter heaven one day. There is no greater hope than that.

#3 Life is short, so don't despair; rather, make it count for the glory of God.

"As for the days of our life, they contain seventy years, Or if due to strength, eighty years, Yet their pride is but labor and sorrow; For soon it is gone and we fly away." (Psalm 90:10)

God limiting our lives on this earth to seventy or eighty years on average could well be evidence of His grace. He knows that sin has marred this world, the creation, and our bodies. He knows that sorrow is very much a part of this life. Thankfully, there are many good things, too, many graces of God to enjoy (e.g. Ecclesiastes 5:18, 9:9, Acts 2:42-47, Psalm 127:3). But the thing for us to remember is that we have a very short window to carry out God's plan for our lives, and rewards in eternity will be dictated upon our faithfulness in this short timeframe. The more we are mindful of how brief this life is, being but a vapor that is here and then vanishes away (James 4:14), the more we will be interested and driven by laying up treasure in heaven that will not rust, decay, or be vulnerable to thieves (Matthew 6:19-20). As we labor with a heavenly purpose, we can look forward to that day when we will fly away to eternal bliss.

#4 In heaven, there will be no more grief, sorrow, death, or pain. So endure to the end, for the end is worth it all.

"And He will wipe away every tear from their eyes; and there will no longer be any death; there will no longer be any mourning, or crying, or pain; the first things have passed away." (Revelation 21:4)

In heaven, there will be no more broken bones, no more infections, no more diseases, no more handicaps, no more dying, and no more grieving because the first things will have passed away. For now, God knows how much we have cried, keeping our tears in a bottle (Psalm 56:8). Then, He will wipe them all away. If that is not a word of encouragement, what is?

Hope is a rare and priceless commodity, but the believer has an infinite supply. Through Christ we can have perfect peace, a meaningful existence, a right perspective, and an enduring hope. Let us not forget the big picture as the storms of this world gain strength.

#92
OBEDIENCE PROVES OUR LOVE FOR GOD

Christianity is becoming really ethereal, touchy-feely, and abstract. For too many professing Christians, it seems that their relationship with God is dictated by how they feel towards God at the time or how they think God feels about them at the time. Closeness to God, according to this way of thinking and believing, is both subjective rather than objective and an experience rather than a reality. "I just feel so close to God today," or "Can't you just sense the Holy Spirit's presence in the room?" become definers of one's spiritual status rather than what the Bible says we should be concerned about. According to the Scripture, if we really want to know where we are at in terms of our relationship with God, we can forget about subjectivity and look at our own fruit. After all, a tree is known by its fruit (Matthew 7:20), not by what the tree thinks about itself or its relation to its Maker. God's opinion is the only opinion that counts, and God knows the heart. And what comes out of the heart dictates fruit or the lack thereof. This is why Jesus said, "If you love me, you will keep my commandments" (John 14:15). *His point is that we ought to forget about how close we think we might feel to God and to rather prove our love for Him by obeying what He has already said to us in His Word.* Obedience is how we prove our love for the Lord, and this is a very concrete, objective measure of the state of our relationship with God.

In Genesis 4, Cain and Abel both brought sacrifices to God. Abel took care of livestock, and he brought an offering of the firstlings of his

286

animals. Cain worked the ground as a farmer, and he brought the produce he had grown as a sacrifice to God. God approved of Abel's sacrifice but not Cain's. The question that comes to our minds is why. Hebrews 11:4 says, "By faith Abel offered to God a better sacrifice than Cain, through which he obtained the testimony that he was righteous, God testifying about his gifts, and through faith, though he is dead, he still speaks." So we know that Abel's sacrifice was better because it was offered by faith. Was it better because it was animals instead of fruit? Perhaps God had given instructions to offer animals, and Cain disobeyed. Or, perhaps Cain brought some leftovers from his crop while Abel brought the best of his flock. Yet the answer to the why question is not directly answered in Scripture, which makes me think that it is the wrong question to ask. The point of Genesis 4 isn't why God didn't accept Cain's sacrifice; rather, it is that Cain didn't bring a sacrifice by faith as his brother Abel did. In other words, God was displeased with Cain because he disobeyed. The primary lesson of the account is that God wants us to obey by faith. If we love Him, we will walk by faith and obey, keeping His commands, as Abel did. Cain failed to obey, and his countenance fell (v. 7). Sadness is thus the result of disobedience, whereas obedience brings joy. This doesn't mean obedience is easy, or Cain wouldn't have struggled. But sin can be mastered (v. 7), and as we do so, we prove our love for God and gain confidence that we are walking closely with our Lord.

Saul also learned about obedience (1 Samuel 15). Samuel's command to him was to conquer the Amalekites, kill their king, and destroy everything, from their livestock to all of their possessions. But Saul disobeyed and kept the king alive. He also brought back all of the good things. When Samuel heard the bleating of the sheep, he confronted Saul about his disobedience. Saul's defense was that he brought the sheep to sacrifice to the Lord. However, he didn't do what God had said. Thus, Samuel said to him,

> "Has the LORD as much delight in burnt offerings and sacrifices As in obeying the voice of the LORD? Behold, to obey is better than sacrifice, And to heed than the fat of rams. For rebellion is as the sin of divination, And insubordination is as iniquity and idolatry Because you

have rejected the word of the LORD, He has also rejected you from being king" (v. 22-23).

When disobedience is called parallel words such as rebellion and insubordination, it seems like more of a severe offense against God. But it doesn't stop there. God likens disobedience to rejection, rebellion, iniquity, idolatry, and divination (witchcraft). In other words, despite Saul's cover story of wanting to sacrifice to God, in God's eyes, his actions made him just as bad as the Amalekites, a people of idolatry, rebellion, iniquity and divination. God wasn't interested in Saul's religious gesture of sacrifice because He would rather have obedience. **Obedience is better than sacrifice- just ask Cain.**

Obedience is a simple proposition to understand, though a very difficult one to carry out. Thankfully, we serve a God Who is faithful to strengthen us to do His will as we put our trust in Him. The more we do so, the greater will be our endurance, character, and hope. Hope implies confidence and a surety that God is pleased and near (James 4:8). Do you want to feel closer to God? Obey and believe.

#93

TRUTHS THAT SUSTAIN
NO MATTER WHAT

What is your greatest fear, your worst case scenario? If it came true, how would you get by? How would you be sustained? How would you endure without compromising or cursing God?

Jesus faced a severe predicament, one of certain death. He knew that He had come to earth for this moment, but still He had a difficult choice to make. Can you imagine knowing the kind of pain that you would be about to experience in being crucified, and yet still going ahead and doing it? Can you imagine having hardly anyone in your court to support you and still making the right decision regardless? Can you imagine submitting yourself to the vices of the very people who hated you and made it necessary for you to be put on the cross in the first place? Can you imagine having all the power to escape and yet being obedient to the will of God anyway? We think that this was a relatively easy thing for our Savior, given that He was God in the flesh. But He was also fully a man, and insomuch as He was human, He suffered greatly. He knew what He was going to have to do, and it was a point of extreme emotional and physical duress to resolve to do it anyway. In Matthew 26:38, Jesus said, "My soul is deeply grieved, to the point of death." Have you ever had such grief over something or someone that you felt like you were going to die? Jesus did, and He understands.

In Luke, we get a medical picture of just how great this internal agony was. Luke 22:41-44 says,

> "And He withdrew from them about a stone's throw, and He knelt down and began to pray, saying, 'Father, if You are willing, remove this cup from Me; yet not My will, but Yours be done.' Now an angel from heaven appeared to Him, strengthening Him. And being in agony He was praying very fervently; and His sweat became like drops of blood, falling down upon the ground" (emphasis added).

The condition of sweating drops of blood is called hematidrosis, and it has been documented to occur in people under extreme stress, say under a death sentence or about to enter battle. We dare not think that Jesus never was under incredible stress, for He was under more stress than most of us can imagine. He was about to face His own agonizing drawn-out death with the prelude of thirty-nine lashes. He prayed that God would offer a way out or another way to redeem mankind, but there was no other way. Christ understood that, and He committed Himself to doing God's will rather than bailing out on God and humanity. What a Savior we have!

It is no coincidence that this section of Scripture is the same passage in which Peter denied Christ three times. Peter boasted in Matthew 26:33, "Even though all may fall away because of You, I will never fall away." In the parallel account in Luke 22, Peter said in verse 33, "Lord, with You I am ready to go both to prison and to death!" Of course, we know how things turned out for Peter. He was greatly humbled in his failure three times over, but eventually he would grow strong such that he would stand for Christ even when it meant his own death.

So how can we learn what Peter learned so that we don't fail as he did? How can we have the strength and resolve to submit to God's will as Christ did even though the stress of the situation could cause us to sweat blood or something analogous, say a panic attack, ulcer, etc.? What would make us choose not to escape with some coping mechanism or compromise rather than face our fears and the call of God upon our lives? We might not ever be given the opportunity to denounce Christ in exchange for living, but then again, maybe we will. Maybe our worst case scenario is not persecution but a loss of a loved one, a job, a home, a meal, etc. We must be ready spiritually to stand if and when the moment of reckoning arrives. Peter thought he was ready, but he wasn't. How can we best prepare ourselves to stand when our faith is put to the test?

If we want to be sustained and endure, we must do what Jesus did by believing that God's will is the best thing for us to do. It certainly wasn't the most enjoyable thing for our Savior in the short term, but long term, it gave Him the name which is above every name such that every knee will bow before Him one day (Philippians 2:9-11). He made it possible for mankind to be saved and go to heaven. This is a wonderful accomplishment that God had planned for Christ to carry out, and it was very, very good. Short term, it was hard, extremely hard, causing Him to sweat blood. But long term, it was worth it. Jesus had an eternal perspective and a faith that what God had called Him to do was best for God, for Him, and for the world. God's will is always best. If we believe that we are living according to God's desire for our lives as we believe and obey, we can be sustained. But if we begin to believe that God's will is too hard or not worth it or that God has made a mistake or bailed out on us, then we will falter. We must trust Him and surrender to His will. Believing that God's will is necessarily the kindest, wisest, and best for us is central to being able to endure faithfully.

We would also do well to remember what Jesus said in the closing words of Matthew: "I am with you always, even unto the end of the age" (28:20). Isaiah 41:10 echoes this truth when God says to His people, "Do not fear, for I am with you; Do not anxiously look about you, for I am your God. I will strengthen you, surely I will help you, Surely I will uphold you with My righteous right hand." Such power and reassurance there are in those words: "For I am with you."

At some point, our faith will be challenged beyond what we thought we could handle. If we want to endure by faith and obey, we must believe that God's will is best and that He is with us, being fully in control, working things for our good, and upholding, helping, and strengthening us. Do you want to be sustained? Believe this.

#94

OVER-COMMITMENT DOESN'T HELP ANYBODY

Exodus 18 provides us with a very important truth about the dangers of over-committing ourselves. On one side of the extreme, we can be prone to laziness and inactivity, and, at such times, we need some prodding to get more involved in life and in ministry. Yet there are other times when we can fall to the other extreme of constant activity and juggling too many responsibilities. This extreme is not any healthier because it leads to high stress for the over-committed individual and an inability on his or her part to be balanced and to give to others what they need. As Exodus 18 will reveal, **even though we might think we are sacrificing for the well-being of others, we can actually be doing them a disservice**. God's desire is that we would use wisdom such that we would make the most of our time and use our lives for the best possible purposes and in the most God-honoring ways (Ephesians 5:15-16). Just how our time is spent and divided up will depend on where we are at in life, what kind of health we are in, what ministry opportunities are available to us, etc (Galatians 6:10, Philippians 4:10). Sometimes certain things will demand an unusual amount of our attention for a period of time, and there is nothing we can do about it whether we like it or not. Other times we will find ourselves with an abnormal amount of time on our hands, and we will need to search out what God would have us do.

Regardless of the specific circumstances, what is certain is that neither laziness nor over-commitment is advantageous to our spiritual success.

Being over-committed is not defined simply by being energetic, purposeful, zealous, or excited about the things of God or about His graces in this life. In fact, we ought to be all of those things. **The danger comes when we do more than God has led us to do or something other than He has led us to do such that we harm ourselves and jeopardize our ability to live faithfully, in holiness, and for the long run.** Zeal must be tempered by wisdom such that it can remain fervent and not die out. 1 Corinthians 15:58 says, "Therefore, my beloved brethren, be steadfast, immovable, always abounding in the work of the Lord, knowing that your toil is not in vain in the Lord." The emphasis for us here is on the idea of "steadfastness" and "immovability" because such characteristics are required in order to be "always abounding in the work of the Lord." Over-committed people abound in activity but not necessarily in the work of the Lord according to how God wants them to spend their time. **There is a significant distinction between being active as compared to doing the work and will of God.** This is why it is so important to seek God's will according to the Scriptures as we go throughout our lives.

In Exodus 18, Moses' father-in-law, Jethro, paid him a visit. Jethro noticed that Moses spent from morning until evening (v. 13) judging the people of Israel. He asked Moses, "Why do you alone sit as judge and all the people stand about you from morning until evening?" (v. 14) Moses replied, "Because the people come to me to inquire of God. When they have a dispute, it comes to me, and I judge between a man and his neighbor and make known the statutes of God and His laws" (v. 15-16). Moses was filling his day with good things (or so he thought) by teaching the people the commands of God. But Jethro saw a problem, and he responded, "The thing that you are doing is not good. *You will surely wear out, both yourself and these people who are with you, for the task is too heavy for you; you cannot do it alone*" (v. 17-18 with emphasis added). Jethro then advised Moses to divide the labor between many other faithful, trustworthy men so that he would only have to decide the most difficult of cases (v. 22). Jethro was absolutely right that Moses would never be able to keep his current schedule going because it was too much for one man to do. His over-commitment was not based in the wisdom of God.

Jethro continued in v. 23, "If you do this thing and God so commands you, then you will be able to endure, *and all these people also will go to their place in peace*" (emphasis added). Moses agreed that Jethro's counsel was indeed wisdom from God, and he made the proper adjustments in how he governed and spent his time. Sometimes we can fall into the trap of thinking that God needs us or that nobody else could fill our shoes such that we choose to take on more than God has asked us to do. This is dangerous for us, and as verse 23 indicates, it harms those we are intending to serve as well. In Moses' case, the people had to wait in line all day to get counsel. Obviously, this wasn't good, and the wisdom of God offered a better way for all.

God's will is that we do the tasks He has given us to do, not more and not less. Our joy will be full as we do these things, and He will supply our needs accordingly. As we walk in wisdom, we will find balance leading to steadfastness and immovability, which, in turn, will enable us to endure. **So, let us not be over-committed; rather, let us be fully committed to what God has asked us to do.**

#95

HOW IS YOUR GENTLE SIDE?

Gentleness is a fruit of the Spirit that is often overlooked. Love, joy, and peace get a lot of attention, but gentleness is not to be ignored. 1 Peter 3:4 says that a gentle spirit in women is precious to God, but the fact of the matter is that gentleness is also a godly trait for men (James 3:13, Titus 3:2). Indeed, we are not walking fully in the Spirit as followers of Christ if we are not gentle. Thus, it is important that we know what gentleness is and how to manifest it in our lives.

The best way to understand gentleness is to look at our God, Who is gentle. Christ had no problem being known as gentle. Matthew 21:5 says, "Say to the daughter of Zion, 'Behold your King is coming to you, gentle, and mounted on a donkey, even on a colt, the foal of a beast of burden.'" His gentleness did not make Him a wimp Who would stand for nothing. His tenderness did not make Him give up His power or authority. His gentleness showed that God had drawn near to mankind so that He would bear the burden of our sin. It showed that He was seeking peace, reconciliation, and restoration. He came not harshly with words of condemnation (except to the proud) but rather with words of salvation. His arms were open, tender, and receptive to children, to foreigners, and to sinners; none was unworthy of His gentle embrace. The God Who is all-powerful is also a God of gentleness. We can thus have absolute confidence that His gentle embrace is soundly unbreakable and totally secure and safe.

When God revealed Himself to Elijah in 1 Kings 19:11-13, He was not in the earthquake or the fire, symbols of judgment and power. Rather, His manifestation to Elijah was that of a gentle blowing wind. Elijah knew God's power and judgment, having just seen God devour a sacrifice with fire from heaven and rid the land of the priests of Baal. But at this point, Elijah was worn down and despairing of life itself. God didn't come to him harshly but gently. God was still powerful and on the throne, as the earthquake and fire indicated, but He was also there to meet Elijah in his time of need. God showed Elijah His gentle side, speaking kindly to him and providing miraculously for him. He didn't baby him, for He told him, in effect, to stop whining and get back to work. But He wasn't harsh about it. He didn't get angry with Elijah, He didn't pour out His wrath upon him for his selfishness, and He didn't penalize him or punish him. He came near to Elijah, spoke tenderly to him, had a meaningful and direct conversation with him, and then exhorted him to get back to business. God was with Elijah in showing forth His power and judgment, and when Elijah needed some gentle encouragement, God was there to minister gentleness to him.

There will be times in life when others will let us down, when we will let them down, and conflicts will erupt. Yet gentleness impacts how conflicts and confrontations are handled. Proverbs 15:1 says, "A gentle answer turns away wrath, but a harsh word stirs up anger." In other words, when somebody insults us, challenges us, or confronts us, we are to respond without raging back at them. Our answer is to be tender, unprovoked, and kind. We are to forgive those who trespass against us... period. We are to pray for those who persecute us and love our enemies (Matthew 5:44). It is kindness that leads us to repentance (Romans 2:4). Such kindness is gentle and does not get provoked to give a harsh response. What we need in times of relational difficulties are gentle words of confrontation, rebuke, exhortation, or encouragement that can lead us to get back on track.

There will be times (or should be) when we are asked about the hope that we have in Christ (1 Peter 3:15). At those times, we are told to give a defense for what we believe, yet gently and reverently. The point is that we can say all of the right things and give a godly explanation for faith, but if we don't do it in a way that shows others that we care about them, we will fail to be and do what God wants us to be and do. We are not to treat others as inferior for not knowing Christ, as outcasts because they are not yet saved, or as those who are intruding on our schedule. Yet let us remember that gentleness doesn't gloss over sin and the truth for the sake of being "friendly." It merely seasons the truth with salt, making is palatable and desirable, so that those whom we confront or exhort experience the grace of God (Ephesians 4:29, Colossians 4:6).

There will be times when a brother or sister is caught in sin, and we are to restore such a one in a spirit of gentleness (Galatians 6:1). It may be tempting to lash out at that person and think or say, "How could you be so stupid or selfish?" It could be tempting to shun him or her, to be maligning, to give a guilt trip, or to make the person earn our acceptance back. These are not God's ways. We must remember that we are just as capable of sinning as others are. Thus we should go to those who have fallen into sin not as those who bring condemnation but as those seek restoration and reconciliation, hoping that they will ask for the forgiveness that we are prepared to offer.

May we be those who are not easily provoked, who make others feel safe, and who are always willing to forgive. How is your gentle side?

#96

THE THRONE OF GRACE

Hebrews 4:15-16 says,

> "For we do not have a high priest who cannot sympathize with our weaknesses, but One who has been tempted in all things as we are, yet without sin. Therefore let us draw near with confidence to the throne of grace, so that we may receive mercy and find grace to help in time of need."

There is great significance to the fact that Christ was born in the likeness of man and lived through adulthood on this earth. That Jesus experienced life from the manger to the cross has great relevance to how we live our lives as Christians. Sometimes we might think that God, being God, could not possibly relate to or understand our incessant needs and weaknesses. Yet the message from Scripture is that Jesus understands and even sympathizes. There is no need to be embarrassed or confounded by our neediness and weakness. Christ wants to show Himself to be strong in our weakness (2 Corinthians 12:9-10), and He promises to meet our needs according to His good and perfect will (Philippians 4:19). When we feel like we can't help but give into sin, He promises to provide a way out (1 Corinthians 10:13). His throne is a place of mercy and grace. He knows that we need help, and He wants us to come and ask Him for it.

He understands pain, for He was beaten and bruised for our transgressions. He understands rejection, for many professing followers abandoned Him. He knows what it is to be fatigued as He spent many long nights in prayer. He endured intense temptation from the devil. He knows the frustration of laboring for the Father when even His own disciples seemed not to understand. He can relate to family life, to the workplace, to the meeting place for worship, and to the everyday issues of life. He hungered and He thirsted. Our God understands, for He has been there.

Yet, despite all that He experienced and endured, He did not sin. This has made it possible for us to be saved and to have the ability in Christ to draw near to God in prayer. We have the awesome privilege of approaching the God of the universe in prayer in the name of Christ. It is not our goodness that makes this possible but His. And given all that He endured on the cross for this to be made possible, how awful it must be to Him when we don't take advantage of this privilege of prayer! He is our intercessor and advocate, and He wants to be there for us. But He won't force us to call out to Him; we need to draw near to Him. Then He will draw near to us (James 4:8). How great is it that we get to approach the very throne of God in prayer, for it is a place of supreme authority and power! It is a place where things can get done, where sin can be forgiven, where requests can be answered, and where hopes can be renewed. And because of Christ, this throne is not a place of the pouring out of God's wrath but a place of grace and mercy for those who believe. Why wouldn't we be willing to trust in our Savior such that we share what is truly going on in our hearts and minds? He already knows, so why not tell Him! As we become convinced that He understands and sympathizes with our condition, we will be more open with our Lord and grow deeper in intimacy with Him. We are safe with Him, and our honest, humble prayers are never too stupid or a waste of His time. Our God cares, and this is why we are to cast our cares upon Him (1 Peter 5:7).

We need to remember that as we approach our Lord in prayer, we need to take care of first things first. If we have unconfessed sin, we must start by setting our hearts right with God (Psalm 66:18). Until we do that, we ought not to expect answers to our prayers or even the ability to pray properly in accordance with God's will. A clean heart enables us to take advantage of the privilege of prayer and to enjoy intimate communion with our Lord.

There are few things as frustrating as opening up to somebody about things that we are feeling and thinking and getting a judgmental reaction, a Christian cliché, a condescending preaching to, or a failure to listen. Or, perhaps the person we open up to is really caring and kind, but he or she just doesn't understand. In either case, there is a sense in which we will go on our way likely feeling abandoned, isolated, or unknown. The beauty of the fact that our Savior is both sympathetic and understanding is that we will always have somebody to lend us an ear, to give us a hand, to offer us forgiveness and freedom, to provide us with the wisdom we need, and to offer us a perfect gift of grace. Taking advantage of the throne of grace is one of the most underestimated and underutilized privileges and graces of the Christian life. There is no better confidant and friend than our Savior. Why wouldn't we take advantage of this?

Sure, sometimes God may provide us with people who do understand us and sympathize with us, and we praise God for these people. Yet even then, we must be sure that we are putting our ultimate trust in the truth of Scripture and in the person of Christ for our comfort and consolation (2 Corinthians 1:3-5). He is fully sufficient to be able to comfort us and help us.

Our hope is that we have a God Who cares and can relate to us because He anticipates our needs and sympathizes with our struggles. He is not a distant, impersonal being, but He is our Comforter (John 14:16 KJV). Let us take full advantage of bringing our petitions, cares, and needs to the throne of grace so that we can receive cleansing when we need it, wisdom when we ask for it, and comfort and understanding each and every time. Will you take your place before the throne of grace?

#97

A LIVING AND HOLY SACRIFICE

In Exodus 12:5, God commanded each household in Israel to take an unblemished lamb and slaughter it on the Passover. The blood of the Lamb was to be put on the doorposts of their homes so that God would pass over them and not strike down their firstborn as He would do to the Egyptians. The picture of blood being shed for saving their children was a clear foreshadowing of Christ who would shed His innocent blood for us as the perfect Lamb of God. Peter reminds us in 1 Peter 1:19 that we have not been bought with perishable things such as silver and gold "but with precious blood, as of a lamb unblemished and spotless, the blood of Christ." Our holy standing before God when judgment day comes is going to be because we have received Christ as the One Who alone could forgive us of our sins and cleanse us from all unrighteousness (1 John 1:9). It is His blood which can set us free, and nothing else, because only He was the unblemished and spotless Lamb of God.

But the imagery of unblemished sacrifices doesn't end here. Jesus refers to those who believe in Him as His sheep (John 10:27), and Paul says in Romans 12:1-2,

> "Therefore I urge you, brethren, by the mercies of God, to present your bodies a living and holy sacrifice, acceptable to God, which is your spiritual service of worship. And do not be conformed to this world, but be

transformed by the renewing of your mind, so that you may prove what the will of God is, that which is good and acceptable and perfect."

There is a sense in which our lives are to resemble the unblemished lamb of the Passover and the holy, unblemished Lamb of God, Jesus Christ. Just as Christ was holy and laid down His life, so, too, are we to grow in holiness and lay down our lives for others. We, the sheep of God, are to be holy sacrifices while we are yet living. This we can do each day as we present our bodies, hearts, and minds as clean and holy to God.

Paul speaks of dying daily (1 Corinthians 15:31, Galatians 2:20), and Jesus says that we must take up our crosses daily (Luke 9:23). Each day, we must offer ourselves to God spiritually, reckoning ourselves dead to sin and alive to God (Romans 6:11). We are alive because Christ has given us new life. We are holy because Christ has made us righteous in His perfect blood. Yet we are also to be sacrifices, living daily in practical holiness as we let God accomplish His good and perfect will in and through us. Paul summarized this mindset in Galatians 2:20 when he said, "I have been crucified with Christ; and it is no longer I who live, but Christ lives in me; and the life which I now live in the flesh I live by faith in the Son of God, who loved me and gave Himself up for me." Galatians 5:24 echoes this theme, saying, "Now those who belong to Christ Jesus have crucified the flesh with its passions and desires." Being holy, living sacrifices means that we are to daily reckon ourselves dead to sin and free to let Christ live out His will in and through us. Being a sacrifice implies a willingness to die. We may never have to physically die for being a Christian, but daily we do need to die to the flesh as we remember by faith that we have been bought with the blood of the perfect Lamb Who is working to perfect us also. When we yield to God, we can see just how alive we really are.

Christ developed this Biblical theme of sacrificial living further when He said in John 12:24-25, "Truly, truly, I say to you, unless a grain of wheat falls into the earth and dies, it remains alone; but if it dies, it bears much fruit. He who loves his life loses it, and he who hates his life in this world will keep it to life eternal." Part and parcel to being a follower of Christ is this concept of dying in order to live. When we first came to Christ, there was a dying in that we became new creations in Christ (2 Corinthians 5:17). Yet, even as believers, there is still a daily dying as we must choose by faith to serve Christ rather than our own selfish interests and fleshly lusts. We cannot love the approval of the world and the things of it more than Jesus. We cannot hold this life dear such that we forget to live with eternal priorities. The only way to bear abundant spiritual fruit is through sacrifice and surrender to Christ.

Paul told Timothy in 2 Timothy 4:6-8,

> "For I am already being poured out as a drink offering, and the time of my departure has come. I have fought the good fight, I have finished the course, I have kept the faith; in the future there is laid up for me the crown of righteousness, which the Lord, the righteous Judge, will award to me on that day; and not only to me, but also to all who have loved His appearing."

Paul lived a life of sacrifice and surrender, pouring his life out like a drink offering. He fought to advance the gospel and to refuse temptation. He finished the course, having done what Christ had asked him to do, and he kept the faith, continuing to believe the truth about Jesus and the promise of eternal life. He had taken his own counsel, having demonstrated what it means to be a holy and living sacrifice. Our goal should be to be able to look back on our lives and say with Paul that we have finished well and stood for righteousness in Christ. As we daily yield to Christ, the Spirit will work through Scripture and through our consciences to transform us so that we are no longer conformed to the ways of this world. He will help us to live and stand for righteousness, working change in our patterns of thoughts, attitudes, and actions.

May we never forget that life in Christ is a life of sacrifice, surrender, service, and sanctification. May He enable us to be holy, living sacrifices, those who die daily so that we can truly live.

#98

GREAT IS HIS FAITHFULNESS

Jeremiah wrote the book of Lamentations, which contains his laments over the state of the people of Israel and over the pain, rejection, and difficulty that he suffered. Jeremiah was faithful, but his ministry was an extremely difficult one because of the hardness of the hearts of those to whom he preached. He took a lot of flack and was severely persecuted, all for the sake of being faithful to God's Word. Speaking of this hurt and frustration, he said in Lamentations 3:19-20, "Remember my affliction and my wandering, the wormwood and bitterness. Surely my soul remembers and is bowed down within me." Jeremiah had great faith, but he had many rough times. He recalled his affliction, his wandering, his alienation, his rejection, and the bitterness and grief that just weighed his soul down. How could Jeremiah continue on with these weights and burdens?

In verses 21-24, he continued, saying, "This I recall to my mind, therefore I have hope. The LORD'S lovingkindnesses indeed never cease, for His compassions never fail. They are new every morning; great is Your faithfulness. 'The LORD is my portion,' says my soul, 'Therefore I have hope in Him.'" Jeremiah had to regularly choose to mentally rehearse the faithfulness of God. He had to actively look for the graces of God to him. They were there despite the suffering, and perhaps, even in and through the suffering. He didn't succumb to doubt and despair because he could look back at all of the good things that God had done. He could believe that God was faithful even when he couldn't see it or understand what God was doing. He recognized that no day had ever gone by without God pouring out new compassions and mercies upon His servants. He affirmed that God's faithfulness remained sure, unchangeable, and eternally and infinitely sizable and significant. It was a remembrance of God's faithful nature, faithful promises, and faithful actions that enabled him to look for the graces of God each day and to believe that they were there in abundance whether he was aware of them or not.

It is extremely easy to meditate upon hurt, struggle, despair, and frustration, but God's desire is that we imitate Jeremiah and choose rather to focus and meditate upon His faithfulness. We each can bear testimony to times in our lives when God was faithful to us. Perhaps He helped us find something we thought we had lost. Perhaps He restored a broken relationship. Perhaps He answered our prayer for salvation for a loved one. Perhaps He graciously opened a door to ministry or supplied a new place of employment. Perhaps he blessed a family with children or provided for an adoption. These are significant memory markers to call to mind when we feel like God has broken His end of the deal. Yet we should even rehearse the "lesser" mercies, such as food to eat, shelter over our heads, clothes to keep us warm, etc. We have His Word, His presence, and the promise of eternal life to top it all off. We have so much more mercy than we tend to see. The key is that we must believe it, look for it, and praise God for it.

We cannot rehearse our trials and temptations over and over again or it will harm our relationship with God because it will distort our perspective. God wants us to praise Him despite the difficulties, glorifying and thanking Him for His faithfulness and that the trials He ordains are purposeful and loving by nature. He cannot deny His own nature. 2 Timothy 2:13 says, "If we are faithless, He remains faithful, for He cannot deny Himself." God was Jeremiah's portion, and He is our portion because His very nature is faithfulness such that He cannot ever be unfaithful. Furthermore, His ability to be faithful is not predicated by our level of faithfulness to Him in return. Even if we succumb to doubt and despair or even rebellion, still God is faithful to honor His love for Christ and therefore to His children as well. There is great hope for us in the unalterable nature of God Who is faithful.

Jeremiah said in verses 25-26 and 32-33, "The LORD is good to those who wait for Him, to the person who seeks Him. It is good that he waits silently for the salvation of the LORD. For if He causes grief, then He will have compassion according to His abundant lovingkindness. For He does not afflict willingly or grieve the sons of men." Jeremiah didn't fall for the devil's trap of doubting God's care and goodness. God does not delight in seeing His people suffer. Yet there will be times when He allows suffering and hardship into our lives. But "if He causes grief, then He will have compassion according to His abundant lovingkindness." We don't know exactly how this compassion and mercy will be experienced as we go through life, but we know that it will be experienced. No matter what happens, we must trust God in difficult times and believe that His compassion and mercies are new every morning. His faithfulness is great, and it will always be.

#99

WHERE TO FIND WISE COUNSEL

There is only one place to find wisdom, namely, in God's Word. And there is only one way to find wisdom, that is, through Jesus Christ. Colossians 2:3 says, speaking of Christ, "In whom are hidden all the treasures of wisdom and knowledge." As we look for wise counsel in life, we need to look no further than Christ and the Scripture. Everything we need to know is contained in His Word. As Romans 15:4 says, "For whatever was written in earlier times was written for our instruction, so that through perseverance and the encouragement of the Scriptures we might have hope." What "wise" men of this world relegate to myth and fables, God says is instructive unto wisdom for today. Only those who are humble enough to receive it will be blessed by it.

1 Corinthians 3:18-20 says,

> "Let no man deceive himself. If any man among you thinks that he is wise in this age, he must become foolish, so that he may become wise. For the wisdom of this world is foolishness before God. For it is written, 'He is THE ONE WHO CATCHES THE WISE IN THEIR CRAFTINESS'; and again, 'THE LORD KNOWS THE REASONINGS of the wise, THAT THEY ARE USELESS.'"

There are many self-proclaimed or media-anointed gurus out there teaching various forms of wisdom, but what is sure is that all of their "wisdom" is foolishness before God because it is not based in Christ or His Word. It is all a waste. Rather than leading to success and prosperity, it leads to eternal loss and destruction. Even in Christian circles, worldly wisdom can sneak in. Just because someone has a lot of people that listen to him or her does not mean that such a person ought to be listened to. Clever words and persuasive speaking do not necessarily mean wisdom is contained therein (1 Corinthians 1:17, 19; 2 Peter 1:16). Too often, the words are mere forms of godliness that are devoid of the power of Christ (2 Timothy 3:5). In life, people will give us all kinds of advice, some of it solicited and some not. Our only hope in identifying true wisdom from worldly wisdom is to be like the Berean Christians who searched out the Scripture on their own to see if what they were being told was indeed true (Acts 17:11). We can trust Christ in us to give us wisdom as we open up His Word and prayerfully seek the truth (Jeremiah 29:13).

The world looks to the strong, the intelligent, the successful, the popular, the famous, and the powerful for wisdom. But according to the Scripture, these folks are the least likely to be true sources of wisdom. 1 Corinthians 1:26-27 says,

> "For consider your calling, brethren, that there were not many wise according to the flesh, not many mighty, not many noble; but God has chosen the foolish things of the world to shame the wise, and God has chosen the weak things of the world to shame the things which are strong."

Paul was not saying that it is impossible for rich or powerful people to have wisdom, just that it is difficult. Christ also alluded to this truth when He spoke of how difficult it is for those with many riches to find and submit to the truth in Christ (Matthew 19:23). Paul was reminding the believers at Corinth that many of them were weak and insignificant in the world's eyes and by the world's criteria, but they were those who had responded to the gospel. God used them to bring shame upon the "wise." Jesus said in Luke 10:21, "At that very time He rejoiced greatly in the Holy Spirit, and said, 'I praise You, O Father, Lord of heaven and earth, that You have hidden these things from the wise and intelligent and have revealed them to infants. Yes, Father, for this way was well-pleasing in Your sight.'" Men cannot get to heaven or find wisdom by their own intellect, strength, power, or influence. Wisdom cannot be bought, discovered, or won in battle. Age and experience of themselves alone do not bring wisdom. Wisdom comes by faith in Christ, something the "wise" of this world tend to miss. As we seek wise counsel, we must look beyond the externals to Christ and His Word. The devil's advice can sound good, and the people giving it can mean well. Yet without Christ, wisdom cannot be present. Helpful hints and wise tidbits are not spiritual wisdom. There is a way that seems right to a man, yet its end is death (Proverbs 14:12). We must always measure everything against the Bible lest we get way off course without even knowing what is happening to us.

David said in Psalm 119:24, "Your testimonies also are my delight; they are my counselors." There is nothing wrong with having wise people as counselors (Proverbs 15:22), but the emphasis ought to be on "wise" as opposed to "counselors." This is because a counselor is only as good as the wisdom he or she possesses. Even in the absence of other human opinions, it is possible to find true wisdom as David did simply by knowing and studying God's Word. In fact, David became convinced that his own study of Scripture gave him more wisdom than those who were supposed to be advising and teaching him. Psalm 119:99 says, "I have more insight than all my teachers, for Your testimonies are my meditation." If we want to find wise counsel, it is not that complicated. We need to be in Christ, and we need to study His Word. The more we study His Word, the better we will be at identifying true wisdom from worldly wisdom. The better we will become at finding people who teach what is right and good.

Godly counsel can be a great blessing, but we must never underestimate the treasure trove of wisdom that we as priests of the kingdom have access to on our own by the Spirit of God opening up God's Word to our hearts and minds. It is in Christ and His Word where true wisdom is found, and counsel is only valuable insomuch as it aligns with God's Word. It is great when others help us grow in learning to follow the Spirit, but ultimately we are responsible for following hard after Him ourselves (Psalm 63:8 KJV).

310

#100

GOD WILL PROVIDE

The concept of need is a very interesting one. We all have needs, though some feel them more severely and acutely than others. Some live with hunger, some live without a roof over their heads, and some live without a loving parent. Others are blessed with the basic necessities of life and yet are consumed with worry about other also valid needs such as harmony in family relationships, problems at work, health complications, etc. The fact of the matter is that even the wealthiest and most powerful people have needs. So why does God allow us to have needs, and why does it seem that many needs go unmet?

Paul says in Philippians 4:19, "And my God will supply all your needs according to His riches in glory in Christ Jesus." Paul rightly understood the concept of need. He says in verse 12 that having needs is a matter of suffering (the exact phrase is "suffering need"). Being in a state of need is not fun or easy. It reminds us that there is nothing that we, by our own human strength, ingenuity, and power can do to change the situation. If we could, we should because such would amount to faithful stewardship. Needs that arise due to our own laziness are our own fault, and we should try to resolve those issues. But inevitably we will encounter needs that we cannot solve and that we are not even meant to be able to solve, and for these needs, we need to learn what Paul learned.

Paul went from times of having an abundance of provisions to times of having next to nothing, including nothing in his stomach and not enough clothing to stay warm. *Never did he accuse God of not meeting his needs in those situations, which is remarkable.* Surely food and shelter are legitimate needs, yet God allowed Paul to be without both at various points in time. Paul, however, did not stumble over this reality and begin to question God's faithfulness. Rather, he spoke of what he learned through these diverse experiences. He says in 4:12-13 that he learned the secret of how to get along regardless of his circumstances, by trusting in Christ who would give him strength to do all things. He would need strength to endure in the suffering, and he would need strength to not grow overconfident when he wasn't suffering. In other words, he learned that he needed divine help at all times and in all circumstances and that Christ would give Him strength to do all the things that God had called him to do. Never would Paul lack what he needed in order to be able to fulfill God's purpose for him in this life. This position of recognizing his own human weakness was how God could show Himself strong by perfecting His power in, through, and even despite Paul's weakness (2 Corinthians 12:9). Paul learned to see need as God sees need, trusting Him absolutely that God would always supply his needs according to His perfect wisdom.

We get into trouble when we try to tell God how to run the universe, and, in particular, the course and events of our lives. Certainly, He cares about our pain and our needs, and He wants us to cast them upon Him (1 Peter 5:7). But we must understand what Paul did, choosing to accept that this life will involve pain and suffering as Jesus said it would (John 16:33). God is not some magic genie who answers to our every beck and call so that we can be instantly removed from any pain and transported to an earthly life full of endless ease and relaxation. Needs are part of this life and part of the human condition, even as believers. God will not always instantaneously spare us of the pain of being in need. *In fact, sometimes what we view as an unmet need might in actuality be a provision in and of itself from God, something that God is using to teach us, mold us, and shape us.* Sometimes, we need to suffer in order to learn, to gain wisdom, and to be able to fully identify and appreciate the good gifts of God when they are given later on. God is good, and

He does provide for and deliver His people. But we must be humble enough to trust Him to ultimately be able to measure and identify our needs and to meet them according to His perfect wisdom and timetable.

Paul goes out of his way in verse 19 to refer to God in a personal, experiential sense by saying "my God." He is saying with full confidence that he has seen firsthand that God does keep His promises, that He does supply our needs, and that He does give us strength to do everything that He has called us to do. If the man who suffered the pangs of hunger and the torment of multiple imprisonments and beatings can say that God never let him down, then so should the Philippians and so should we. *Rather than getting bitter at God about an unmet need, we should eagerly look forward to how God will cause a particular difficulty to work for good (Romans 8:28).* Rather than asking in a faithless manner "Why is God allowing this?" we should think "I can't wait to see how God is going to work this out for good!"

God may allow us to come to a place of utter helplessness, hopelessness, and desperation before acting mightily on our behalf. This reminds us of our weakness and inability and of His strength and absolute power. It is not God holding out on us or keeping something good from us. There is always purpose behind His methods, and there is always goodness filling His heart.

The more we see God continue to meet our needs and come through for us in perfect wisdom, even sometimes despite our doubt (2 Timothy 2:13), we will begin to learn, like Paul, the secret of how to get along no matter the circumstances, being filled with joy, contentment, strength, and peace. Of those things, praise God, there never has to be any lack. May God increase our faith in His eternal supply and may we believe that He will indeed give us strength to do all that He has given us to do.

For more teaching by Brent Barnett, please visit www.relevantbibleteaching.com for free, downloadable Bible lessons, articles, commentaries, and more. Brent can be reached via e-mail at brentbarnett7@yahoo.com.